A Future of Lousy Jobs?

THE CENTER FOR ECONOMIC PROGRESS AND EMPLOYMENT
 within the Brookings Economic Studies program is devoted to studies in growth, productivity, and employment opportunities. Its goal is to encourage and coordinate research on these topics in order to inform the policy debate. In addition to the studies listed below, the Center produces an annual Microeconomics issue of the *Brookings Papers on Economic Activity.*

American Living Standards: Threats and Challenges
Robert E. Litan, Robert Z. Lawrence, and Charles L. Schultze, eds.

Estimates of Productivity Change by Industry:
An Evaluation and an Alternative
Edward F. Denison

Paying for Productivity: A Look at the Evidence
Alan S. Blinder, ed.

A Future of Lousy Jobs? The Changing Structure of U.S. Wages
Gary Burtless, ed.

A Future of Lousy Jobs?

The Changing Structure of U.S. Wages

GARY BURTLESS
editor

The Brookings Institution
Washington, D.C.

Copyright © 1990 by

THE BROOKINGS INSTITUTION

1775 Massachusetts Avenue, N.W., Washington, D.C. 20036

Library of Congress Cataloging-in-Publication data:

A Future of lousy jobs? : the changing structure of U.S. wages /
Gary Burtless, editor.
    p.   cm.
    Includes bibliographical references.
    ISBN 0-8157-1180-8 (alk. paper)—ISBN 0-8157-1179-4 (pbk.)
    1. Wages—United States.   I. Burtless, Gary T., 1950–
HD4975.F87   1990
331.2'973—dc20   89-77414
                                                       CIP

9 8 7 6 5 4 3 2 1

Set in Linotron Times Roman
Composition by NK Graphics Inc.
  Baltimore, Maryland
Printed by R.R. Donnelley and Sons Co.
  Harrisonburg, Virginia

THE BROOKINGS INSTITUTION

The Brookings Institution is an independent organization devoted to nonpartisan research, education, and publication in economics, government, foreign policy, and the social sciences generally. Its principal purposes are to aid in the development of sound public policies and to promote public understanding of issues of national importance.

The Institution was founded on December 8, 1927, to merge the activities of the Institute for Government Research, founded in 1916, the Institute of Economics, founded in 1922, and the Robert Brookings Graduate School of Economics and Government, founded in 1924.

The Board of Trustees is responsible for the general administration of the Institution, while the immediate direction of the policies, program, and staff is vested in the President, assisted by an advisory committee of the officers and staff. The by-laws of the Institution state: "It is the function of the Trustees to make possible the conduct of scientific research, and publication, under the most favorable conditions, and to safeguard the independence of the research staff in the pursuit of their studies and in the publication of the results of such studies. It is not a part of their function to determine, control, or influence the conduct of particular investigations or the conclusions reached."

The President bears final responsibility for the decision to publish a manuscript as a Brookings book. In reaching his judgment on the competence, accuracy, and objectivity of each study, the President is advised by the director of the appropriate research program and weighs the views of a panel of expert outside readers who report to him in confidence on the quality of the work. Publication of a work signifies that it is deemed a competent treatment worthy of public consideration but does not imply endorsement of conclusions or recommendations.

The Institution maintains its position of neutrality on issues of public policy in order to safeguard the intellectual freedom of the staff. Hence interpretations or conclusions in Brookings publications should be understood to be solely those of the authors and should not be attributed to the Institution, to its trustees, officers, or other staff members, or to the organizations that support its research.

Foreword

In recent years there has been growing public concern over the decline—or perceived decline—in middle-class jobs. The U.S. economy
has produced more than 35 million jobs since 1973, a record that is the
envy of other industrialized nations. But many citizens and policymakers
are convinced that too many of these jobs pay too little to sustain a
middle-class living standard.

This book addresses two main issues. It examines the changing distribution of U.S. jobs and seeks to determine whether recent employment growth has been disproportionately concentrated in low-wage jobs.
And it attempts to establish the main economic causes behind the drift
in the American wage structure.

The authors conclude that U.S. wages have become more unequal
over the past decade, largely because of the steady rise in wage inequality
among men. Young men and men with little formal education have been
particularly affected by the changing structure of wages. Several groups
actually suffered substantial losses in real earnings. Two factors seem
to be important. First, the changing industrial structure of the labor
force has seriously harmed the job prospects of less skilled men, particularly those with little previous work experience. Second, in industry
after industry employers have changed the way work is done. As a result,
workers with extensive skills, formal education, and prior work experience have prospered; workers with limited skills, education, and experience have suffered. A long-range solution to this imbalance will
require upgrading the skills of workers now sunk at the bottom of the
wage structure.

This book is a result of a two-day conference organized by Gary
Burtless and held at the Brookings Institution in March 1989. Five papers
were commissioned, each prepared by one or more labor economists
knowledgeable about recent wage patterns. The papers were discussed
on the first day by formal commentators, whose revised remarks are

included in the volume. On the second day, the conference included participants from industry, government, and organized labor as well as from academia.

Nancy D. Davidson, Caroline Lalire, and Brenda B. Szittya edited the manuscript; Victor M. Alfaro and Roshna Kapadia checked it for factual accuracy; and Susan L. Woollen prepared it for typesetting. Florence Robinson prepared the index. The Brookings computation staff, especially Christine C. de Fontenay and Brian Sayer, provided valuable assistance in preparing data files for some of the analysis.

Brookings gratefully acknowledges financial support from the following for its Center for Economic Progress and Employment, the sponsor of this effort: Donald S. Perkins, American Express, AT&T, Chase Manhattan Bank, Cummins Engine, Ford Motor Company, Hewlett-Packard, Morgan Stanley, Motorola, Prudential Insurance Company of America, Springs Industries, Union Carbide, Warner-Lambert, Xerox Corporation, Aetna Foundation, Ford Foundation, General Electric Foundation, Smith Richardson Foundation, Institute for International Economic Studies, and Alex C. Walker Education and Charitable Trust.

The views expressed here are those of the authors and should not be attributed to the trustees, officers, or staff members of the Brookings Institution.

BRUCE K. MAC LAURY
President

January 1990
Washington, D.C.

Contents

Figures

Introduction and Summary

Gary Burtless

INCOME inequality is rising in the United States. Over the last twenty years the share of all income received by the richest one-fifth of families has grown by 3.3 percentage points, to 43.7 percent, whereas the share received by the poorest one-fifth has fallen one point, to 4.6 percent (table 1). The income shares of families in the second and third quintiles also fell, and the share received by the fourth quintile—the fifth of families just beneath the richest—rose slightly. These shifts in the income distribution may not appear sizable, but they have reversed the trend that prevailed over much of the postwar period, when income inequality was shrinking.

Though inequality has grown for many reasons, one cause has sparked particular comment: the purported decline in the number of middle-class jobs and the associated rise in the proportion of jobs paying meager wages. The main source of income for most American families is wage earnings. If the labor market offers fewer jobs that pay good or moderate wages, fewer families will be able to enjoy the middle-class life style that is widely held to be a hallmark of American life. According to a popular view, the bulk of American wage earners once worked in offices and on factory assembly lines, earning enough to feed, clothe, and shelter their families in reasonable comfort. A growing proportion now work in fast food restaurants, theme parks, and other low-paying service industries where they cannot earn enough to achieve a middle-class living standard. Instead of making steel or cars, the typical new worker now flips burgers or sweeps the office floor, producing too little to justify a middle-class wage.

Economists writing about this issue have hotly debated two kinds of questions. First, they disagree on whether the U.S. labor market has indeed produced a disproportionate number of poorly paid jobs. Second, those analysts who acknowledge a trend toward bad jobs disagree about the causes of the trend.

Table 1. Share of Aggregate Income Received by Each Fifth of U.S. Families, Selected Years, 1947–87
Percent

| | Quintile | | | | |
Year	Lowest	Second	Middle	Fourth	Highest
1947	5.0	11.9	17.0	23.1	43.0
1957	5.1	12.7	18.1	23.8	40.4
1967	5.5	12.4	17.9	23.9	40.4
1977	5.2	11.6	17.5	24.2	41.5
1987	4.6	10.8	16.9	24.1	43.7

Source: U.S. Bureau of the Census, *Money Income of Households, Families, and Persons in the United States, 1987*, series P-60, no. 162 (February 1989), p. 42.

To noneconomists it may seem surprising that economists cannot agree about the existence of a trend that should be readily observable.[1] But the reasons for the disagreement are fairly straightforward. Economists cannot agree on the definition of either a lousy or a middle-class job. In their analyses they do not always select the same population of jobs or workers for examination, and they sometimes measure labor market trends over different periods. Moreover, analysts have differed on whether the quality of jobs should be measured by using an absolute standard—one that does not vary from one year to the next—or by using a relative standard, which varies depending on the average or median earnings in a given year. If economists disagree on the standards used for measurement, it can hardly be surprising if their conclusions sometimes diverge.

On one point all analysts agree: average earnings growth among production workers has ceased in recent years after rising strongly over the early postwar period. In the two and a half decades from 1947 through 1973, the inflation-adjusted hourly earnings of an average production worker in private employment rose more than 70 percent, or about 2.1 percent a year. During the next fourteen years, from 1973 through 1987, average real hourly earnings *fell* 5.4 percent, or about 0.4 percent a year.[2] Even during the economic recovery after 1982, real

1. For evidence in favor of the proposition that the number of low-wage jobs is rising, see Barry Bluestone and Bennett Harrison, *The Great American Job Machine: The Proliferation of Low-Wage Employment in the U.S. Economy*, study prepared for the Joint Economic Committee (GPO, December 1986). The opposing view is presented by Marvin H. Kosters and Murray N. Ross, "A Shrinking Middle Class?" *Public Interest*, no. 90 (Winter 1988), pp. 3–27.

2. Average hourly earnings are converted into constant dollars using the implicit price deflator for personal consumption expenditures. *Economic Report of the President, 1989*, pp. 313, 358.

hourly wages continued to fall nearly half a percentage point each year. If the quality of production jobs in the private sector is measured according to an absolute standard tied to real hourly wages, there is little doubt the average quality of jobs has failed to improve since 1973. For some production workers job quality has clearly deteriorated.

At one level the reason for the sharp decline in average wage growth since 1973 is no mystery. The growth of productivity has slowed sharply and in some years stopped altogether. From 1948 until 1973 output per hour worked in the business sector rose 2.8 or 2.9 percent a year. Since 1973 business productivity has risen just 1.0 percent a year. Because gains in average compensation are ultimately tied to gains in productivity (at least over the long run), the drop in productivity growth has caused a predictable drop in the growth of wages. Economists and noneconomists have argued about the sources of the productivity slowdown but have not reached any consensus.[3] If the slower pace of productivity growth could be explained, we would have a far better understanding of the anemic wage growth in recent years.

But explaining the productivity slowdown does not resolve all the mysteries about recent wage trends. The drop in productivity growth can account for a drop in average wage gains. It cannot explain the growing inequality of wages around the average. The papers in this book focus on the changing pattern of wage inequality around average U.S. wages. The authors attempt to answer both of the questions mentioned earlier: Have wages grown more unequal? And if so, why?

Measuring and Explaining
the Wage Structure

Inequality can be calculated in various ways. An ideal measure of worker compensation would include money wages and the employer's contribution to fringe benefits, and it would show compensation over some standard unit of time, such as an hour or a forty-hour workweek. Unfortunately, the Census Bureau does not collect enough information from individual workers to calculate such a measure. As their yardstick of compensation, most analysts of wage inequality use annual wage and salary earnings reported every March in the Current Population Survey (CPS). Analysts sometimes restrict their sample of workers to wage

3. For one view, see Edward F. Denison, *Accounting for Slower Economic Growth: The United States in the 1970s* (Brookings, 1979), and Denison, *Trends in American Economic Growth, 1929–1982* (Brookings, 1985).

earners who work all year round on a full-time schedule, because annual
earnings in this group are not affected by variations in unemployment
experience and marked differences in weekly work schedules. In the
summary statistics described immediately below, however, I consider
annual earnings of *all* wage and salary workers, whether they work on
part-time or full-time schedules or work year round or fewer than fifty-
two weeks a year.[4]

One way to see what has happened to the distribution of wages is to
calculate the trend in earnings of workers at selected points in the earnings distribution. This calculation can be performed back through 1967
by using publicly available CPS files. Figure 1 shows trends in inflation-
adjusted wages for workers aged 25–64 at five different points in the
earnings distribution, the 20th, 40th, 60th, 80th, and 95th percentiles of
annual wages. Annual wage gains are shown for two different periods,
1967 to 1979 and 1979 to 1987, with trends for men and women displayed
separately.[5] If wage gains have been faster at the top of the earnings
distribution than in the middle and bottom, wage inequality is rising; if
gains have been faster at the bottom and middle of the distribution,
inequality is falling.

Data in the figure clearly show that inequality is rising among men
but falling or remaining fairly stable among women. The perception that
middle-class jobs are disappearing in the United States might be true
for men; it is plainly untrue for women. Women near the middle and
at the bottom of the female wage distribution have enjoyed sizable
earnings gains over the last twenty years, though the gains were a little
faster in the first half of the period than in the second. At the top of
the wage distribution women have enjoyed faster earnings gains in recent
years than they did between 1967 and 1979, but in neither period were
their wage increases substantially higher than those of women nearer
the bottom of the distribution. Of course, it is somewhat misleading to
discuss earnings gains among women as though the same women held

4. Wage and salary workers are excluded from the calculations if they have net income
from self-employment that exceeds their wage earnings. The conclusions are not particularly sensitive to the exclusion of the self-employed from the analysis sample. Nor are
they especially sensitive to the inclusion or exclusion of workers on part-time or part-year
work schedules.

5. Inflation-adjusted earnings were obtained by deflating nominal earnings amounts
by the CPI-UX, an experimental version of the consumer price index for urban consumers
or clerical and wage workers which uses a rental equivalence measure for homeowners'
costs. This index is available back through 1967 and provides a more reliable measure of
long-term inflation than the standard CPI series.

Figure 1. Growth of Annual Earnings at Selected Points in the Earnings Distribution, 1967–79 and 1979–87

Percent change a year

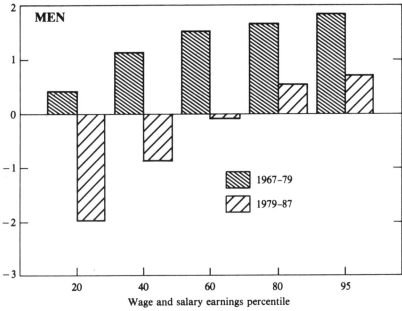

Wage and salary earnings percentile

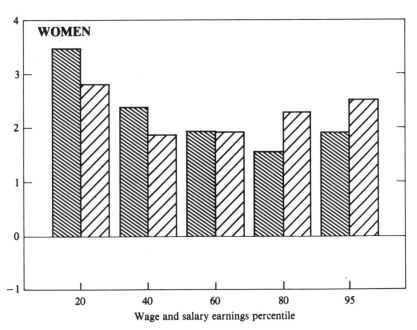

Wage and salary earnings percentile

jobs throughout the two decades covered by the figure. The labor force participation rate among women rose almost 40 percent over the period, from 40 percent in 1967 to 56 percent in 1987. Female wage earners in 1987 had better educational qualifications and previous work experience than women did in 1967. Moreover, women worked longer hours in 1987 than in 1967, so some improvement in wages would be expected. Nonetheless, the pattern of earnings gains shown in the figure suggests that wages were more tightly concentrated around the average earnings level in 1987 than they were in 1967.

The pattern for men is starkly different. During 1967–79 real annual earnings among men above the 80th percentile rose 1.8 percent a year. For the worker at the 20th percentile, earnings rose just 0.4 percent a year. Real earnings growth dropped sharply for workers over the entire distribution during 1979–87. Wages rose only 0.5 percent a year for a man at the 80th percentile and 0.7 percent a year for one at the 95th percentile. But real earnings actually *fell* 0.9 percent a year for a male worker at the 40th percentile, and 2.0 percent a year for one at the 20th percentile. After reaching a peak in 1973, real earnings at the 20th percentile of the wage distribution fell 20 percent, and earnings at the 40th percentile fell 10 percent. From 1973 through 1987 real earnings at the 60th percentile were essentially unchanged, whereas earnings at the 80th and 95th percentiles rose 6 and 8 percent, respectively. The implications for male inequality are clear. The earnings gaps between well-paid and moderately paid workers and between moderately paid and poorly paid workers have grown over time, especially in the last decade, while the number of men with earnings close to the median wage level has shrunk. Jobs near the middle of the male distribution have disappeared.

In seeking reasons for these changes in the wage structure, economists have examined two broad classes of explanations. The first links changes in relative wages to shifts in the composition or aggregate level of labor supply. The most obvious compositional changes arose because of the entry of the large baby boom generation into the work force starting in the late 1960s and because of the unprecedented influx of women into the labor force over the last thirty years. Less striking compositional shifts have occurred because of immigration, changes in educational attainment among new labor market entrants, and slow trends in the racial makeup of the working-age population.

A second class of explanations focuses on the changing pattern of demand for U.S. workers. The wage structure is affected by the general level of demand for workers, the relative demand within high-wage and low-wage industries, and the relative demand for workers in different skill classes or occupational groups. A naive view of recent history might link the rise in the number of poorly paid jobs to a surge in the utilization by employers of less skilled, poorly paid workers. Whether because of changes in production techniques or shifts in the demand for workers among different kinds of industries, employers now offer more jobs that require relatively few skills and consequently offer low wages.

While this kind of diagnosis might seem plausible to many noneconomists, it is in fact inconsistent with the evidence. If employers were creating a disproportionate number of jobs that required few skills and little education, we would anticipate that the wages of less skilled workers would be bid up relative to those received by better skilled, more educated workers. The opposite pattern has occurred in the 1980s. We would also expect joblessness among less skilled workers to fall relative to joblessness among the more skilled. But unemployment rates of the less skilled have risen relative to those experienced by more skilled workers.

The declining wages of less skilled men could be due to a variety of shifts in the structure of labor demand. Demand for less skilled workers could have fallen because of collapsing demand for the goods or services produced by industries in which less skilled labor is concentrated. Unskilled workers displaced by this shift would be forced to seek employment in other industries, forcing down the wages paid to unskilled labor in those industries.

Alternatively, changes in the technology of production might have depressed the demand for less skilled labor in selected industries or across the industrial spectrum. If technological changes were concentrated in a handful of industries, unskilled workers would suffer disproportionate employment and wage losses in those industries and wage losses in most other industries. If technological changes were widespread, wage losses would be visible across a wide variety of industries, but the distribution of unskilled labor across industries might be little affected.

Finally, it is possible that the drop in average wages received by unskilled workers has been due to sharp employment losses in such industries as mining and durable manufacturing that pay particularly high wages to less skilled workers. The loss of this kind of employment affects average wages in two ways. It reduces the average wage paid to less skilled workers because fewer of these workers are employed in high-wage industries. And by driving displaced workers into low-paying industries, it could depress the average wage received by less skilled workers in those low-wage industries. Analysts have been particularly concerned with shifts in demand among high-wage goods-producing industries and low-wage service-producing industries. By analyzing shifts in the industrial composition of skilled and less skilled workers and changes in the wage premium paid for greater skill in different industries, it may be possible to confirm or rule out some of the demand-side explanations just mentioned.

Changes in the supply of labor can have two kinds of effect on the wage structure. A rise in the number of less skilled workers, such as new entrants and women with little recent work experience, will raise the proportion of all workers who receive low wages. And heightened competition for less skilled jobs might drive down their wages relative to those paid in more skilled occupations. Both these effects are observable to some degree over the the last twenty years. The proportion of male workers who are less well paid because they are new entrants has risen, and the wages of younger male workers have fallen relative to those received by older workers. On the other hand, the number of years of schooling obtained by male workers has risen. Older men are less likely than younger ones to have completed either college or high school. As these men retire, they are gradually replaced by younger men, who typically have more schooling. Despite the rise in the proportion of college graduates among males, the relative earnings of college graduates has not fallen; it has risen. The relative supply of different kinds of female workers can similarly account for certain trends in the female wage structure, but not for all.

Figure 2 shows trends in relative earnings by age and educational attainment, separately for men and women. The lightly shaded bars show the ratio of median earnings among 45-to-54-year-olds to median earnings among 25-to-34-year-old workers. As one would expect, older workers typically earn higher wages than younger workers. The earnings premium received by older males rose as the number of older workers relative to younger workers declined. In 1967 the number of 45-to-54-year-old workers was about the same as the number of 25-to-34-year-olds. By 1987 there were only half as many 45-to-54-year-old workers as there were 25-to-34-year-olds. Older males have prospered—and younger workers suffered—as the baby boom generation entered the work force.

The age profile of earnings among women contrasts strongly with

Figure 2. Trends in Relative Earnings, by Age and Education, 1967–87

Ratio of median earnings [a]

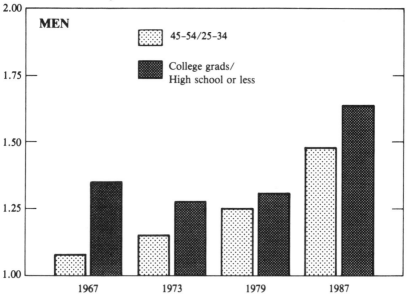

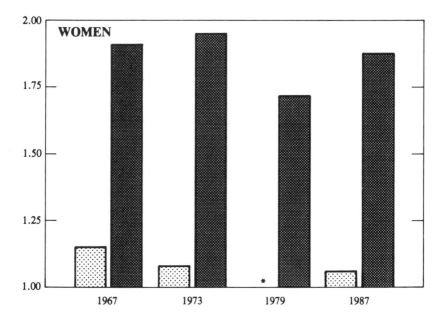

*Ratio is 1.00.

that among men, and the trend in the age profile differs as well. Between 1967 and 1987 the earnings of older women fell in comparison with those received by younger workers, even though the relative scarcity of older women increased at about the same pace as the scarcity of older men.

The dark bars in figure 2 show the earnings of young college graduates as a fraction of the earnings received by young workers who have no education beyond high school. Earnings within each group are calculated as the median earnings level among 25-to-34-year-olds in the respective educational categories. Among men the relative earnings of college graduates fell slightly from 1967 through 1979 but then jumped sharply in the 1980s. The earnings premium received by a male college graduate jumped from 31 percent to 64 percent in the eight years after 1979. By contrast, the earnings premium for a female college graduate in 1987 was below the premium she would have received in either 1967 or 1973. The increased relative supply of college-educated women might account for the shrinkage of the college premium. But it is curious that male college graduates, who are also relatively more plentiful, did not see a diminution in the premium they enjoy relative to less educated men. Their premium has exploded.

Some of the differences between men and women might be explained by sex segregation in the labor market and disparate trends in labor demand. If moderately well paid men are concentrated in declining industries, middle-class jobs could be disappearing for men even as the distribution of wages among women remains virtually unchanged.

Figure 3 shows changes in the distribution of male and female employment across broad industrial categories over the last two decades. Each bar reflects the percentage point change in the proportion of male or female workers employed in a particular industry during a given ten-year period. In 1967 slightly more than 50 percent of male wage and salary workers were employed in the traditionally well paid goods-producing, transportation, communications, and utilities industries.[6] By 1977 slightly less than 47 percent of men were employed in the same industries, indicating a drop in the proportion employed there of 4.2 percent. By 1987 the proportion employed in those industries had shrunk an additional 3.1 percentage points, to just 43.7 percent of male wage

6. The goods-producing industries are mining, construction, and manufacturing. Agriculture, a traditionally poorly paid industry, is excluded. Since typical earnings in the transportation, communications, and utility industries are more similar to those in the goods-producing industries than to those in the service sector, I have included those industries with the goods-producing sector.

Figure 3. Change in the Industry Mix of the Work Force, 1967–87[a]

Change in percent of work force

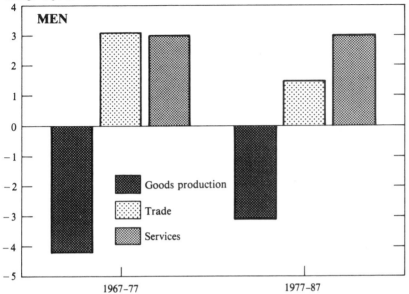

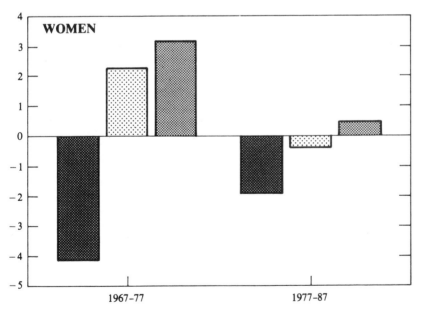

Source: March CPS tapes.

a. Trade: wholesale and retail; goods production: mining, manufacturing, transportation, communications, and utilities.

and salary employment. In contrast, male employment in wholesale and retail trade and in selected service industries, which historically pay low wages, grew in both decades.[7] Contrary to a popular view, not all jobs in these industries are poorly paid. But the average earnings of workers in trade and in services are well below typical earnings received by employees in the goods-producing, transportation, and communications industries. For example, in 1977 the median earnings level of men engaged in wholesale and retail trade was just 63 percent of median earnings in goods production; median earnings in service industries was 79 percent of median earnings in the goods-producing sector.[8]

The pattern of employment gains and losses shown in figure 3 confirms the popular perception that the number of jobs in better paid industries has shrunk relative to the number in the worse paid trade and service sectors. Between 1967 and 1977 this pattern of employment gains and losses was similar for both men and women. From 1977 through 1987 the loss of goods-producing jobs continued, but it was more rapid among male than among female workers. That may partly explain the diverging patterns of wage gain for men and women shown in figure 1, though the differences do not appear large enough by themselves to account for much of the divergence.

If simple supply and demand explanations for wage trends are unsatisfying, analysts sometimes look to more eclectic explanations of change. An obvious candidate is the declining influence of labor unions in American economic life. Unions help raise the earnings of moderately paid workers and often reduce the inequality of wages of organized workers. Their waning influence on wages may contribute to growing inequality. Similarly, the erosion in the value of the minimum wage has affected the relative earnings of people at the extreme lower tail of the wage distribution.

The authors represented in this volume examine a wide variety of explanations for recent trends in earnings inequality. Their conclusions cannot be summarized easily, because no analyst (or combination of analysts) finds that simple explanations can satisfactorily account for recent changes in the wage structure.

7. The industries included among services are business and repair services, private household services, personal services (such as hairdressing), entertainment and recreation, and professional and related services.

8. Relative earnings across industries are similar for women. Among women in wholesale and retail trade, median earnings in 1979 were 47 percent of median earnings in goods production, transportation, and communications; median earnings in services were 75 percent of earnings in the goods-producing sector.

The Deteriorating Position
of Less Skilled Men

A striking trend in the wage structure over recent years has been the continuing and pronounced drop in earnings among less educated men. This trend is illustrated in figure 2, and its effects on the earnings distribution are easily visible in the top part of figure 1. McKinley L. Blackburn, David E. Bloom, and Richard B. Freeman analyze the causes behind this disturbing trend. To keep the presentation as simple as possible, they restrict their analysis to white men who are at least 25 and no more than 64 years old. In some cases they further limit their estimation sample to young men between 25 and 34 years of age, since unskilled workers in this age group have been the ones most affected by the drop in real wages.

Blackburn, Bloom, and Freeman begin by documenting the magnitude of the earnings losses sustained by less skilled workers. These workers are defined both by their limited educational attainment and by their occupation. The least skilled workers obviously include those who have not completed high school. In an era in which an increased fraction of the work force has some schooling beyond high school, workers who have gone no further than high school also appear to face growing handicaps in the labor market. In addition, the authors identify operatives, handlers, and service workers as employees with limited skills and compare their wages with those earned by managers and professional workers. Unskilled workers have fared poorly over the last twenty years, especially since 1979. Their wages fell in absolute terms and during the 1980s dropped substantially relative to those received by highly skilled workers. To understand this drop in earnings, the authors propose a simple framework in which wage changes over time are divided into changes due to shifts in labor demand and those due to shifts in labor supply.

The first demand-side factor they examine is the shift in labor demand across industries. One way to analyze the effects of changing industrial composition is to apply a technique known as shift-share analysis. In this analysis the change in average wages received by less skilled workers is arithmetically apportioned into three different components. The first reflects the change in average wage that has occurred because the distribution of unskilled workers across high-wage and low-wage industries has changed over time. The second reflects the change in average wages paid to less skilled workers *within* each of the major industries. And the last component measures the interaction between changes in the industrial distribution of less skilled workers and the changes in their wages within different industries.

Shift-share analysis suggests that most of the earnings losses suffered by less skilled workers have been caused by changes in the distribution of wages *within* various U.S. industries. Only 20 to 30 percent of their losses have been due to the first and third components, the two that might be associatied with deindustrialization in the United States. The authors also use a regression approach to explain the size of wage changes, an approach that permits them to take explicit account of the influence of age, geographical region, and other factors on earnings. This second technique yields a similar estimate of the effect of industrial shifts on the relative earnings of less skilled workers. Such shifts are found to account for roughly one-sixth to one-third of the widening wage gap between skilled and less skilled workers.

The authors next investigate the influence of three supply-side factors on the declining earnings of less skilled workers. The first of these is the shift in the relative supply of male workers with differing educational qualifications. As noted earlier, the proportion of college graduates in the male work force has risen strongly over the last two decades. Among men between 25 and 64 the ratio of college graduates to high school dropouts rose from 0.82 in 1973 to 2.39 in 1987. If all other factors remained fixed, one would expect the rise in the supply of skilled labor to have resulted in a drop in the wage differential between college-educated and less well educated men. Surprisingly, however, among men aged 25–34 the ratio of college-educated to less well educated workers actually *declined* after 1979, suggesting that a falling supply of college-educated young men might explain part of the growing earnings gap between young skilled and unskilled men during the 1980s. According to the authors' estimates, this factor alone can explain one-eighth of the increased earnings gap between college graduates and high school dropouts aged 25–34 and it can explain 30 percent of the growing gap between college graduates and high school graduates.

It seems unlikely, however, that other factors remained constant after 1973. Between 1973 and 1979 the earnings gap between skilled and less skilled workers remained fairly stable in spite of the burgeoning size of the college-educated population. It seems reasonable to infer that the demand for college-educated workers was rising fast enough to hold the college premium constant. After 1979 the proportion of college-educated 25-to-34-year-old men declined, and the rate of increase in the proportion of college-educated 25-to-64-year-olds slowed. Blackburn, Bloom, and Freeman suggest that the slower rise in the proportion of college-educated men can account for part of the rise in skill-related wage differentials. If the demand for highly skilled workers continued to rise at the same pace both before and after 1979, then a slowdown in the rate of increase in skilled labor supply could have produced a twist in the earnings distribution favoring the more highly skilled. If this inference is valid, the authors believe they can explain roughly half the growing gap in wages between college-educated and less well educated 25-to-64-year-olds since 1979. Under the same assumption they can explain virtually all the widening gap between skilled and less skilled 25-to-34-year-olds. The explanation in both cases is the same. A continuing rise in demand for better educated men was not matched in the market by a continued rise in the supply of men with college degrees.

The authors are less successful in their attempts to determine the effects on the male wage structure of the influx of women into the job market and of fluctuations in the number of men under 25 seeking work. Though these supply-side factors may be important, their influence cannot be reliably measured by using the data and techniques applied in the paper.

Blackburn, Bloom, and Freeman next examine the effects on the wage structure of two notable changes in wage-setting institutions, the minimum wage rate and U.S. labor unions. The minimum wage fell substantially during the 1980s, measured either by purchasing power or by average economy-wide wages. If the real value of the minimum wage had remained constant over the 1980s, the minimum wage rate in 1988 would have been $4.34 an hour. The actual minimum was $3.35, or about 23 percent lower. Since unskilled workers are virtually the only ones paid the minimum wage, the decline in the minimum has reduced their earnings relative to those of more skilled workers. The authors find that the declining real value of the minimum accounts for a small but perceptible part of the decline in relative wages received by high school dropouts. It has played almost no part in the fall in relative wages of high school graduates over 25, however, because very few workers with a high school diploma are paid the minimum wage.

Of greater significance in explaining the declining fortunes of the less skilled is the continuing decline in unionization among unskilled workers. As is well known, the share of the U.S. work force belonging to a union has fallen over time. This trend continued through the 1970s and 1980s. The trend was especially concentrated among workers without a high school diploma and without any schooling beyond high school. The authors find that this trend is particularly significant for younger men, since less educated young men have historically received the largest wage dividend from membership in a union. Declining unionization might account for 15–20 percent of the drop in relative wages received by the less skilled during the 1980s.

Blackburn, Bloom, and Freeman conclude that a large share of the change in relative wages can be explained by observable changes in demand and supply and changes in labor market institutions. The relative importance of the individual factors is hard to pin down, however, and depends on assumptions about the nature of unobservable trends in the structure of labor demand. But whatever our assumptions, certain factors seem to be important in driving up wage differentials between less skilled and more skilled workers. Of these the most significant are changes in the industrial structure, declining rates of unionization, and the fact that, after 1979, the number of college-educated young men entering the work force failed to keep pace with the rising demand for highly educated workers.

Business Cycle and Demographic Effects

Economists have long known that the income distribution is affected by the business cycle. Relative to the affluent, the poor prosper in good times and fall behind in bad. Because so much of the income received by poor families is derived from labor earnings, it seems reasonable to surmise that the cyclical income position of the poor is connected to fluctuations in their labor income over the business cycle. During prolonged periods of high unemployment, such as the span from 1975 through 1985, earnings inequality may rise solely because of this connection. And if a strong relationship exists between unemployment and earnings inequality, much of the recent trend toward greater wage inequality might be explained by the trend in unemployment. The unemployment rate of 25-to-54-year-old men averaged only 3.0 percent in the 1960s and 3.7 percent in the 1970s. Between 1980 and 1987 the average rate jumped almost two-thirds, to 6.1 percent.

In the second paper Gary Burtless assesses the contribution of high unemployment to trends in earnings inequality over the past two decades. Because the influence of the business cycle can be understood only in the context of recent wide swings in the demographic structure, he also provides a detailed analysis of demographic trends and their impact on the wage structure. He examines the distribution of annual earnings within a variety of groups of wage and salary workers, but always analyzes trends among men and women separately because of the marked differences in the wage structures of these two populations.

Unlike other recent analysts, Burtless declines to classify jobs or workers into "poor," "middle class," and "high wage" categories. Instead he relies on traditional measures of inequality drawn from the income distribution literature to calculate the level and trend of earnings inequality. The measures he uses include the Gini coefficient, the Theil inequality index, and the variance of the natural logarithm of individual earnings. Because none of these statistics has a simple intuitive interpretation, he also calculates the share of earnings received by each quintile in the earnings distribution and the ratios of average earnings in the top and bottom quintiles relative to average earnings in the middle fifth of the population.

Using historical wage distribution statistics published by the Census Bureau, Burtless shows that the trend toward greater inequality among men is not a recent phenomenon. It dates back at least to the early postwar period. In fact, according to Census Bureau statistics, earnings inequality as measured by the Gini coefficient rose faster between 1947 and 1961 than it has risen during any comparable period since. By the early 1960s, however, male inequality reached a plateau and actually declined during the long economic expansion of the 1960s. The gradual upward drift of inequality resumed in the 1970s and then accelerated during the early 1980s.

Simple statistical analyses suggest that the historical pattern of male inequality is at least partly attributable to fluctuations in the rate of joblessness. Burtless finds, for example, that a 1 percentage point rise in the overall unemployment rate is associated with a 1.2 percent to 1.6 percent gain in average earnings among workers in the top quintile relative to wages received by workers in the middle quintile. The same change in unemployment is associated with a small drop in average earnings in the bottom quintile relative to earnings in the middle.

The relation between unemployment and inequality explains only a small part of the recent rise in male inequality, however. Burtless estimates that the upward drift in unemployment between the late 1960s and middle 1980s accounts for only one-seventh to one-fifth of the rise in inequality that occurred in that period. Even when the effects of unemployment are discounted, the trend toward greater inequality among men accelerated in the 1980s. Controlling for the influence of the business cycle, the author finds that the share of all earnings received by men in the top fifth of the earnings distribution rose nearly 0.3 percent a year between 1980 and 1987. The share received by the bottom three quintiles shrank at a comparable rate. The gap between earnings in the top and middle quintiles rose by about 3 percent a year.[9]

The female wage structure has changed much more gradually than the male wage distribution, and it is much less affected by fluctuations in unemployment. Depending on the measure of inequality used, female inequality in the mid-1980s was either slightly below or about the same as the level of inequality in the late 1960s. Inequality among women wage and salary workers rose in the 1980s, but it fell during most of the 1970s. Trends in unemployment seem to play almost no role in explaining these shifts in the pattern of wage inequality among women.

If business cycle effects explain only a small part of the trend in male inequality and little if any of the trend among women, the reason could be that wide demographic swings have swamped the effects of other factors. One notable demographic trend has been the rise in female labor force participation. This trend is not a recent phenomenon, however; female participation has been rising fairly steadily since the middle 1950s.

The most important recent demographic swing has been the entry of the large baby boom generation into the job market. Burtless distinguishes two potential effects of the baby boom on the wage structure. First, the influx of new labor market entrants would be expected to swell the number of workers holding low-paying jobs, thus tilting the employment distribution toward jobs with low annual earnings. Second, increased competition for unskilled jobs might drive down wages on those jobs relative to wages paid in more skilled occupations.

The first of these effects can be analyzed in a straightforward way. If inequality has risen solely because of an influx of young workers who are paid low average wages, one should be able to eliminate the effect of this demographic swing on the earnings distribution by disregarding the earnings reports of some new entrants into the work force. For example, if the proportion of 20-to-24-year-old workers in the labor force doubled between 1965 and 1975, the effect of the greater number of young workers could be eliminated by ignoring the reports of exactly

---

9. In 1979 the average earnings of a male worker in the top quintile was 119 percent above the average earnings of workers in the middle quintile. The trend rise in the earnings gap is 3.0 to 3.3 percentage points a year.

one-half the 20-to-24-year-olds when calculating earnings distribution statistics for 1975. If half the 20-to-24-year-olds are ignored in 1975, the age profile of the population used in calculating the earnings distribution would be the same in 1975 as in 1965. Earnings inequality might still turn out to be higher in 1975 than it was in 1965. But none of the rise in inequality would be attributable to the increased proportion of young workers in the analysis sample.

Burtless finds that a small part of the rise in male inequality during the 1970s could have been avoided if the demographic profile of the working population had remained constant over that decade. Surprisingly, however, demographic shifts since 1979 should have contributed to a growing equalization of earnings among men. Most of the changes in the age distribution, the education distribution, and the distribution of work experience occurring in the 1980s raised the proportion of workers who should be near the middle of the earnings distribution. The same pattern holds for female workers in the 1980s. Inequality among women rose slightly after 1979, though it should have fallen in view of the evolving distributions of age, educational experience, and work experience among women. Rather than explain the trend of inequality in the 1980s, demographic factors only deepen the mystery.

Demographic changes have also affected the relative earnings of different population groups, as Blackburn, Bloom, and Freeman show in their paper. The influx of young entrants reduced the earnings of young men relative to those of older men with greater skill and experience. It is simple to calculate the contribution toward greater inequality that occurred because of the rising gap in earnings between identifiable categories of workers, defined, for example, on the basis of age and education. Using the Theil index of inequality, Burtless divides the trend in overall inequality into the part due to trends in wage inequality *between* different population categories and the part due to trends in wage inequality *within* each of these categories. If the categories are defined by both age and education, he finds that less than 40 percent of the rise in male inequality from 1967 to 1987 is due to changes in the relative earnings of different population groups. More than 60 percent is attributable to growing inequality within groups of workers of the same age and educational attainment.

Burtless concludes from this analysis that the baby boom may have contributed modestly to rising inequality in the 1970s and even more trivially to inequality in the 1980s. But the main explanation for increased male inequality cannot be connected to swings in the demo-

graphic changes, because so much of the rise has occurred within identifiable population groups, including groups—such as older, well-
educated workers—who should have benefited from the influx of young
unskilled workers.

The findings in the Blackburn, Bloom, and Freeman study should be
interpreted in light of this conclusion. Blackburn, Bloom, and Freeman
sought to explain why earnings of one class of workers—less educated
men—fell so dramatically compared with earnings of another class—men
with college degrees. Even if their analysis fully explained this growing
wage gap, as well as all other wage gaps that arose during the last two
decades, they would not have accounted for the major source of growing
inequality among males. Most of the growth has occurred because the
pay of men with similar characteristics has become more unequal over
time.

In the last section of his paper, Burtless tries to determine whether
the changing variability of individual earnings is due to a change in the
variability of hours at work or to changes in the variability of hourly
wage rates. Although the CPS wage data are imperfect, he concludes
that most of the rise in the variance of annual earnings stems from the
rising variance of hourly wage rates. Among women the variability of
annual weeks at work and weekly hours of work has actually fallen,
while among men the rise has been small. Since the hourly wage represents the best approximation to the pure price of labor, this finding
implies that the price of labor rather than the level of individual work
effort has become more unequal over time. Burtless speculates that the
rising variance of wage rates is associated with the rising wage premiums
that worker ability and skill now command.

The Role of Part-Time Jobs

Part-time jobs account for a growing share of U.S. employment.
Because part-time work is widely perceived to be poorly compensated
and unpleasant, the rise of part-time employment is sometimes linked
to the trend toward declining quality in U.S. jobs. The problem with
this view is that most part-time workers voluntarily choose jobs with
limited weekly hours. They do not desire full-time jobs, and they could
suffer serious welfare losses if part-time jobs disappeared. Rather than
reflect a deterioration in American job opportunities, the rise in part-
time employment might reflect a healthy response of employers to the
demands of a new generation of workers.

Rebecca M. Blank investigates the development of part-time employment in the third paper in this volume. She is primarily interested in determining whether and to what extent part-time jobs are bad jobs, that is, jobs with low wages and few fringe benefits.

She begins by tracing the growth in part-time employment over the last two decades. Notwithstanding the perception that part-time employment is mushrooming, Blank finds that the percentage of workers on part-time schedules is rising slowly though erratically over time. Twelve percent of adult employment in 1968 consisted of part-time workers; by 1987 the percentage had risen to just 15 percent. The fraction of female workers on part-time schedules—about one-quarter—remained fairly stable over that period, while the fraction of men working part time rose about 3 percentage points, to 8.5 percent in 1987. The rise in the share of workers on part-time schedules is thus due to a growing participation of women in the work force and the increased probability that men will work less than full-time hours. Though most workers on part-time schedules voluntarily choose part-time over full-time work, much of the rise in part-time employment among men has been caused by a growth in involuntary part-time work. If they could find jobs offering longer hours, many men on part-time schedules would accept them.

Part-time workers receive lower wages than full-time workers, but the difference is not terribly large. In 1987 the hourly wage of women on part-time schedules was 8 percent below the wage received by women on full-time schedules; the part-time differential among men amounted to just 6 percent. In some occupations the differential is of course much larger. But Blank also finds occupations in which part-time workers are better paid than workers on a full-time schedule and still others in which workers on part-time and full-time schedules receive roughly equal pay. What drags down the average wage of part-time jobs is the distribution of these jobs across occupations. Part-time work is disproportionately concentrated in service occupations, where low pay is common for all workers.

If the difference in money wages between part-time and full-time jobs is modest, the difference in fringe benefits is considerable. Slightly more than half the women on full-time schedules are covered by a pension plan; less than a sixth on part-time schedules are covered by a pension. The difference in pension coverage between full-time and part-time men is even wider. Among single women who head families and work on a full-time schedule, about three out of four are covered by employer-provided health insurance; only one out of four single women on a part-time schedule is provided with health insurance. If part-time jobs are bad jobs, they are bad because they do not offer fringe benefits.

Blank refines her estimates of the impact of part-time hours on wage rates in several ways. She uses multiple regression to determine the difference between full-time and part-time wages, controlling for the influence of age, educational attainment, marital status, union membership, the local unemployment rate, and other individual and regional characteristics. When these factors are taken into account, the estimated difference between part-time and full-time wages rises considerably. Women on part-time schedules are estimated to receive wages about 20 percent below those received by otherwise identical women on full-time schedules; men on part-time schedules receive nearly 30 percent less than men on full-time schedules.

This approach to estimating the gap between part-time and full-time wages is unsatisfying, however, because it fails to account for unmeasurable differences between workers on part-time and full-time schedules. Workers who choose or are forced to work on a part-time schedule may receive lower wages than similar workers on a full-time schedule because they differ in some systematic but unmeasurable way from full-time workers. Blank tries to account for these unmeasurable differences by using a more sophisticated statistical methodology. The results of this analysis indeed suggest that part-time workers would receive lower wages on full-time jobs than do similar workers who actually hold full-time jobs. Once this difference is taken into account, Blank estimates that women on part-time schedules are not really penalized for working short hours, while for men the penalty is much smaller than 30 percent. In fact, she finds that women in part-time jobs may actually be paid higher hourly wages than they would receive if they instead chose to work full-time hours.

If the wage penalty for part-time work is small or nonexistent, the penalty in terms of lost fringe benefits remains very large. Blank finds that statistical corrections to control for differences between part-time and full-time workers do not eliminate this large penalty. Part-time workers are much less likely to be covered by health insurance or a private pension than they would be if they became full-time workers.

The author concludes that part-time jobs are not bad jobs from the point of view of many women who hold them, but may be poor jobs from the vantage point of workers forced to accept them because of either family or economic circumstances. For many women the hourly wage available on part-time jobs appears comparable to the wage on full-time jobs, and the lack of certain fringe benefits, such as health insurance, is not troubling if the spouse's job already provides these benefits. For single women forced to accept part-time work because of child care responsibilities, the lack of fringe benefits is far more troubling. And for both men and women compelled to work part time because of the scarcity of full-time jobs, part-time jobs are clearly undesirable: they pay lower hourly wages and offer fewer fringe benefits than the jobs these workers could expect to obtain if they found full-time work.

Although Blank's paper helps us understand the relative quality of part-time jobs in the late 1980s, it does not shed any direct light on whether part-time employment is contributing to a deterioration in the quality of U.S. jobs or even to a decline in typical annual earnings. Part-time jobs today pay slightly lower hourly wages than full-time jobs, and they may provide year-round earnings that are substantially below earnings on full-time jobs. It might therefore seem plausible to conclude that the 3-percentage-point rise in part-time employment between 1968 and 1987 caused average job quality to deteriorate. But this inference is wrong if part-time jobs improved in quality relative to full-time jobs during that period.

In fact, results in the papers by Burtless and Robert A. Moffitt suggest that part-time work has contributed very little to the trend toward low-paying jobs among men. Both Burtless and Moffitt find that earnings inequality among men has risen because wage rate inequality has risen, not because there has been a rise in inequality of annual hours of work. Thus, even though the number of part-time jobs has increased, the gain in part-time employment has not significantly raised the variance of yearly hours of work. This finding, together with the results in Blank's paper, should lay to rest many fears about the adverse effects of part-time employment on the quality of U.S. jobs.

The Effect of the Baby Boom
on Educational Attainment

The entry of the baby boom and subsequent baby bust generations into the work force caused wide swings in the supply of young, less skilled labor. In 1960 the population of 15-to-24-year-olds was just 19 percent larger than the population of 45-to-54-year-olds. Two decades later the ratio of 15-to-24-year-olds to 45-to-54-year-olds had risen to

1.86. But this ratio started to fall in the 1980s as the baby boom generation began to enter middle age and the baby bust generation entered the work force. The swings in the age profile of the population directly affected the overall earnings distribution and the relative earnings of less skilled workers, as shown in the papers by Burtless and Blackburn, Bloom, and Freeman. But these swings also produced some indirect effects that may have enduring consequences for the future distribution of earnings.

Linda Datcher Loury examines one of the most important of these indirect effects, that of demographic swings on average educational attainment. The effect arises because of the direct impact of cohort size on the relative earnings of young people. Loury distinguishes among several theories linking cohort size and educational attainment. All these theories are based on the reasonable proposition that young people will invest more or less in schooling depending on the expected rate of return from additional schooling. By affecting the rate of return from a college degree and from other post–high school training, the cycle of baby boom and baby bust has affected the attractiveness of obtaining education beyond high school.

On this much all economists can agree. They disagree, however, on how the demographic cycle has affected the rate of return from schooling. Loury begins her paper with a thorough review of the past literature on this subject. According to one theory, the influx of young, unskilled workers will cause the relative earnings of less skilled labor to tumble. This will reduce one of the main costs of additional schooling, namely, the wages that are forgone while a student is sitting in a college classroom. Since baby boom workers will be plentiful throughout their careers, a worker born in this cohort might reason that it would be beneficial to persuade employers that he or she is different from most baby boom workers and similar to workers in the relatively scarce older cohort. That can be accomplished by collecting educational credentials beyond a high school degree. By this line of reasoning, baby boom workers should obtain more training beyond high school than workers born in smaller cohorts.

Other theorists have suggested the opposite. Although the influx of young workers depresses the wages of all young people relative to those of old people in the market, it depresses the wages of college-educated workers more than it does those received by less well trained workers. The reason for this pattern is that young unskilled workers are reasonably close substitutes for older unskilled workers, while young college-educated workers are not close substitutes for older, more experienced college graduates. When young workers surge into the market, the wages of young and old unskilled workers fall, with the decline greater for younger than for older unskilled workers. But the wages of young, college-educated workers fall sharply, because there are so many of them and because they are such imperfect substitutes for older college graduates. If this were true, the rate of return from schooling beyond high school would fall, and college attendance would decline.

It should be obvious that economic theory offers no clear guidance about the impact of cohort size on the rate of return from postsecondary training. The analyst is thus forced to examine empirical evidence to draw reliable inferences. The traditional source of evidence on this question has been time-series data. Economists have analyzed aggregate trends in college attendance, relative earnings, and relative labor supply to infer the effects of cohort size.

Loury's approach to estimation is very different. Instead of using time-series data, she uses data from a cross-sectional survey, the National Longitudinal Study of the High School Class of 1972 (NLS72). Young people interviewed in this survey were drawn from communities all across the United States. In some of these communities the effects of the baby boom on relative cohort size were very large; in others the effects were virtually nonexistent. That is, in some communities the number of young people relative to older people was very high, while in others it remained fairly low. If relative cohort size exercises a profound influence on the schooling and training choices of young people, the influence should be visible in the schooling choices of young people in these communities.

The author finds that large cohort size significantly reduces college attendance rates and postsecondary training among men but not among women. It is not obvious why the effect of cohort size should differ for men and women, although this cross-sectional finding is consistent with the time-series pattern of postsecondary education.

Loury finds that the effect of relative cohort size is best captured by the relative sizes of older generations of workers. She measures cohort size by the ratio of 25-to-29-year-olds to 35-to-39-year-olds in a given community. Interestingly, this measure of cohort size seems to produce more reliable results than an alternative measure based on the ratio of 15-to-17-year-olds to 35-to-39-year-olds. This finding suggests that high school graduates are myopic in deciding whether to pursue further schooling. They pay more attention to the relative earnings received by cohorts a little older than their own than they do to the relative earnings they can expect to receive as a result of the size of their own cohort. That seems sensible, for new high school graduates cannot directly observe their own future earnings, though they can observe the relative earnings of workers just a bit older than themselves.

Although Loury concludes that cohort size plays an important role in determining the educational choices of young men, the effect is not particularly large. The tail end of the baby boom generation received less education in 1980 than it would have received if the age profile of the population had remained fixed. Similarly, the tail end of the baby bust generation will receive more education than it would receive if the age profile were to remain constant. According to Loury's estimates, this swing will cause a rise in male college attendance rates of 2.7 percentage points between 1980 and 2000. (About half of 18-year-old males go on to college.) The change is statistically significant and will perceptibly improve the average quality of the future work force, but it will hardly create a revolution in the U.S. job distribution.

The Effects of Welfare State Programs

One popular explanation for the declining fortunes of low-income families is the growth of government income support programs that permit wage earners to survive with low levels of annual earnings. Crude versions of this argument sometimes appear in the popular press. A more sophisticated version was recently advanced by Charles Murray, who argues that social programs for the poor have on balance done harm.[10] They have worsened the condition of the people they were designed to help by undermining recipients' incentives to behave in a socially responsible way—within the family, in school, and at work. Public income support programs have encouraged socially undesirable activities, such as idleness and malingering, by greatly reducing their cost. If these effects are important, they should be especially significant for workers in the lower tail of the income distribution, because these are the workers most likely to receive public transfers.

Although Murray's thesis has been widely debated in the popular press and in the social science literature, it has never been linked to the controversy over the disappearance of moderate-income jobs. Yet the

10. Charles A. Murray, *Losing Ground: American Social Policy, 1950–1980* (Basic Books, 1984).

connection between the two debates should be obvious. If welfare state programs, which have grown in size and availability, discourage low-income earners from working up to their full potential, the earnings of such workers will fall relative to those of middle-income and affluent workers; earnings inequality will rise. Robert A. Moffitt investigates and rejects this hypothesis in the last paper of the volume.

Like Blackburn, Bloom, and Freeman, Moffitt restricts his analysis to men, arguing that earnings inequality has risen among men, whereas the availability of middle-class jobs has not fallen for women. Moffitt measures inequality by using the variance of the natural logarithm of individual annual earnings. The variance of earnings might fluctuate in response to changes in the composition of male workers. To account for this possibility, the author analyzes inequality trends separately for white and nonwhite men and statistically adjusts his estimate of earnings variance within each group to reflect different socioeconomic characteristics, such as education and prior work experience. Moffitt finds, as expected, that the variance of male earnings has risen over time and that the rate of rise accelerated in the early 1980s.

To see whether trends in assistance programs can explain the rise in earnings variability, the author considers developments in the major assistance programs in recent years. The most significant programs he considers are aid to families with dependent children (AFDC), food stamps, and medicaid. All three programs have grown explosively over the last twenty-five years, but none grew especially fast during the 1980s, when earnings inequality rose among men. In fact, most growth in these programs was concentrated in the late 1960s and early 1970s, when inequality was fairly stable. The patterns of inequality growth and transfer program growth thus fail to correspond.

Moffitt also finds that the percentage of working-age men who receive transfers is small. Only 20 percent of husband-wife couples received any transfers at all in 1984, and of these many received only unemployment compensation benefits. Unlike AFDC, food stamps, or medicaid, unemployment compensation has not exploded in the last two decades; instead, it has declined. Workers becoming unemployed during the 1980s were less likely to receive unemployment insurance than they were at any time during the previous two decades. Nor does Moffitt find that rising benefit levels can explain the recent spurt in male inequality. AFDC benefits have generally declined since the early 1970s, and real benefit levels in the food stamp and medicaid programs have failed to rise. Overall, the level of benefits relative to earnings was about the same in 1985 as it was in 1969. Real benefits and real wages have both declined over the period.

Moffitt reviews the empirical literature on the effects of AFDC and food stamps on earnings and concludes that the empirical magnitude of the male response is too small to matter. This is true in part because too few men receive benefits for the behavior of men to be much affected, and in part because the estimated size of the effect even on program participants is fairly small.

The author offers several further reasons for believing that transfer benefits have played little role in the recent rise in male inequality. First, he finds that much of the rise is due to a rapid gain of earnings at the very top of the earnings distribution relative to earnings both in the middle and at the bottom. The hypothesis that transfer benefits have played an important role would be supported only if earnings at the bottom dropped relative to earnings in the middle and at the top of the distribution. Like Burtless, Moffitt finds that the rise in earnings inequality is due to a growing inequality in wage rates, not to a growing inequality in annual hours of work. If Murray is correct that transfer programs are undermining the work ethic, we would anticipate that inequality of work effort would rise, not inequality of wage rates.

Transfer programs may have undermined the institution of marriage by reducing women's dependence on men. In fact, divorce and births out of wedlock have risen over the last twenty years. Since single men typically earn less than married men, the decline of marriage might contribute to growing earnings inequality among men by raising the proportion of unmarried males. This would occur, for example, if unmarried men feel less need to earn high incomes than similar married men because they are not required to support dependents. Moffitt argues, however, that even if all the decline in marriage is due to transfers—which is doubtful—the maximum potential effect on male earnings inequality is quite modest.

Finally, Moffitt explores the relation between wage inequality within different states and the level of transfer benefits in the several states. Since AFDC and medicaid benefit levels are set by state legislatures rather than by the federal government, transfer generosity varies quite widely from state to state. If generous benefits cause earnings inequality to rise, one would anticipate that high-benefit states would be ones with a high degree of earnings inequality. This hypothesis is not confirmed in the data. Moffitt also finds that the diversity of benefit levels across states has fallen with time. The growing equality of benefit levels should thus contribute to a convergence of overall earnings inequality. As noted earlier, however, inequality has grown, especially in the last decade.

Moffitt's analysis leaves little reason to believe that welfare state programs have contributed appreciably to the rise in male earnings inequality of the last two decades. If they have contributed to the trend at all, the contribution has been elusive and indirect. The historical record provides no evidence that inequality has jumped when welfare state programs expanded or were made more generous. Nor is there any evidence that inequality has fallen when benefits have been scaled back.

The Future

The papers in this volume demonstrate that it is easier to disprove a plausible but flawed hypothesis than to validate a correct one. On several points the evidence seems persuasive. Wage inequality has risen among men, but not among women. It is extremely unlikely that part-time jobs or welfare state programs have contributed much to changes in the wage structure in recent years. The direct and indirect effects of supply-side demographic trends have contributed in a noticeable way to wage developments, as the papers by Blackburn, Bloom, and Freeman, Burtless, and Loury show. And the long-term trend toward higher joblessness, particularly among prime-aged men, has contributed a bit to earnings inequality. But even if the demographic structure of the working-age population had remained unchanged and the rate of unemployment had held steady, the level of wage inequality among men would have risen. Part of the growing gap between skilled and unskilled and between well-paid and poorly paid men can be attributed to changes in the industrial structure and the decline in unionization. But the evidence assembled by Blackburn, Bloom, and Freeman suggests that these factors can account for only a small part of the steadily widening gap.

Since measurable changes in the structure of supply and demand for labor cannot account for the entire trend in the wage structure, analysts are naturally inclined to speculate about changes that are less easy to quantify. Blackburn, Bloom, and Freeman investigate the recent suggestion that the deteriorating quality of American schools has left a generation of workers ill equipped to deal with the challenges of modern employment.[11] They find some evidence to support this idea. Less ed-

11. See John H. Bishop, "Is the Test Score Decline Responsible for the Productivity Growth Decline?" *American Economic Review*, vol. 79 (March 1989), pp. 178–97.

ucated men have suffered greater earnings losses than better educated men, regardless of their age. But among less educated men, the largest losses were sustained by younger men, precisely the ones who would be most affected if the quality of schools had recently dropped. Unfortunately, this pattern of earnings loss can also be explained by other hypotheses.

Burtless as well as Blackburn, Bloom, and Freeman suggests that the structure of demand for skilled and unskilled male workers *within* industries has been changing over time. Many of the trends in the male wage and employment structure can be explained if demand for skilled workers has been growing faster than supply and the demand for less skilled workers has fallen faster than supply. This has occurred not so much because of a shift in the level or distribution of demand across different companies and industries, but because companies and industries have tried to change their production techniques in a way that requires more able and highly skilled workers. Because skilled workers remain scarce, their wages have been bid up, raising the gap between them and workers with lower educational attainment and more limited abilities.

Less skilled men have suffered from this shift in two ways. Their earnings have fallen relative to the wages received by better educated and more skilled men, and their joblessness has risen. The problem they face is not an overabundance of bad jobs, as suggested in the title of this book, but a surplus of unskilled workers in a market requiring more skill than ever. Ironically, their labor market position could be improved if the U.S. economy produced *more* not fewer jobs requiring limited skill. Their wages might then be bid up and the wage gap reduced.

This diagnosis is speculative. But it seems plausible in comparison with other hypotheses that have been shown to be incomplete or wrong. If the demand for unskilled labor has dropped, the obvious policy response is to improve the qualifications of less skilled workers to match the developing requirements of the job market. If the nation has too many unskilled workers, rather than too many bad jobs, both efficiency and equity will be served by improving the skills of workers now lodged at the bottom.

The Declining Economic Position of Less Skilled American Men

McKinley L. Blackburn, David E. Bloom, and Richard B. Freeman

FROM 1900 through the 1960s the real earnings of less skilled American workers grew substantially. In some periods the earnings of the less skilled also improved relative to the earnings of their more skilled counterparts. Natural labor market forces—increased productivity per worker and the declining ratio of less skilled to more skilled workers—in conjunction with the pressures imposed by wage-setting institutions—minimum wage laws and unionism—seemed to promise a bright economic future for the less skilled.

The 1970s and 1980s mark a striking break with this historic pattern for men. The earnings of less skilled American men began dropping in real terms after 1973 and fell precipitously during the 1980s, when young male high school graduates and dropouts suffered exceptional losses relative to their college graduate peers.[1] Handlers and service workers, factory operators, and blue-collar workers as a group lost ground relative to managers and professionals and to white-collar workers as a group. Workers in low-wage industries had smaller increases in earnings than workers in high-wage industries.[2] The wage distribution of male workers widened, with the lowest-paid workers falling further below the median than in years past.[3]

We would like to thank John Bound, Gary Burtless, John Chilton, Lawrence Katz, Jacob Mincer, Kevin Murphy, and Aloysius Siow for helpful discussions and David Beede for research assistance. This research was supported by the Brookings Institution, by a grant from the Economic Development Administration, by a Sloan Research Fellowship, and by the Russell Sage Foundation and the Smith-Richardson Foundation.

1. Kevin Murphy and Finis Welch, "Wage Differentials in the 1980's: The Role of International Trade," paper presented at the September 1988 Mont Pelerin Society General Meeting.

2. Linda A. Bell and Richard B. Freeman, "The Facts about Rising Industrial Wage Dispersion in the United States," in *Proceedings of the Thirty-Ninth Annual Meeting* (Madison, Wis.: Industrial Relations Research Association, 1987), pp. 331–37.

3. McKinley L. Blackburn and David E. Bloom, "Earnings and Income Inequality in the United States," *Population and Development Review*, vol. 13 (December 1987), pp.

Table 1. Real and Relative Annual Earnings, White Male Full-Time, Year-Round Workers, by Age and Skill Class, 1973, 1979, 1987
Earnings in 1987 dollars; differentials in log points

Item	Ages 25-64			Ages 25-34		
	1973	1979	1987	1973	1979	1987
By years of schooling						
Real earnings[a]						
High school dropouts (LTHS)	22,134	21,353	19,169	20,128	18,693	15,922
High school graduates (HS)	26,822	26,155	24,651	24,719	23,440	21,420
College graduates (CG)	35,371	33,815	35,848	30,034	27,583	30,132
Earnings differential[b]						
CG to LTHS	.47	.46	.63	.40	.37	.62
CG to HS	.28	.26	.38	.20	.15	.33
Earnings differential, regression-corrected[c]						
CG to LTHS	.49	.51	.64	.41	.39	.62
CG to HS	.29	.26	.36	.20	.16	.33
By occupation[d]						
Real earnings[a]						
Handlers and service workers (H&S)	18,703	17,912	16,844	19,226	17,931	15,699
Operators (OP)	23,300	23,412	22,260	22,307	21,926	19,908
Managers and professionals (MP)	34,613	33,495	35,817	25,951	27,514	29,537
Earnings differential[b]						
MP to H&S	.62	.63	.76	.48	.43	.63
MP to OP	.39	.35	.48	.28	.23	.39
OP to H&S	.22	.27	.28	.20	.25	.24
Earnings differential, regression-corrected[c]						
MP to H&S	.58	.58	.71	.48	.43	.63
MP to OP	.39	.33	.44	.28	.20	.35
OP to H&S	.19	.27	.27	.20	.22	.24

Source: March 1974, 1980, and 1988 CPS public use samples.
a. The numbers reported are geometric means for annual earnings over the calendar year preceding the survey.
b. The earnings differentials are measured using the difference in the logarithm of the mean incomes for the two groups of workers.
c. The regression-corrected differentials are estimates from logarithmic earnings equations that include nine age dummies (one age dummy for the 25–34-year-old sample), eight region dummies, three marital status dummies, and a dummy for workers with 13–15 years of school completed. Regressions were fit separately for each year.
d. See note 5 of the text for a description of the occupational categories.

Why? What happened to rescind the American promise of rising earnings for the less skilled?

In this paper we explore these questions by analyzing the earnings and employment of white male workers aged 25–64, and of a younger subgroup of that population—those aged 25–34. Focusing on white males eliminates considerations of how race or gender affects earnings and employment. Focusing on workers 25 and over eliminates considerations having to do with the volatile youth labor market, where military service and schooling decisions make it difficult to interpret changes in earnings and employment. Finally, focusing on men aged 25–34 isolates a group whose economic position is more sensitive to current labor market realities than is the position of older workers already ensconced in enterprises.

Our primary source of data is the annual March Current Population Survey (CPS), which provides information both on workers' annual earnings for the calendar year preceding each survey and on workers' current labor force status. We also analyze data on "usual" hourly earnings contained in the May and in some of the March CPS samples.

We begin by documenting the post-1970 decline in the relative and absolute earnings of less skilled American men and the concomitant increase in their unemployment rate and drop in their employment-to-population ratio. Then we look for explanations. We look first at shifts in labor demand and labor supply for workers with different levels of skill and then at the declining importance of two major wage-setting institutions: the minimum wage and labor unions. We use a sources-of-change accounting analysis to assess the extent to which these factors have contributed to the observed decline in the economic position of less skilled men. We conclude with speculations about the future economic prospects of these workers.

The Growing Wage Gap

Table 1 documents the deterioration in the real and relative earnings of less skilled American men that began in the early 1970s. It reports summary statistics derived from March CPS data on real annual wage

575–609; Marvin H. Kosters and Murray N. Ross, "The Quality of Jobs: Evidence from Distributions of Annual Earnings and Hourly Wages," AEI Occasional Papers (American Enterprise Institute, July 1988); and Barry Bluestone and Bennett Harrison, "The Growth of Low-Wage Employment, 1963–1986," *American Economic Review*, vol. 78 (May 1988, *Papers and Proceedings, 1987*), pp. 124–28.

and salary income in 1973, 1979, and 1987 for six groups of full-time, year-round white male workers aged 25–64 and 25–34.[4] We distinguish three educational groups: high school dropouts, high school graduates, and college graduates; and three occupational groups: handlers and service workers, operators, and managers and professionals.[5] The numbers presented in table 1 and depicted in figure 1 reveal substantial declines in the average level of real earnings among less skilled men, particularly among those aged 25–34. From 1973 through 1987 the natural logarithm (log) of real earnings among high school dropouts aged 25–64 fell by .14 log points, while the logarithm of earnings among dropouts aged 25–34 fell by .23 points.[6] Similarly, among handlers and service workers, there was a .10 log point drop for those aged 25–64 and a .20 log point drop for those aged 25–34. By contrast, the real earnings of the more skilled—college graduates, and managers and professionals—remained roughly constant over the period, recovering rapidly in the 1980s from a 1973–79 drop.

With earnings of the less skilled falling and those of the more skilled rising during the 1980s, the earnings gap between the groups, which had

4. Our samples exclude agricultural and private household service workers, workers with any self-employment earnings, and workers with a real wage below $1.00 an hour (in 1985 dollars) in any year. In addition, earnings in each year are top-coded on the basis of a consistent real dollar value ($50,000 in 1979 dollars); see Blackburn and Bloom, "Earnings and Income Inequality," for a discussion of top-coding in the CPS. Finally, CPS sample weights are used in all calculations.

We use the personal consumption expenditure deflator in the GNP accounts to translate all earnings figures into constant dollars. Had we used the consumer price index (CPI) as our deflator, our estimates of real wage declines would have been somewhat larger, mainly because the CPI overstated housing price inflation in the late 1970s and early 1980s. Of course, the earnings differentials shown are invariant to our choice of a deflator.

5. The educational grouping of the sample is actually based on completed years of schooling. High school dropouts have less than twelve years; high school graduates have twelve years; and college graduates have at least sixteen years. People may be misclassified if they did not advance one grade with each year of school completed (for example, someone who completed four or more years of college but did not graduate). Also, high school dropouts will include some people who never attended high school.

The three occupational categories we use are defined as follows: handlers and service workers comprise handlers, equipment cleaners, helpers, laborers, service workers (except protective service), and forestry and fishing occupations. Operators comprise machine operators, assemblers, inspectors, and transportation and material moving occupations. Managers and professionals comprise executive, administrative, managerial, and professional specialty occupations.

6. Log points are roughly comparable to percentage differences. Most differentials and changes in differentials are reported in log points in the paper rather than as percentage changes. In the case of earnings differentials, this convention facilitates comparisons with our regression results, since they are based on logarithmic earnings equations.

Figure 1. Changes in Real Earnings of White Male, Full-Time, Year-Round Workers, by Education, Occupation, and Age, 1973–87

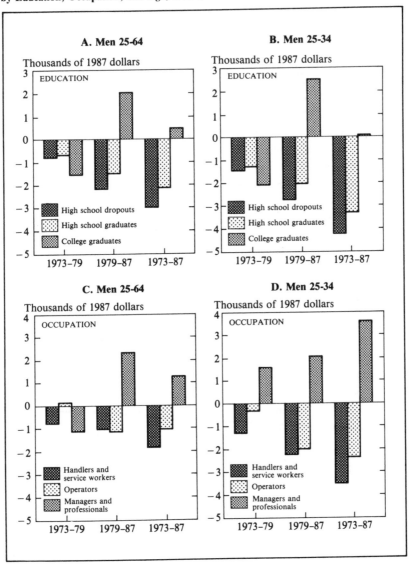

remained fairly stable after the early 1970s, increased dramatically. Table 1 measures the magnitude of this change by the difference in the natural logarithm of the mean incomes of the various groups at different points in time. The gap between the earnings of college graduates and the earnings of high school dropouts increased from a .47 log point difference in 1973 and a .46 log point difference in 1979 to a .63 log point difference in 1987. For workers aged 25–34 the gap grew even more, from .40 log points in 1973 and .37 log points in 1979 to .62 log points in 1987.[7] The earnings gap between men in more and less skilled occupations also grew from 1979 to 1987.

To make certain that the changes in differentials are not due to changes in the composition of the broadly defined groups we study, we also estimated earnings differentials that control for workers' age, region, and marital status.[8] The results of these regressions, which are shown in table 1, confirm the pattern of rising earnings gaps in the 1980s. For those aged 25–64 the changes over time in the differentials are reduced modestly by the introduction of controls, with most of the changes that do occur being due to the inclusion of age controls; the levels and changes in the differentials for those aged 25–34 are scarcely affected by the control variables.

A second useful set of earnings figures is the usual hourly earnings series collected in the May CPS, and in the March CPS in recent years.[9] The hourly earnings data permit us to focus on all workers, not just full-time, year-round workers, without having to adjust for differences in hours and weeks worked to eliminate labor supply effects. The May CPS data also contain information on union membership, which figures prominently in the analyses performed later in the paper. Note, how-

7. Similar findings are reported in several other recent studies. See Murphy and Welch, "Wage Differentials in the 1980's"; John Bound and George Johnson, "Changes in the Structure of Wages during the 1980's: An Evaluation of Alternative Explanations," Working Paper 2983 (Cambridge, Mass.: National Bureau of Economic Research, May 1989); and Lawrence F. Katz and Ana L. Revenga, "Changes in the Structure of Wages: The U.S. versus Japan," Working Paper 3021 (NBER, July 1989). A decline in earnings differentials between educational groups that occurred in the early 1970s is documented in Richard B. Freeman, *The Overeducated American* (Academic Press, 1976).

8. We treat marital status as a possible indicator of labor quality on the assumption that marriage increases the labor market productivity of men; for evidence supporting this assumption, see Sanders Korenman and David Neumark, "Does Marriage Really Make Men More Productive?" unpublished paper, 1988.

9. For salaried workers, usual hourly earnings is calculated as the ratio of usual weekly earnings and usual hours per week.

Table 2. Hourly Earnings Differentials, All White Male Workers, by Age and Skill Class, 1974, 1980, 1988

Log points

Item[a]	Ages 25–64			Ages 25–34		
	1974	1980	1988	1974	1980	1988
Earnings differential						
CG to LTHS	.39	.40	.56	.32	.41	.61
CG to HS	.21	.23	.36	.17	.28	.36
MP to H&S	.53	.52	.59	.46	.38	.54
Earnings differential, regression-corrected						
CG to LTHS	.34	.38	.49	.34	.40	.60
CG to HS	.18	.20	.28	.19	.26	.35
MP to H&S	.51	.50	.57	.45	.36	.54

Source: The usual hourly earnings data were drawn from the May CPS for 1973 and 1980 and from the March CPS for 1988. The regression controls consist of nine age dummies, eight region dummies, two marital status dummies, and a dummy for workers with 13–15 years of schooling completed. Regressions were fit separately for each year.
a. See table 1 for definition of abbreviations.

ever, that the usual hourly earnings data focus on slightly different years and smaller samples than the annual earnings data do.

Table 2 reports the estimated earnings gaps among white males between college graduates and high school dropouts, between college graduates and high school graduates, and between managers and professionals and handlers and service workers in the hourly earnings data. In each case the gap rises in the 1980s; and though there are some differences between tables 1 and 2 in the size of the increase in the gap (for example, the increase in the gap between managers and professionals and handlers and service workers is smaller in the usual hourly earnings data than in the annual earnings data), the overall picture of change is the same in the two tables. Both show that the relative economic position of less skilled workers worsened dramatically in the 1980s.

Other tabulations using the March and May CPS data reveal increases in overall earnings inequality among male workers that correspond closely to the increased skill premiums given in tables 1 and 2. For instance, in the annual earnings data that we use, the standard deviation of the logarithm of earnings among 25–64-year-old male workers increased from 0.44 to 0.50 from 1979 through 1987. Blackburn and Bloom present similar results based on a variety of inequality measures. In addition, Blackburn finds that roughly 20 percent of the increase from

Table 3. Unemployment Rates, Labor Force Participation Rates, and Employment-to-Population Ratios for White Male Workers, by Age and Skill Class, 1974, 1980, 1988

	Ages 25–64			Ages 25–34		
Item[a]	1974	1980	1988	1974	1980	1988
Unemployment rate (percent)						
LTHS	4.4	7.4	9.2	6.2	11.8	12.1
HS	2.7	4.7	5.4	3.6	7.1	6.7
CG	1.4	1.5	1.5	2.1	2.2	2.1
Unemployment rate difference (percentage points)						
CG to LTHS	3.0	5.9	7.7	4.1	9.6	10.0
CG to HS	1.3	3.2	2.9	2.1	4.9	4.6
Unemployment rate difference, regression-corrected (percentage points)						
CG to LTHS	3.5	6.7	7.9	4.5	9.9	10.1
CG to HS	1.5	3.4	3.9	1.6	4.7	4.5
Labor force participation rate (percent)						
LTHS	84	79	76	94	91	88
HS	94	89	89	97	96	95
CG	96	94	94	96	96	96
Employment-to-population ratio (percent)						
LTHS	80	73	69	88	80	77
HS	91	85	84	94	89	89
CG	95	93	93	94	94	94

Source: The figures reported were calculated using March CPS data from 1974, 1980, and 1988. The regression-corrected differentials are derived from estimates of a linear probability model with nine age dummies, eight region dummies, three marital status dummies, and a dummy for workers with 13–15 years of schooling completed.
a. See table 1 for definition of abbreviations.

1979 to 1985 in the variance of log earnings for white males can be attributed to increased returns to schooling.[10]

Although it is apparent that the average wage received by less skilled workers has worsened in the 1980s, it does not necessarily follow that the overall economic position of the less skilled has worsened. In particular, the decline in wages received by the less skilled could have been associated with the increased hiring of these workers; had more men among the less skilled obtained jobs (albeit ones that pay lower wages), the change in the economic welfare of all less skilled men—including both those employed and those not employed—would not be clear. To see whether the decline in earnings has been "traded off" for higher employment, we focus on changes over time in the employment and unemployment status of male workers by skill group.

Table 3 reports unemployment rates, labor force participation rates,

10. Blackburn and Bloom, "Earnings and Income Inequality"; and McKinley L. Blackburn, "What Can Explain the Increase in Earnings Inequality among Males?" *Industrial Relations* (forthcoming).

and employment-to-population ratios for various skill groups, aged 25–64 and 25–34. Between the early 1970s and late 1980s the unemployment rate of less educated men rose relative to that of more educated men. Although the U.S. unemployment rate for all workers was approximately the same in 1988 (5.4 percent) as in 1974 (5.5 percent), the unemployment rates for high school dropouts and for high school graduates roughly *doubled* between 1974 and 1988 for both age groups. In contrast, the unemployment rate for college graduates in both age groups remained essentially unchanged—1.5 percent for those aged 25–64 and 2.1 percent for those aged 25–34. The labor force participation rates in table 3 also exhibit a widening gap between more educated and less educated workers. With both their unemployment and labor force participation rates worsening, the less educated necessarily suffered declining employment-to-population ratios.[11] Moreover, in contrast to the pattern of changes in earnings differentials, the deterioration in employment prospects was more severe during the 1970s than during the 1980s. The unemployment gap between 25–34-year-old college graduates and high school dropouts rose, for example, by 5.5 percentage points during the 1970s compared with a 0.4 percentage point rise during the 1980s.

As a result of the changes shown in tables 1 through 3 and in figure 1, the earnings and chances of holding a job were markedly worse for less skilled men in the late 1980s than they had been in the early 1970s—a remarkable break with the historic pattern of economic improvement for U.S. workers. The conjunction of falling earnings and the declining use of less skilled labor implies that analyses which concentrate on changes in earnings as we do in this paper understate the economic problems now faced by less skilled men.

In the remainder of the paper we focus primarily on educational differentials, for two reasons: one, the occupational codes cannot be matched precisely before and after the January 1983 CPS; and two, estimates of earnings equations that control for both education and occupation indicate that the phenomenon of widening skill differentials is primarily associated with education.

---

11. The employment-to-population ratio can be expressed as the labor force participation rate times one minus the unemployment rate; if the labor force participation rate falls and the unemployment rate increases, the employment-to-population ratio will by definition decrease.

Assessing Causes: Shifts in Demand and Supply

As a framework for analyzing how demand and supply shifts have affected the relative earnings of the less skilled, we apply a simple partial-equilibrium model of the labor market. Let η_s (≥ 0) be the elasticity of labor supply and η_d (<0) be the elasticity of labor demand, and let L_d and L_s measure the location of the loglinear labor demand and labor supply curves (that is, their x-intercepts, on a logarithmic scale). Using an asterisk to denote the time derivative of the natural logarithm of a variable (that is, to transform the variables into instantaneous rates of change), this model has the following reduced-form expression for wage changes:

$$(1) \qquad W^* = \frac{1}{(\eta_s - \eta_d)} (L_d^* - L_s^*).$$

According to this expression, the rate of wage change for a particular skill group is proportional to the difference between the rates at which the labor demand and the labor supply curves are shifting for workers in that group, with the factor of proportionality equal to the inverse of the difference in the supply and demand elasticities.

An equation for the rate of change in the relative wage ratio for workers from two different skill groups can be derived if we assume a constant elasticity of substitution production technology.[12] In doing so, we assume that the relative supply of workers from the two skill groups is predetermined in the short run (that is $\eta_s = 0$), which would be the case if a lengthy period is required for increasing one's training or education. The rate of change in the relative wage ratio is given by

$$(2) \qquad RW^* = (-1/\sigma)RS^* + RD^*,$$

where RW is the logarithm of the ratio of the wage received by the two skill groups, RS is the logarithm of the ratio of the numbers of workers in the two skill groups, RD is an index of relative demand changes, and

---

12. It is difficult to derive a relative wage equation from equation 1 directly without making a number of strong assumptions (including the fact that equation 1 already assumes that labor demand for each skill group is independent of the other group's wage).

$\sigma \geq 0$ is the "aggregate" elasticity of substitution between the two groups.[13]

Equation 2 provides a framework for evaluating labor demand and supply forces that cause the rate of change of earnings differentials to differ between two periods of time as well as factors that influence the rate of change of earnings differentials in a single time period. Consider, for example, the question why the relative wages of the less skilled declined in the 1980s after being reasonably stable during the middle and late 1970s. If the factor of proportionality in equation 2 is stable over time, the difference between the rates of change in earnings differentials across the two time periods must be due to differential shifts in relative demand and relative supply:

(3) $\Delta RW^* = (-1/\sigma)\Delta RS^* + \Delta RD^*,$

where Δ refers to the change across time periods. This equation relates the *acceleration* or *deceleration* of relative wage growth to the acceleration or deceleration of relative shifts in labor demand and labor supply. It is especially useful for analyzing changes when there are important unmeasured factors that shift relative demand or relative supply at a roughly similar pace in the two different time periods. That is because the differencing will eliminate the effect of such unmeasured factors on relative earnings.[14]

Given the framework of equations 1 through 3, what can we say

13. The "aggregate" elasticity of substitution reflects the effect of wage changes on relative employment, holding constant shifts in demand for the two groups. In the case where there is a single output and each skill group is paid its marginal product, the elasticity of substitution can be written:

$$\sigma = d\ln(L_2/L_1)/d\ln(w_1/w_2);$$

cross-multiplying and integrating both sides provides the following:

$$\ln(w_1 w_2) = \frac{-1}{\sigma}[\ln(L_1/L_2) - C_2] - C_1.$$

Since supply is assumed to be perfectly inelastic, $RS = \ln(L_1/L_2)$; the constants of integration, C_1 and C_2, reflect changes in the relative efficiency of the two kinds of labor. In equation 2, $RD = C_2/\sigma - C_1$.

14. It is important to recognize that equation 3 entails comparisons of the rate of change of earnings differentials in two different periods, like the 1980s relative to the 1970s, and not the analysis of changing earnings differentials in a single period, like the 1980s.

about the factors that have shifted demand and supply for workers with different levels of skill and thus altered their relative earnings?

Demand-Side Shifts

We begin by considering three factors that arguably have shifted relative labor demand in the 1980s: normal cyclical shifts in demand; changes in the mix of employment by industry; and technological changes.

The Business Cycle

Because skill differentials historically widen in recessions, shifts in labor demand associated with normal business cycle fluctuations can plausibly explain the declining relative economic position of less skilled male workers from 1979 to 1983. They cannot, however, explain the decline that occurred after 1983. If the business cycle was the main reason for the decline, the relative position of the less skilled should have improved substantially during the economic recovery of the middle and late 1980s. As is evident from figure 2, it did not.[15] Moreover, the calculations in tables 1 through 3 cover years that represent roughly similar stages of the cycle, and they show a significant deterioration in the earnings and employment of the less skilled. Forces other than the business cycle were evidently at work in reducing the relative earnings and employment of these workers.

The Effect of Industrial Shifts

Many observers attribute the declining fortunes of less skilled men to changes in the industrial composition of employment, in particular to the shift of jobs from manufacturing industries that tend to be high-wage sectors for the less skilled to lower-wage service industries. We use two related techniques to estimate the effect of industrial shifts on the growing earnings gap. The first technique is a shift-share decomposition of changes in earnings differentials, with the changes divided

15. Figure 2 contains a time series of logarithmic earnings differentials between more educated and less educated men, both among those aged 25–64 and among those aged 25–34. The numbers are taken from various issues of the Current Population Reports P-60 series; a more complete discussion of these data is presented in the section of the paper concerned with supply-side shifts.

Figure 2. Ratios of Mean Earnings of White Male Full-Time, Year-Round Workers, Aged 25–34 and 25–64, 1967–87

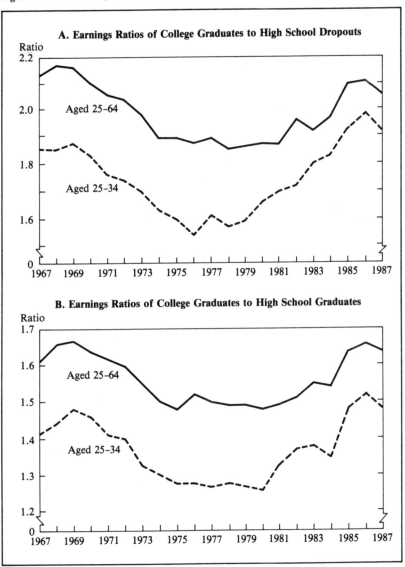

A. Earnings Ratios of College Graduates to High School Dropouts

B. Earnings Ratios of College Graduates to High School Graduates

Source: See note 15.

into the following three components: the effect of changes in the allocation of labor in different skill groups across forty-three two-digit industries, the effect of within-industry changes in wages for workers in each skill group, and the interaction of the two changes.[16]

The first component measures the effect on the average earnings of a skill group of shifts in the distribution across industries of that group's workers. Shifts toward higher-wage industries raise earnings and shifts toward lower-wage industries reduce earnings. The shifts themselves can result from changes in the overall distribution of employment across industries or from changes in each skill group's share of employment within industries. For instance, the proportion of less skilled workers in high-wage manufacturing jobs can fall because of a general decline in manufacturing employment or because technological change induces manufacturing firms to demand relatively fewer less skilled workers.[17] In our decomposition both effects show up as an industry shift, although only the former is due to the aggregate shift in employment among industries.

The second component measures changes in relative wages that occur within industries, and we thus exclude it from our industry shift explanation of the growing wage gap. Excluding all within-sector changes in wages should lead to a downward bias in our estimation of the "true" effect of industrial shifts on skill differentials if, as seems reasonable given the time periods we analyze, industrial shifts produce changes in skill differentials that are transmitted across all industries.[18] The interaction component in our decomposition measures the extent to which changes in industry employment tend to be correlated with changes in earnings within industries for each skill group. We do not include it as part of our industry shift explanation of changes in earnings.

Table 4 reports the results of decomposing the changes in earnings differentials during 1979–87 into the three components. The decom-

16. The decomposition follows from the fact that the average log wage for workers in a particular skill group is a weighted average of the average log wages received by workers in that skill group within different industries, with industry employment shares for the skill group providing the weights.

17. Assuming that all workers in a given skill group are employed, a general employment decline in an industry in which that group is concentrated will increase the share of those workers employed in other industries. Thus changes in the skill distribution within industries are not independent of overall changes in industry employment, motivating our focus on the industry employment shares of different skill groups.

18. A rough calculation suggests that this particular spillover is likely to be small, since the growing industries were only slightly more skill intensive than the industries that declined in relative size.

**Table 4. Shift-Share Decompositions of Changes in Earnings Differentials,
White Male Workers, 1979–87**
Log points

| | | Portion due to | | |
| | Change in earnings differential | Changes in industrial allocation of labor | Changes in earnings within industry | Interaction effect |
Workers[a]				
Ages 25–64				
CG to LTHS	.17	.03	.12	.02
CG to HS	.12	.02	.09	.01
Ages 25–34				
CG to LTHS	.25	.03	.20	.02
CG to HS	.18	.05	.12	.01

Source: These calculations are based on data contained in the March CPS for 1980 and 1988. The decomposition uses a forty-three–industry classification of the labor force; the base year is 1979.
a. See table 1 for definition of abbreviations.

positions are performed separately for white males aged 25–64 and for those aged 25–34. The first column reports the actual changes in earnings differentials for the groups (taken from table 1 and measured in log points). The second through fourth columns apportion those changes among the different components. The calculations show that the widening of the earnings gap for the work force as a whole was associated largely with growing gaps *within* industries. For example, about 70 to 80 percent of the increase in the earnings gap between college graduates and high school dropouts from 1979 through 1987 occurred within industries. Still, the contribution of changes in the allocation of labor across industries is far from negligible, accounting for .02 to .05 log points of the changes. This reallocation of labor has affected relative earnings in part because employment for all skill groups has shrunk in the industries in which the less skilled are relatively well paid, but more important because the shrinkage in employment in high-wage industries has involved a disproportionately large share of less skilled jobs.[19] Finally, an additional .01 to .02 log point increase results from the interaction effect—the tendency for less skilled workers to shift dispropor-

19. Taking the decomposition one step further, one can measure the extent to which the observed changes in the distribution of wages across industries are associated with changes in overall industry employment as opposed to changes in the skill distribution within industries. Such a decomposition shows that our measured industry effects are largely due to less skilled workers becoming more concentrated in industries that pay low wages to less skilled workers. This result implies that the changes in earnings differentials attributed to overall shifts in industry employment (and not changes in the skill composition of employment within industries) might be too high.

tionately into industries in which the relative wages of less skilled workers have been falling over time.

Our second technique for assessing the effect of industrial shifts on the growing earnings gap uses a logarithmic earnings regression model. Here we estimate earnings equations in which we pool all the men in our CPS samples for 1979 and 1987. Explanatory factors in the regression include the level of education, age, region, marital status (all of which were used in our table 1 regression-corrected estimates of earnings differentials), and in some specifications dummy variables for the industry of the worker. We allow all the variables except for the industry dummy variables to have separate coefficients for the two years. Formally, let w_i be the log of the wage for worker i; I_i a vector of forty-two industry dummy variables that are equal to one if the person works in the particular industry and zero otherwise; E_i a vector of three dummy variables for education group; X_i a vector of additional explanatory factors; and D_i a dummy variable equal to one if the observation appears in the 1987 sample. The equation we estimate is

$$(4) \quad w_i = b_0 + b_1 I_i + b_2 E_i + b_3(D_i E_i) + b_4 X_i + b_5(D_i X_i) + e_i,$$

where b_0 through b_5 are vectors of coefficients to be estimated, and e_i is an error term. The coefficients b_3 for the interaction of the year dummy variable and the education dummy variables will reflect changes from 1979 to 1987 in the wages premiums associated with different levels of education. These estimated coefficients can also be used to measure changes in earnings differentials over these years; for example, the change in the college graduate–high school graduate differential is the element of b_3 associated with the college graduate group minus the element of b_3 associated with the high school graduate group.

Comparing these estimated differentials across specifications without, and then with, the industry dummy variables allows us to assess the impact of changing industry employment on educational differentials. Insofar as the relative earnings decline of the less educated results from their employment becoming relatively more concentrated in industries that pay low wages to workers in all educational groups, the change over time in earnings differentials in a regression that includes industry dummy variables should be smaller than the change in the (regression-corrected) differentials in table 1. We restrict the industry coefficients to be equal in the two years so as to limit the measured industry impact to changes in industry employment, and thereby to exclude changes

Table 5. Effect of Including Industry Controls on Regression-Corrected Earnings Differentials, White Male Workers, 1979–87
Log points

| Workers[a] | Change in differential from regressions | | Change due to industry controls |
	Without industry controls	With industry controls	
Ages 25–64			
CG to LTHS	.13	.10	.03
CG to HS	.10	.07	.03
Ages 25–34			
CG to LTHS	.23	.19	.04
CG to HS	.17	.13	.04

Source: These calculations were performed using data contained in the March CPS for 1980 and 1988. The regressions restrict the coefficients for the industry dummy variables to be the same in the two years, but allow the coefficients on all other variables to vary across years. For the other controls, see note c to table 1.
   a. See table 1 for definition of abbreviations.

over time in average industry wages from being part of the industry effect.

The regression method of taking account of industry differs from the decomposition analysis of table 4. It controls for the influence on earnings of age, region, and marital status, which we did not hold constant in the decompositions. On the other hand, it imposes similar industry effects on each educational group, whereas the decomposition analysis allowed for separate industry effects for each group. This difference could be consequential, since it implies that the regression method does not capture the effects of industrial shifts that operate through cross-industry differences in education-related wage differentials.

Table 5 summarizes the results of our analysis. The first column reports the 1979–87 regression-corrected changes in earnings differentials, as seen in table 1. The second column reports the change in earnings differentials when dummies for forty-two industries are included in the regressions, as in equation 4. The differences between the numbers in the first and second columns reflect the effect of industrial shifts in employment on educational earnings differentials. These estimates are similar to those from the table 4 decompositions, suggesting that .03 to .04 log points of the growth in the relevant earnings gaps is associated with changes in the industrial composition of employment for workers with different levels of schooling. They indicate that the differential change in the industrial composition of employment between less skilled and more skilled men can account for 23–30 percent of the change in earnings differentials for men aged 25–64, and 17–24 percent of the change in earnings differentials for men aged 25–34.

The Effect of Technological Change

A third potential demand-side influence on skill differentials is the speed of technological change, which has been hypothesized to increase the relative demand for more educated workers. This hypothesis is premised on the notion that education enhances a worker's ability to adapt to a changing work environment.[20] Studies that explore the link between technological change and the return to education find that industries with rapid technological progress tend to exhibit relatively wide earnings gaps between educational groups.[21] If the 1980s were a period of rapid technological improvement relative to earlier periods, that could potentially be an important determinant of the changed pattern for earnings differentials evident in the 1980s.

Multifactor productivity statistics from the Bureau of Labor Statistics show that productivity growth was greater from 1979 to 1987 (0.6 percent a year) than from 1973 through 1979 (0.1 percent), implying some potential shift in demand toward the more educated during the 1980s compared with the 1970s. However, the rate of productivity growth in the 1980s was smaller than in earlier postwar decades and too slight to have a substantive effect on relative earnings.[22] Changes in the nature

20. Richard R. Nelson and Edmund S. Phelps, "Investment in Humans, Technological Diffusion, and Economic Growth," *American Economic Review*, vol. 56 (May 1966, *Papers and Proceedings, 1965*), pp. 69–75; Finis Welch, "Education in Production," *Journal of Political Economy*, vol. 78 (January–February 1970), pp. 35–59; Theodore W. Schultz, "The Value of the Ability to Deal with Disequilibria," *Journal of Economic Literature*, vol. 13 (September 1975), pp. 827–46; and Zvi Griliches, "Capital-Skill Complementarity," *Review of Economics and Statistics*, vol. 51 (November 1969), pp. 465–68.

21. Lee A. Lillard and Hong W. Tan, "Private Sector Training: Who Gets It and What Are Its Effects?" R-3331-DOL/RC (Santa Monica, Calif.: Rand Corp., March 1986); Ann P. Bartel and Frank R. Lichtenberg, "Technical Change, Learning, and Wages," Working Paper 2732 (NBER, October 1988); Indermit Gill, "Technological Change, Education, and Obsolescence of Human Capital," paper presented at the 1988 NBER Summer Labor Institute, 1988; Jacob Mincer and Yoshio Higuchi, "Wage Structures and Labor Turnover in the United States and Japan," *Journal of the Japanese and International Economies*, vol. 2 (June 1988), pp. 97–113; and Jacob Mincer, "Labor Market Effects of Human Capital and of Its Adjustment to Technological Change," working paper of the Institute on Education and the Economy, Teachers College, Columbia University, February 1989.

22. We assessed the contribution of technological change to the widening of educational wage differentials in the 1980s by simulating the effects of technological change using regression results obtained by Lillard and Tan, "Private Sector Training." The Lillard-Tan results indicate that the return to schooling in a given industry depends positively on multifactor productivity growth in that industry. Calculations using Lillard and Tan's CPS-based estimates show that the contribution of productivity growth to the widening of the earnings gap between male college graduates and high school dropouts and between college

of technology might have twisted the relative demand for labor toward more skilled workers, but we do not have good measures of these possible changes.

In sum, our demand-side analyses find that measured changes in labor demand associated with shifts in the industrial composition of employment of workers with different skills explain a nonnegligible fraction of the growth in the earnings gap. But these changes are not as dominant a factor as many believe, and there is little evidence that several other measured changes in demand have had a substantial impact on the rising gap.

Supply-Side Shifts

We now consider the extent to which shifts in labor supplies contributed to the decline in the earnings of less skilled male workers, focusing on the importance of changes in the relative number of less skilled to more skilled male workers, changes in the relative quality of less skilled men due to the quality of their schooling, and changes in the supply of other workers who might be relatively close substitutes for the less skilled.

Changes in the Relative Supply of Less Skilled Workers

Table 6 records the ratios of the number of college graduates to high school dropouts and of college graduates to high school graduates in 1973, 1979, and 1987; the average annual changes in the log of those ratios in 1973–79 and in 1979–87; and the difference in the annual changes in the two periods. For men aged 25–64, the table shows that

---

graduates and high school graduates was relatively modest—0.4 and 0.2 percentage points, respectively. A similar calculation using Lillard and Tan's National Longitudinal Survey–based estimates suggests that the rising trend in productivity growth explains a 0.6 percentage point widening in both differentials. Averaging these estimates, we attribute .005 points of the 1980s increase in the differential between college and high school graduates and .004 points of the increase in the differential between college graduates and high school dropouts to technological advance. We note that these estimates should be considered lower-bound estimates, since more rapid technological change within an industry should have spillover effects for other industries resulting from an increase in the aggregate demand for skilled labor (and thereby an increase in the price that must be paid for skilled labor in all industries, and not just in the industry in which technological change is occurring).

Table 6.   Ratios of White Male College Graduates to High School Dropouts and High School Graduates and Implied Changes in Relative Earnings, 1973, 1979, 1987[a]
Log points except for ratios

	Ages 25–64		Ages 25–34	
Item	CG/LTHS	CG/HS	CG/LTHS	CG/HS
Ratios				
1973	0.82	0.56	1.69	0.66
1979	1.46	0.76	3.00	0.90
1987	2.39	0.87	2.75	0.76
Annual rate of change in ratios				
1973–1979	.10	.05	.10	.05
1979–1987	.06	.02	−.01	−.02
Difference in annual rates of changes	−.04	−.03	−.11	−.07
OLS estimates of $1/\sigma$[b]	−.08	−.25	−.26	−.22
Effect of changes in relative labor supply on 1979–87 change in differentials	−.04	−.04	.02	.04
Effect of changes in annual growth of relative labor supply on change in differentials, 1979–87 versus 1973–79[c]	.02	.07	.22	.13

Source: Raw data from the March 1974, 1980, 1988 CPS.
a. The figures in this table refer to full-time year-round workers.
b. From table 7.
c. Calculated by multiplying the estimated difference in annual growth rates by the OLS estimate of $1/\sigma$ by 8, so that the figures relate to an eight-year change.

the supply of college graduates increased relative to that of high school dropouts and graduates in both periods, though at a rate that was lower in the 1980s than in the 1970s. In 1973 the ratio of college graduates to high school dropouts was 0.82; in 1979 it was 1.46, and in 1987 it was 2.39. The annual rate of increase dropped from .10 log points a year in the 1973–79 period to .06 points a year in the 1979–87 period. The increase in the relative number of the more educated in the 1980s implies that labor supply shifts alone cannot account for the 1980s rise in the earnings gap. However, the decelerating rate of growth of relative supply between the 1970s and 1980s can help to explain why relative earnings fell in the 1980s while remaining roughly stable in the 1970s, an idea we develop further below.

During 1973–79 the pattern of relative supply growth for men aged 25–34 was almost identical to that of the full sample of men. But, as Katz and Revenga have pointed out, among 25–34-year-olds in the 1980s the number of male college graduates actually fell relative to the number of high school dropouts and graduates.[23] This decline was the result of

23. Katz and Revenga, "Changes in the Structure of Wages," p. 4.

enrollment decisions made in the 1970s which were probably affected by the falling return to college education in the early years of that decade. For 25–34-year-old men, changes in supply can help explain the rise in the earnings gap in the 1980s as well as the change in the rate of increase in the gap from the 1970s to the 1980s.

One way to assess the quantitative impact of changing relative supplies on changing relative earnings is to perform time-series regressions of the log of relative earnings on the log of relative labor supply and measures of shifts in relative labor demand. Estimated coefficients on the relative supply variable can be used, in conjunction with the observed changes in relative supply, to calculate how much of the change in relative wages is attributable to shifts in relative labor supplies. Freeman used equations of this form to explain the falling relative earnings of college graduates in the early and mid-1970s.[24] Katz and Revenga use such equations to explore the rising relative earnings of college graduates in the 1980s. We estimate such models for 25–64-year-olds and 25–34-year-olds using time-series data for all full-time male workers (white and nonwhite) from 1967 through 1987.[25] We model relative labor demand as a function of time (quadratic), the logarithm of real GNP (to control for the business cycle), and the ratio of net exports to GNP (to allow trade factors to affect the relative demand for skilled and less skilled labor).[26]

24. Richard B. Freeman, "The Effect of the Increased Relative Supply of College Graduates on Skill Differences and Employment Opportunities," in Zvi Griliches and others, eds., *Income Distribution and Economic Inequality* (Frankfurt: Halsted Press, 1978), pp. 240–55.
25. Both nonwhite and white males are included in these calculations because our data come from the Current Population Reports P-60 series, in which separate figures for whites and nonwhites are not presented before 1975. Also, the numbers refer to the logarithm of the ratio of the arithmetic means, and not the ratio of the geometric means, for any two education groups. In both of these ways, these numbers differ from those reported in table 1.
Two corrections were necessary in constructing the time series of differentials. First, numbers for income (and not earnings) were available before 1975, while both were available afterward; an adjustment for this difference was made to the pre-1975 numbers so that they correspond to earnings rather than income. Second, the income imputation procedure was changed in 1975, with the result that education was included as one of the characteristics used in imputing income. This served to raise artificially the earnings differentials in 1975 (relative to those that would have been found if the old imputation procedure had been used); therefore, another adjustment was made to the pre-1975 numbers so that they are comparable to numbers that would be reported if the new imputation procedure had been used. Both these corrections are rough, but should serve to reduce biases in the original series. Details of the corrections are available upon request.
26. We also fit our equations using various measures of technological change as ad-

Table 7. Least-Squares Estimates of Supply and Demand Effects on Relative Wages, All Male Full-Time Workers, 1967–87[a]

	Ages 25–64[b]		Ages 25–34[b]	
Independent variable	CG/LTHS	CG/HS	CG/LTHS	CG/HS
Intercept	1.01	0.60	1.20	0.68
	(0.17)	(0.13)	(0.22)	(0.21)
Log relative supply	−0.08	−0.25	−0.26	−0.22
	(0.14)	(0.12)	(0.09)	(0.09)
Trend	−0.010	0.004	0.032	0.013
	(0.022)	(0.010)	(0.024)	(0.014)
Trend squared	0.0010	0.0006	0.0004	0.0004
	(0.0002)	(0.0002)	(0.0005)	(0.0004)
Log real GNP	−0.35	−0.38	−0.83	−0.61
	(0.28)	(0.20)	(0.31)	(0.26)
Ratio of net exports to GNP	−0.010	−0.011	0.001	−0.010
	(0.005)	(0.004)	(0.007)	(0.006)
R^2	0.90	0.91	0.91	0.88

a. The dependent variable is the log of relative earnings. Numbers in parentheses are standard errors.
b. See table 1 for definition of abbreviations.

Table 7 reports our estimates of these time-series models. The regressions show a negative association between earnings differentials and relative labor supply for all age and skill groups. The negative associations are substantial and statistically significant for three of the four groups (the exception is for the differential between college graduate and high school dropouts aged 25–64). Other studies using different specifications and data, or analyzing different time periods, report similar inverse relations between relative supplies and relative earnings.[27] Nevertheless, with limited variation in a short time series, the estimated elasticities are sensitive to the variables chosen to measure demand shifts, and to the particular years covered in the sample.[28] They provide, at best, "orders of magnitudes" of the relevant response parameters.

---

ditional regressors (in particular, the BLS multifactor productivity series, and the ratio of R&D expenditures to GNP). However, the estimated coefficients for these variables were often insignificant and were not stable across age and educational groups. Thus we have found no convincing evidence that technological change accounts for widened earnings differentials in the 1980s.

27. Freeman, *Overeducated American*; Freeman, "Effect of the Increased Relative Supply of College Graduates"; and Katz and Revenga, "Changes in the Structure of Wages."

28. A more appropriate economic model would include the supply or prices of other kinds of labor, capital, and raw materials, using a consistent cost function framework. Estimation of such a model is beyond the scope of this study.

To see what the estimates imply for the potential impact of relative labor supply shifts on relative earnings in the period under study, we multiply the parameter estimates by the measured change in relative supplies from 1979 to 1987. We report these figures in the line labeled "Effect of changes in relative labor supply on 1979–87 change in differentials" in table 6. For workers aged 25–64, among whom the relative supply of the more educated increased during 1979–87, the estimated parameters imply that supply-side factors *reduced* the earnings of college graduates relative to those of high school dropouts, and relative to those of high school graduates, by .04 log points. Far from helping explain the 1980s fall in the relative earnings of the less skilled, the changes in supply make an explanation more difficult, since they raise the amount of change to be explained by shifts in relative labor demand, or in wage-setting institutions, compared with the changes shown in table 1.

For men aged 25–34, by contrast, the parameter estimates suggest that the decline in the relative supply of college graduates during 1979–87 can account for .02 to .04 log points of the 1979–87 increase in earnings differentials.

These calculations are based on the assumption that there were no shifts in relative demand in the 1980s (that is, if RD^* from equation 2 was zero). This is a sensible counterfactual for assessing the effect of relative supply changes on changes in earnings differentials. But it is not the only interesting counterfactual to use as a reference case. Another involves assuming that the rate at which demand was increasing the relative wage ratio was the same in the 1980s as in the 1970s (namely, that $\Delta RD^* = 0$ in equation 3). The impact of supply changes on earnings differentials would then depend on the change in the growth rate of relative labor supply across the two time periods (that is, its acceleration or deceleration).

The Deceleration of Relative Supply Growth between the 1970s and 1980s

To what extent can the *slowing growth* of the relative supply of more educated workers shown in table 6 account for the rising wage gap in the 1980s compared with the 1970s? To answer this question, we multiplied our ordinary-least-squares estimates of the labor-supply coefficients by the *difference* between the growth rate in relative labor supplies from 1979 to 1987 and the growth rate in relative labor supplies from

1973 to 1979.[29] These estimates are given in the line in table 6 labeled "Effect of changes in annual growth of relative labor supply on change in differentials, 1979–87 versus 1973–79." For 25–64-year-old men this calculation suggests that deceleration in the growth of the relative supply of the more educated contributed .02 to .07 log points to the increase in the growth of wage differentials between the periods. For 25–34-year-olds the calculation suggests that the enormous deceleration in the growth of the relative supply of the more educated accounts for .22 log points of the increased growth in the wage gap between college graduates and high school dropouts and .13 log points of the increased growth in the wage gap between college and high school graduates. By these calculations the changed growth of relative labor supplies represents a major difference in the labor market for more and less educated 25–34-year-old men between the two periods, implying that the increased differential between college graduates and high school dropouts among men aged 25–34 was largely supply driven.

Since our estimates of the impact of deceleration on the growth of relative supply of the more educated fall short of fully explaining the changed growth of three of the four earnings differentials (the exception is the differential between college graduates and high school dropouts among 25–34-year-old men), it is natural to infer that shifts in relative demand toward more skilled workers accelerated in the 1980s. Indeed, a combination of the decelerating growth of relative labor supply and the accelerating growth of relative labor demand offers the most plausible economic interpretation of the increase in earnings differentials for all our age and education groups.

Changes in Labor Quality

Another potential supply-side factor that could have reduced the relative earnings of less skilled American men is a decrease in their relative quality or ability, associated, say, with falls in standardized test scores over time.

To examine the possible impact of changes in labor quality on relative earnings, we calculated earnings differentials between college graduates and high school dropouts for specific age cohorts in 1973, 1979, and

29. These are eight-year growth rates. Because the number of years in the two intervals 1973–79 and 1979–87 differs, we transform the 1973–79 changes to an eight-year basis for ease of comparison by multiplying them by 1.33 (8 years/6 years).

Table 8. Relative Earnings Differentials between White Male College Graduates and High School Dropouts, by Age Cohort, 1973, 1979, 1987
Differentials in log points

Cohort age in			Relative earnings differential for specified cohort in		
1973	1979	1987	1973	1979	1987
11–18	17–24	25–32	. . .	. . .	.62
19–24	25–30	33–38	. . .	.34	.68
25–30	31–36	39–44	.36	.45	.73
31–36	37–42	45–50	.48	.63	.59
37–42	43–48	51–56	.58	.55	.63
43–48	49–54	57–62	.55	.53	.69
49–54	55–60	63–68	.54	.62	.66
55–60	61–66	69–74	.56	.62	. . .
61–64	67–70	75–78	.47	. . .	. . .

Source: The earnings differentials are based on data from the 1974, 1980, 1988 March CPS. The numbers refer to full-time year-round workers.

1987. Table 8 reports these differentials. This table allows us to compare changes in wage gaps within cohorts over time as well as changes over time in wage gaps for workers within given age groups.

Reading the table horizontally, we see how differentials changed for a given cohort as it aged. For example, the numbers in the third line of the table show that college graduates aged 25–30 in 1973 had a .36 log point advantage over high school graduates in that year, a .45 log point differential six years later when the cohort was 31–36, and a .73 point differential in 1987 when the cohort was 39–44.

If the rise in the wage gap between college graduates and high school dropouts was due entirely to a deterioration in the quality of primary and secondary schooling (with no change in the quality of higher education), what would one expect to find in table 8? To begin, one would expect to find that the wage gap is higher (in both 1979 and 1987) for the two youngest age cohorts, since they attended high school after the late 1960s, when the educational achievement of high school students began to fall.[30] In addition, one would expect to see no greater change in the wage gap, for each individual cohort, in the 1980s than would be expected to occur on the basis of increasing age alone.

The numbers in the table do not generally accord with these expec-

30. John H. Bishop, "Is the Test Score Decline Responsible for the Productivity Growth Decline?" *American Economic Review*, vol. 79 (March 1989), pp. 178–97.

tations. First, the differentials for the cohorts that completed their schooling after the late 1960s are not uniformly higher than the differentials for the older cohorts when they were at similar ages. The wage gap for 25–30-year-olds in 1979 was .34 log points, which is very close in magnitude to the .36 log point wage gap for 25–30-year-olds in 1973. In contrast, the 1987 wage gaps among the 25–32- and 33–38-year-olds are larger in size than the 1973 and 1979 wage gaps among comparable age groups. However, any support this latter observation might contribute to the declining quality hypothesis is confounded by the fact that changes in the relative supply of more educated young workers appear to have also led to increased wage gaps for these age groups. Second, the wage gaps tended to increase more in the 1980s for individual cohorts than would be expected on the basis of increases in age alone (judged by comparing the 1979–87 change in each wage gap to the 1973–79 change for similarly aged cohorts, data permitting).[31] Both these findings are inconsistent with the view that declining school quality can account for the entire widening of earnings differentials.

Changes in Other Sources of Labor Supply

To what extent might changes in the relative supply of less skilled women or of men below age 25 (both of whom are likely to be good substitutes for less skilled adult males) have adversely affected the relative wages of less skilled men in the 1980s? To answer this question, we estimated two time-series cross-sectional regression equations linking the relative earnings of male workers in forty-three two-digit industries in 1973, 1979, 1985, and 1987 to the shares of women and younger men in those industries. In the first regression equation, our dependent variable, E_{it}, is the (regression-corrected) estimated annual logarithmic earnings differential (for full-time year-round males) between college graduates and high school dropouts in industry i in year t. In the second regression equation, our dependent variable, R_{it}, is the effect of an additional year of schooling on earnings in industry i in year t, obtained

31. To illustrate, from 1979 to 1987 the wage gap for 43–48-year-olds (in 1979) increased by .08 log points (from .55 to .63). In contrast, the wage gap for 43–48-year-olds actually declined by .02 log points (from .55 to .53) from 1973 to 1979. This is the sense in which we view the 1979–87 increase in the wage gap as being larger than would be expected on the basis of normal age effects.

from estimating a standard log earnings equation separately for each industry in each of the four years. Our regression equations are

$$(5a) \qquad E_{it} = c_0 + c_1 X_{it} + c_2 T + \epsilon_{1it}$$

$$(5b) \qquad R_{it} = d_0 + d_i X_{it} + d_2 T + \epsilon_{2it},$$

where X_{it} is a vector that includes the following industry characteristics: the percentage of the industry's work force comprised of women in various educational classes; the percentage of the work force comprised of men less than 25 years old; and the industry's unionization rate (obtained from the May CPS data for 1973 and 1980, and the March CPS for 1985 and 1987). T is a vector of year dummies.

The parameter estimates—reported in table 9—indicate that earnings differentials tend to be narrower in industries that have large shares of skilled women and wider in industries that have large shares of less

Table 9. Least-Squares Estimates of the Effect of Industry Characteristics on Relative Earnings

	Dependent variable	
Independent variable[a]	Earnings differential (CG to LTHS)[b]	Return to schooling
Men under 25	0.034	−0.016
	(0.161)	(0.016)
Women		
High school dropout	0.165	0.018
	(0.128)	(0.014)
High school graduate	0.228	0.019
	(0.170)	(0.022)
Some college	0.053	−0.003
	(0.214)	(0.026)
College graduate	−0.161	−0.020
	(0.200)	(0.021)
Unionized	−0.298	−0.044
	(0.097)	(0.010)
R^2	0.357	0.402

Source: The dependent variable refers to a particular industry (forty-three in total) in a particular year (1973, 1979, 1985, and 1987). All variables were calculated using the relevant March CPS, with the exception of the union variable in 1973 and 1979, which was calculated using the relevant May CPS. Year dummies were also included as regressors. Numbers in parentheses are standard errors.
a. Measured as percentage of industry work force.
b. See table 1 for definition of abbreviations.

skilled women. But the imprecision of these estimates clouds their use-fulness in accounting for cross-industry variations in skill differentials.[32] The potential usefulness of these results in explaining widening earnings gaps is further limited by the small changes in the skill distribution of working women during the 1980s; in fact, some simple calculations sug-gest that changes in other sources of labor supply had a (very small) negative effect on male wage differentials in the 1980s (since educational attainment among women in the labor force continued to increase in the 1980s). The only variable that appears to help explain the growing earnings gap is union density, which is estimated to have a sizable neg-ative effect on both earnings differentials and the return to schooling. This finding is consistent with other studies showing that unions reduce wage differences between white- and blue-collar labor.[33] Given the large 1979–87 drop in union density, these results suggest that deunionization may be a significant factor in the worsening position of the less skilled, a point explored in the next section.[34]

Changes in Wage-Setting Institutions

The declining importance of two wage-setting institutions that have historically raised the earnings of less skilled workers may have con-tributed to the 1980s rise in the wage gap. The minimum wage is a prime candidate for explaining some of the growing gap because it decreased 23 percent in real terms from 1980 through 1988, lowering the legal barrier to paying low wages. Unionization is a prime candidate for

32. Since the equations in table 9 are based on dependent variables that we estimated and that do not have constant variance, we report "white standard errors" below the coefficient estimates (that is, standard errors that are asymptotically robust to hetero-skedasticity).

33. Richard B. Freeman, "Unionism and the Dispersion of Wages," *Industrial and Labor Relations Review*, vol. 34 (October 1980), pp. 3–23.

34. In specifications for X_{it} not reported in table 9, we included the rate of growth of total factor productivity and the ratio of net imports to domestic shipments as independent variables. The former variable was included as a measure of technological change, while the latter was included to capture any effects associated with increased foreign trade. The coefficients on both variables were small in magnitude and statistically insignificant. These results are perhaps not that surprising, since the rate of productivity growth is an error-ridden measure of technological change, and since Freeman and Katz have shown that increases in net imports have tended to reduce the wages of all workers in industries in which the less skilled are concentrated. See Richard B. Freeman and Lawrence F. Katz, "Industrial Wage and Employment Determination in an Open Economy," paper pre-sented at NBER Conference on Immigration, Trade, and the Labor Market, September 1987.

explaining some of the growing gap because the proportion of workers that are unionized fell sharply in the 1980s—especially among the less skilled, for whom unions have traditionally won the most substantial wage gains.

The Fall in the Minimum Wage

To assess the effect of the decline in the real minimum wage on the wages of the less skilled, we compare the actual distribution of hourly earnings in 1988 with a simulated distribution constructed under the assumption that the nominal minimum wage increased by the rate of inflation (40 percent from 1980 to 1988) so that it had the same real value in 1988 as it did in 1980. Specifically, we simulated what the 1988 earnings distribution would have been if the wages of workers earning between $3.35 (the minimum wage in 1988) and $4.34 an hour (the 1988 value that would maintain the real minimum at its 1980 level) increased to $4.34 an hour, and if the 1988 wages of workers earning less than $3.35 an hour increased at the same rate (40 percent), maintaining the real value of their earnings at a constant percent below the hypothetical 1988 minimum wage. Our simulation uses usual hourly earnings data reported in the March 1988 CPS, because these provide more reliable information on hourly pay than the data on annual earnings and annual hours worked that are also collected in the March CPS.

Although this simulation has the virtue of simplicity, it ignores several ways in which the declining real minimum might affect the average earnings of less skilled workers. For example, our simulation ignores any negative employment effects of increases in the minimum. If these employment effects are concentrated among the least productive members of the less skilled segment of the work force, our estimate will understate the impact of the fall in the real minimum wage on earnings differentials. At the same time, the earnings calculation does not allow for the likely effect of changes in the minimum on unemployment among the less skilled (which we know from table 3 did not worsen in the 1980s when the real value of the minimum fell). The simulation will also understate the impact of a falling real minimum wage on earnings differentials insofar as it ignores any potential positive spillover effects of a higher minimum on the wages of less skilled workers who earn marginally above the minimum. But these downward biases may be partly offset, or even reversed, by the countervailing effect of a declining real minimum wage on the demand for skilled labor.

These shortcomings aside, the results of our simulations suggest that the decline in the real value of the minimum wage had a small effect on the relative earnings of high school dropouts. Among men aged 25–64 and 25–34, it accounts for .01 log points of the increase in the wage gap between college graduates and high school dropouts. On the other hand, it accounts for none of the increase in the gap between college and high school graduates because so few male high school graduates above age 25 received wages below the hypothetical minimum wage in 1988.[35]

Deunionization

We estimate the effect of changes in union density on earnings differentials using a three-stage analysis.

First, we calculated the average within-industry change in unionization rates for each educational group. We calculated within-industry changes in unionization to avoid double-counting the effects on earnings differentials of the changes in industry composition that we analyzed in tables 4 and 5. We used a standard shift-share analysis for this calculation. To begin, we tabulated from the May 1980 and March 1988 CPS unionization rates for educational groups within industries. We then calculated what the changes in unionization rates would have been if *overall* industry employment shares had remained at their 1973 levels.[36] Because the bulk of the decline in union density occurred within industries, our estimates of the decline in density that control for industrial shift are just 10–15 percent lower than raw tabulations of the decline in density.

Our estimates of the within-industry changes in unionization rates are presented in the first column of table 10. They show that the 1980–88 decline in unionization was highly concentrated among the less educated. The proportion of high school dropouts and graduates who belonged to

35. Although our analysis indicates that the relative earnings of high school dropouts would have declined less had the nominal minimum wage increased during the 1980s, their relative unemployment would probably have increased. See the elasticities for younger workers reported in Charles Brown, Curtis Gilroy, and Andrew Kohen, "The Effect of the Minimum Wage on Employment and Unemployment," *Journal of Economic Literature*, vol. 20 (June 1980), pp. 487–527. Under these circumstances, raising the minimum wage would have replaced one symptom of the declining economic position of the less skilled with another.

36. The method used in correcting for industry shifts involves a three-level decomposition of the education-group-specific unionization rate; an exact description is available from the authors on request. The 1973 shares were used to facilitate the computation of similar adjusted unionization rates for the 1970s, used in constructing table 12.

Table 10. **Effect of Deunionization on Average Earnings within Educational Groups, White Male Workers, 1980–88**

Workers[a]	Fall in proportion unionized, 1980–88, holding constant industry shares	Union premium in 1980 (log points)	Effect on average earnings (log points)
Ages 25–64			
LTHS	−.13	.20	−.03
HS	−.13	.10	−.01
CG	−.04	−.01	0
Ages 25–34			
LTHS	−.13	.20	−.03
HS	−.13	.30	−.04
CG	−.06	−.02	0

Source: The calculations are based on data contained in the May CPS for 1973 and 1980, and the March CPS for 1988. The union premiums are based on a 1980 log earnings equation that includes forty-two industry dummies, nine age dummies, eight region dummies, three marital status dummies, four schooling dummies, and interactions between union status and the schooling dummies.
a. See table 1 for definition of abbreviations.

unions fell 13 percentage points within industries from 1980 through 1988, both among those aged 25–64 and among those aged 25–34. By contrast, the proportion of unionized college graduates fell only 4 percentage points among those aged 25–64 and 6 points among those aged 25–34.

Second, we estimated union wage premiums for each educational group by fitting a standard log earnings equation that includes separate dichotomous union membership variables for each group and industry dummy variables to control for overall industry effects on earnings. We used May 1980 CPS data to perform the estimation; the results are in the second column of table 10.[37] In line with other studies of union wage premiums, the results reveal large union wage effects for the less educated and small insignificant (actually negative) effects for college graduates.[38]

37. Measuring union wage premiums in 1980 ignores the increases in those premiums that are indicated by CPS data since 1980. For example, the change in earnings differentials that we attribute to union decline would be even larger than that in table 10 if we used 1988 estimates of union wage premiums in our calculations. However, we did not use 1988 estimates of union wage premiums for two reasons. First, the increased premiums are not consistent with the prevalence of concession bargaining in the 1980s. Second, increases in union wage premiums in the 1980s are not generally confirmed in other data sets. See Richard B. Freeman, "In Search of Union Wage Concessions in Standard Data Sets," *Industrial Relations*, vol. 25 (Spring 1986), pp.131–45.

38. See Richard B. Freeman and James L. Medoff, *What Do Unions Do?* (Basic Books, 1984); and H. Gregg Lewis, "Union Relative Wage Effects," in Orley C. Ashenfelter and Richard Layard, eds., *Handbook of Labor Economics*, vol. 2 (Amsterdam: North-Holland, 1986), pp. 1139–81.

Finally, we multiplied the decrease in the proportion unionized by the relevant union wage premium to estimate the effect of the decline in unionization on average earnings for the different educational groups.[39] These estimates, reported in the third column of table 10, indicate that deunionization in the 1980s substantially widened the earnings gap. For example, union decline can account for .03 log points of the .16 point increase in the gap between college graduates and high school dropouts among those aged 25–64 and .03 points of the corresponding .20 point increase among those aged 25–34 (see table 2).[40]

In sum, although deunionization does not appear to be the overriding determinant of the deterioration of the economic position of the less skilled, it is clearly an important one.

Summary

How far do our estimates of the effect of changes in relative labor demand, in relative labor supply, and in wage-setting institutions take us toward understanding the 1980s decline in the earnings of less skilled American men? And what does our analysis imply for the future economic well-being of these workers?

There are two methods for organizing our estimates to assess the causes of the growing earnings gap.

The first method examines how changes in measured demand, supply, and wage-setting institutional variables contributed to the change in the earnings gap during the 1980s, *all else held fixed*. This is the type of calculation suggested by equation 2. For instance, if one asks the counterfactual question "what might have happened to relative earnings had the level of unionization stabilized in the 1980s at its 1980 level?" this method provides an answer. To see the extent to which these changes account for 1979–87 changes in differentials, we bring together our earlier findings and summarize them in table 11. There we report figures from both techniques used to estimate the impact of industry shifts.

39. Estimating the effect of unionism in this way ignores the effect that declining union density may have on the wages of all less skilled workers (including nonunion workers) because of spillover or union threat effects.

40. It is worth noting that the estimated effects of union decline on earnings differentials are of similar magnitude in tables 9 and 10. For example, the product of the coefficient on the percentage unionized in table 9 (-0.298) and the .08 point drop in the within-industry percent unionized during 1979–87 suggests that union decline explains, on average, a .024 point increase in the earnings differential—a figure that is close to corresponding figures reported in table 10.

Table 11. Sources-of-Change Accounting for Increased Earnings Differentials, White Male Workers, 1979–87
Log points

Item	Ages 25–64[a]		Ages 25–34[a]	
	CG to LTHS	CG to HS	CG to LTHS	CG to HS
Change in demographic-corrected differential[b]	.13	.10	.23	.17
Explanatory factors				
Shift in relative labor demand associated with changes in industrial composition				
Decomposition	.03	.02	.03	.05
Regression	.03	.03	.04	.04
Shift in relative labor supply	−.04	−.04	.02	.04
Changes in wage-setting institutions				
Minimum wage	.01	.00	.01	.00
Unionization	.03	.01	.03	.04
Overall change accounted	.03	−.01/.00	.09/.10	.12/.13
Percent of overall change accounted for	23	. . .	39/43	71/76

Source: Calculated from tables 1, 4, 5, 6, and 10, as described in text.
a. See table 1 for definition of abbreviations.
b. Between 1979 and 1987.

This table tells a markedly different story about our ability to explain changes among 25–64-year-old men and among 25–34-year-old men. For male workers aged 25–64 the analysis accounts for just 23 percent of the increased differential between college graduates and high school dropouts, and none of the increased differential between college graduates and high school graduates. In both these cases, shifts in relative demand and changes in wage-setting institutions contribute importantly to the rise in the differential, but they are offset (in part or in full) by the increase in the relative supply of college graduates, which acts to reduce earnings differentials. The implication is that the relative demand for less skilled labor must have declined in ways that are not captured by either our measures of shifts in the industry composition of employment or by our measures of changes in wage-setting institutions.

For 25–34-year-olds, the numbers in table 11 show that we do a better job of accounting for observed changes. The reason is that the relative supply of the more educated 25–34-year-old male workers fell during the 1980s, contributing to, rather than offsetting, the effect of shifts in industry demand and changes in wage-setting institutions in raising relative earnings. Our calculations explain roughly 40 percent of the rise in the differential between college graduates and high school dropouts

Table 12. Sources-of-Change Accounting for the Increase in Differentials in 1979–87 Compared with 1973–79, White Male Workers
Log points

Item	Ages 25–64[a]		Ages 25–34[a]	
	CG to LTHS	CG to HS	CG to LTHS	CG to HS
Change to be explained[b]	.10	.14	.26	.22
Explanatory factors				
Acceleration of shift in relative labor demand associated with changes in industrial composition				
Decomposition	.02	.01	− .01	.02
Regression	.00	.03	.00	.00
Deceleration in growth of relative labor supply	.02	.07	.22	.13
Changes in wage-setting institutions				
Minimum wage	.01	.00	.01	.00
Unionization	.02	.01	.00	− .01
Overall change accounted	.05/.07	.09/.11	.22/.23	.12/.14
Percent of overall change accounted for	50/70	64/79	85/88	55/64

Source: Same as table 11 for 1979–87 changes. The 1973–79 effects were obtained by replicating the calculations in tables 4, 5, 6, and 10 for the 1973–79 period. The numbers reported are the difference between the 1979–87 effects and the 1973–79 effects.

a. See table 1 for definition of abbreviations.

b. This change is the difference between the 1979–87 change in differentials and the 1973–79 change in differentials adjusted to correspond to a comparable number of years. The adjustment simply multiplies the actual 1973–79 change by 8/6, or 1.33. A similar adjustment was made to the estimated 1973–79 effects from the explanatory factors.

and three-quarters of the rise in the differential between college and high school graduates. In both cases the explanation is divided about equally among changes in relative supply, shifts in industry composition, and changes in wage-setting institutions.

The second method of assessing the deterioration in the earnings of the less educated is to contrast changes during the 1980s with changes during the 1970s. This method focuses on *differences in the changes* in variables between the two periods, as in equation 3. For instance, if one asks the counterfactual question, "how much has the accelerated decline in unionization between the 1970s and the 1980s contributed to the growing earnings gap?" this method provides an answer.

Table 12 presents our analysis of the contribution of differences in the changes in demand, supply, and wage-setting institutions between 1973–79 and 1979–87 to the difference in the change in differentials between those periods. The change in differentials we seek to explain—the increase in the growth of demographic-corrected earnings differentials from 1973–79 to 1979–87 (with the 1973–79 change adjusted to an eight-year basis so as to be comparable to the 1979–87 change)—is reported in the first line of the table. For example, the regression-corrected earnings differential between high school dropouts and college graduates increased by .03 log points from 1973 to 1979 (on an eight-year basis) and by .13 log points from 1979 to 1987 (see table 1). The difference between these changes is .10 log points, the first entry in table 12.

The estimates in table 12 illustrate that the factors that have changed most in the 1980s relative to the 1970s are those associated with relative labor supply.[41] For men aged 25–64 the deceleration in the growth of relative supply explains .02 points of the increase, from the 1970s to the 1980s, in the (eight-year) growth rate of the earnings gap between college graduates and high school dropouts and .07 points of the college graduate to high school graduate increase for that age bracket. The deceleration in the growth of supply has an even more marked effect among men aged 25–34, where it explains .22 points (college to less than high school) and .13 points (college to high school) of the increase in the growth rate of the wage gap. Both the industrial shift and unionization effects appear to have had similar effects on wage differentials in the 1970s and 1980s, and so help little in explaining why changes in wage differentials in the 1980s were so different from changes in the 1970s. In total, for men aged 25–64 we can account for 50 percent to 70 percent of the increased growth rate of the college graduate to high school dropout differential and two-thirds to three-quarters of the increased growth rate of the college to high school graduate differential. For men aged 25–34 we explain nearly 90 percent of the increase in the former differential from 1973–79 to 1979–87 and 55 percent to 64 percent of the increase in the latter differential.

Our sources-of-change analyses support three main conclusions. First, we are moderately successful in explaining the growth in wage differentials in the 1980s for men aged 25–34 but are largely unsuccessful in

41. To obtain the estimates in this table, we performed the same calculations for 1973–79 as we did for 1979–87. We estimated the effect of unionization, changes in industry composition, and changes in the real minimum wage on earnings for 1973–79 using the same procedures as in our earlier tables. We report in table 12 the differences between our estimates of (1) the impact on relative wages of 1979–87 changes in variables and (2) the impact on relative wages from 1973–79 changes in variables. For example, deunionization accounts for about .01 log points of the increase in the college graduate to high school dropout differential (among men aged 25–64) during 1973–79, and .03 log points during 1979–87. In our sources-of-change analysis, the changing rate of deunionization therefore accounts for .02 log points of the change in the growth rate of relative earnings between the two time periods. To make the estimates comparable, we calculated the annual rates of change for the variables from 1973 to 1979 and multiplied them by 8.

explaining the growth in wage differentials for men aged 25–64. Second, our analysis achieves greater success when we focus our aim on a different, but related, target: the *change* in the rate of growth of wage differentials between the 1970s and the 1980s. The main finding here is that relative supply movements, which differed sharply between the 1970s and 1980s, can account in large part for the accelerated pace of change in the wage gaps. Third, it is also clear from table 12 that the 1970s and 1980s differ importantly in ways not captured by our analysis. Since labor supply and institutional changes seem reasonably well measured, we can infer that relative demand shifts, caused by factors we were unable to measure, accelerated in the 1980s.[42]

Implications

Given our assessment of the causes of changes in earnings differentials, is the deterioration in the real and relative earnings of less skilled male workers likely to continue into the 1990s?

Over the long run, educational investments and occupational choice responses by young men to the increased differentials should slow or partly reverse the pattern of the 1980s.[43] Indeed, an increasing proportion of young white males have been enrolling in college in the 1980s. If supply factors are as important in raising differentials as our calculations for young men suggest, the direction of change is likely to reverse itself in the next decade, at least for new labor market entrants.

Still, we are not especially sanguine about the near-term economic prospects for those less skilled workers whose wages have already been substantially depressed. We see no sign of a turnaround in any of the other developments that have widened the earnings gap. Modest increases in the minimum wage will do little for 25–64-year-old men, and a large increase will improve real and relative earnings only at the cost of decreased employment. We anticipate that the world economy will

42. To understand more fully the deterioration in the relative economic position of the less skilled, one should go beyond the analysis of changes in relative earnings to examine the reasons for the increase in unemployment-rate differentials. Although we do not explore this issue in any depth, we offer two suggestions for why these changes were less severe for the less skilled in the 1980s than in the 1970s. First, the more rapid fall in unionization rates in the 1980s may have lessened the contribution of unions to unemployment. Second, the fall in the real value of the minimum wage over the 1980s may have helped in keeping the unemployment rate from increasing.

43. Freeman documents the supply responses of young men to changes in relative earnings in terms of choosing to enroll in college and selecting a major field when in college.

grow increasingly competitive, perhaps further reducing employment of the less educated in high-wage sectors. We also expect union density to continue to fall. Finally, the concentration of future labor force growth among Hispanics, blacks, and non-Hispanic white women—groups competitive with less skilled white males—may hinder the latter's chances for an economic rebound.[44]

The best hope for stemming the economic decline of the less skilled is increasing tightness in the overall U.S. labor market. During the 1970s the civilian labor force in the United States grew at an annual rate of 2.6 percent, largely because of the rapid entry of women and baby boomers into the labor market. The deceleration of women's labor market activity and the arrival of smaller cohorts at work-force-entry ages should lead to considerably slower future labor force growth, only slightly in excess of 1 percent a year, until 2000. If labor demand grows at a reasonable pace, the result of this supply change will be a tighter labor market, which should improve the employment and earnings of less educated men. Freeman presents evidence that the real and relative earnings of 16–24-year-old male high school dropouts and graduates increased from 1983 to 1988 in low-unemployment areas.[45] These findings suggest that the possible transformation of the U.S. labor market from a buyer's to a seller's market over the next decade could be exceptionally beneficial to the less skilled. Nonetheless, the uncertainty inherent in this scenario leaves us doubtful that without social and economic changes more general and far-reaching than those we anticipate, less skilled males will enjoy large enough economic gains to restore their 1970s relative earnings position or to return to their historic path of rapid real earnings growth.

44. See David E. Bloom and Neil G. Bennett, "Future Shock," *New Republic*, June 19, 1989, pp. 18–22.

45. See Richard Freeman, "How Do Young Less Educated Workers Fare in a Labor Shortage Economy?" paper presented at the 1988 annual meetings of the American Economic Association, December 1988. Murphy and Welch in "Structure of Wages," Katz and Revenga in "Changes in the Structure of Wages," and our estimates in table 7 also provide evidence that skill differentials narrow in tight labor markets.

Comment by Barry Bluestone

AFTER several years of haggling over whether real wages have declined in absolute terms and whether wage differentials have actually increased, analysts now largely agree that both have occurred in the United States, at least among male workers.[46] Since the late 1970s the level of earnings dispersion has accelerated, despite the economic recovery that began in 1983. The once established association between tighter labor markets and more equal wage distributions is no longer in evidence, even under the current 5 percent unemployment rate regime. Hence one must ask what is driving the widening earnings gap, especially between the skilled and the less skilled, between the college educated and those with a high school education or less, and between those in professional occupations and those in manual ones. Here Blackburn, Bloom, and Freeman have made a valiant effort at statistically identifying from among a host of supply and demand suspects the factors responsible for the increasing earnings dispersion among white men aged 25 through 64. Their investigation suggests a conclusion not unlike that in Agatha Christie's *Murder on the Orient Express*: virtually everybody on the train had a part in the crime.

From time-series data, the authors demonstrate that the ratio of mean earnings between white male college graduates and white male high school dropouts (as well as the ratio between college graduates and high school graduates and between distinct occupation categories) followed a U-turn pattern between 1967 and 1987, a pattern that has become familiar in the recent literature on U.S. wage distributions.[47] The ratios

---

46. Among the early studies of earnings inequality are those by Peter Henle and Paul Ryscavage, "The Distribution of Earned Income among Men and Women, 1958–1977," *Monthly Labor Review*, vol. 103 (April 1980), pp. 3–10; and two by Martin Dooley and Peter Gottschalk, "Does a Younger Male Labor Force Mean Greater Earnings Inequality?" *Monthly Labor Review*, vol. 105 (November 1982), pp. 42–45, and "Earnings Inequality among Males in the United States: Trends and the Effect of Labor Force Growth," *Journal of Political Economy*, vol. 92 (February 1984), pp. 59–89. More recent studies include Bennett Harrison, Barry Bluestone, and Chris Tilly, "Wage Inequality Takes a Great U-Turn," *Challenge*, vol. 29 (March–April 1986), pp. 26–32; Kevin Murphy and Finis Welch, "The Structure of Wages," University of Chicago working paper, August 1988; and Gary Burtless's paper in this volume.

47. See, for example, Bennett Harrison and Barry Bluestone, *The Great U-Turn: Corporate Restructuring and the Polarizing of America* (Basic Books, 1988); and Sheldon Danziger, "Education, Earnings, and Poverty," Discussion Paper 88-881 (University of Wisconsin—Madison, Institute for Research on Poverty, August 1989).

declined from 1967 to the mid-1970s, stagnated until 1979, and rose steeply thereafter. The increases are proportionally higher for the earnings ratio between college graduates and high school dropouts and for younger workers aged 25 to 34. Essentially the growing wage gaps reflect this time-series structure because mean real earnings have continuously declined for those without a high school degree and for those with a secondary school diploma, whereas the real average wage for white male college graduates had reverted to its 1973 level by 1987 after a dip during the late 1970s. The rising wage differentials are consequently a post-1979 phenomenon.

Using shift-share and regression analysis, the authors find that the rise in the *level* of the wage gap between 1979 and 1987 can be attributed partly to industrial shift on the demand side, partly to a relative shortage in the supply of college graduates, and partly to declines in union density. Technological progress and the declining value in the statutory minimum wage had a decidedly smaller, though not negligible, effect. Combining several of the authors' analyses produces a breakdown of the following rough proportions (in percentages):

Demand related
    Industrial shifts   16–33

Supply related
    Changes in education   13–30

Institutionally related
    Deunionization   15–20
    Technological progress   5
    Decline in minimum wage   0–4

In short, changes in labor supply, shifts in labor demand, and changes in the structure of wage-setting institutions contribute about equally to explaining the wage gap between college educated men and those who have a high school diploma or less.

Yet when the analysis turns to explaining the rate of *acceleration* in the wage gap between 1973–79 and 1979–87 rather than in the differences in the levels per se, the apparent weight of the evidence shifts decidedly to the supply side. A post-1979 decline in the ratio of the number of college graduates to those with less education—a growing undersupply of college-trained recruits—takes the blame for the sharp rise in wage disparity. The authors claim that 50 percent of the growing earnings gap among 25-to-64-year-olds and virtually 100 percent of the growing gap among 25-to-34-year-olds can be explained by this particular supply-side phenomenon.

A (Slight) Reinterpretation

What is one to make of these intriguing results? In particular, do they provide a reasonably complete account of how supply and demand phenomena are affecting wage dispersion?

To be sure, the results do provide some new evidence to support the controversial "deindustrialization" thesis—the hypothesis that the shift from manufacturing employment to "postindustrial" service work has had a negative effect on average wages and wage equality.[48] The reported estimates, however, do not fully reflect the impact of demand-side phenomena, as the authors freely admit, for deindustrialization narrowly defined as interindustry shift fails to account for the various forms of industrial restructuring that have been taking place *within* industries and that conceivably dominate the effect of interindustry shifts themselves.

Indeed, when Blackburn, Bloom, and Freeman decompose changes in earnings differentials for 1979 to 1987, they find that 70 to 85 percent of the increase in the earnings gap between college graduates and high school dropouts occurred within industries.[49] Yet it would be incorrect to attribute all the measured intraindustry growth in earnings disparity to supply-side factors, or for that matter to changes in union density. Many unmeasured demand-side restructuring efforts were clearly at

---

48. In my own research using time-series regression analysis on annual data for 1963 to 1987, I found other evidence for the deindustrialization hypothesis. The elasticity of the variance in the logarithm of annual earnings for year-round, full-time workers with respect to the percentage of employment in the manufacturing sector was estimated to be -0.67 and statistically highly significant after controlling for changes in productivity, changes in the age structure of the labor force, and the growth in female labor force participation. See Barry Bluestone, "The Changing Nature of Employment and Earnings in the U.S. Economy, 1963–1987," paper presented at the conference on Job Creation in America, University of North Carolina at Chapel Hill, April 1989.

49. An almost identical estimate is found in an earlier source of growth analysis prepared by Chris Tilly, Bennett Harrison, and myself. We found that only a fifth of the overall growth in wage inequality since 1978—as measured by the variance in the logarithm of annual earnings for all workers aged 16 and over—can be explained by the shift in employment from the generally high-paying durable goods manufacturing sector to the lower-paying service sector. The other four-fifths of the increase in wage inequality occurred within industries. See Chris Tilly, Barry Bluestone, and Bennett Harrison, "What Is Making American Wages More Unequal?" in Barbara D. Dennis, ed., *Proceedings of the Thirty-Ninth Annual Meeting*, (Madison, Wis.: Industrial Relations Research Association, 1987), pp. 338–48.

Table 13. **Annualized Percentage Point Change in the Ratio of Manufacturing and Service and Trade Employment to Total Employment and in the Ratio of College Graduates and Those with Some College Education to All Workers Aged 16 and Over**

Item	1973–79	1979–87
Manufacturing/total	−0.26	−0.43
Services and trade/total	0.37	0.56
College graduates/total	0.41	0.23
Some college/total	0.44	0.32

Source: March CPS for 1974, 1980, and 1988.

work during the 1980s.[50] Wage concession bargaining, the imposition of two-tier wage structures, the substitution of contingent labor for full-time regular workers, and the allocation of jobs to smaller subcontractors no doubt affected wage levels and wage disparity in many industries, both unionized and nonunionized.[51] Clearly, research is needed to develop quantitative estimates of these restructuring efforts, which could then be used to study their impact.

The supply-side explanation of the earnings gap acceleration after 1979 also fails to give the demand side its due. According to an untested assumption made by the authors, "relative demand shifted at the same annual rate" during the 1973–79 and 1979–87 periods. My own calculations, using the March Current Population Surveys for 1973, 1979, and 1987, suggest that the annual rate of decline in manufacturing and the annual growth rate of service and trade employment accelerated sharply in the latter period (table 13).

Table 13 confirms the decelerating growth in the relative supply of college graduates and those with some college, as suggested by Blackburn, Bloom, and Freeman. But to ignore the change in the rate of deindustrialization surely leads to an overestimate of the pure supply-side effect. Table 13 hints of the possibility of a strong interaction between supply-side and demand-side phenomena, particularly after 1979.[52]

50. For a discussion of these mechanisms, see Harrison and Bluestone, *Great U-Turn*, especially chaps. 2 and 3.

51. For a detailed examination of the spread in concession bargaining as one aspect of industrial restructuring, see Daniel J. B. Mitchell, "Shifting Norms in Wage Determination," *Brookings Papers on Economic Activity, 2:1985*, pp. 575–99.

52. Tables 13–15 were prepared from March CPS samples for all workers aged 16 and over (men *and* women) who had positive annual wage and salary earnings in the previous year. The reason for using all workers rather than subsamples for full-time, year-round white male workers aged 25 to 64 is that each of these tables attempts to approximate the number of *jobs* in the economy exhibiting particular characteristics. Thus in table 13

Table 14.   Inequality within and among Industrial Sectors, 1979, 1987

Industry	Variance in the log of annual wages and salaries		Percent change
	1979	1987	
Mining	0.862	0.750	−13.0
Construction	1.491	1.526	2.3
Durable manufactured goods	0.849	0.809	−4.7
Nondurable manufactured goods	1.220	1.251	2.5
Transportation, communications, and utilities	1.028	1.112	8.2
Wholesale and retail trade	2.013	2.085	3.6
Finance, insurance, and real estate	1.274	1.364	7.1
Business and repair services	1.933	2.241	15.9
Entertainment and recreation services	2.208	2.613	18.3
Professional services	1.584	1.661	4.9

Source: Calculations from Annual Demographic File of *Current Population Survey*, March 1980 and March 1988. Sample includes all workers aged 16 and over who had some wages during the year.

Evidence for this conjecture is found in tables 14 and 15. Table 14 contains estimates of the variance in the logarithm of annual wages (VARLNWAGE) for all workers (aged 16 and over) by broad industry grouping for both 1979 and 1987. Inspection of the table shows two things. One is that, in general, the goods-producing industries (mining, construction, and durable and nondurable manufacturing) have traditionally had more equal wages than the service industries. The second is that wage inequality is rising significantly faster in the service sector. The VARLNWAGE actually declined in mining and durable manufacturing during the 1980s and rose only modestly in construction and nondurable manufacturing. In contrast, *all* the service sector industries had larger proportional increases in their wage dispersions than any of the goods-producing sectors.

It would therefore not be surprising that a growth in wage dispersion has accompanied the shift in aggregate employment from goods production to services. Employment has been stable or declining in the manufacturing industries, where wage inequality is relatively low, while

---

the annualized percentage point changes in the industry-specific employment levels reflect the size of the manufacturing sector itself, not the proportion of the industry comprised of a particular type of worker. Similarly, in table 14 my concern is with the distribution of *jobs* in an industry, not the distribution of a particular type of worker. In table 15 the numbers refer to the average wage of *jobs* filled by workers with specific amounts of formal schooling.

it has been growing rapidly in the service sector, where it is considerably higher. Although this shift does not automatically result in higher overall earnings variance, it could explain at least some of the growth in inequality during the 1980s.

A clue to a possible interaction between demand-side industrial shifts and supply-side educational requirements is found in table 15. Here I measured the mean real annual earnings for all workers aged 16 and over for the years 1963, 1973, 1979, and 1987 and disaggregated the findings by education and by industry. Consistent with Blackburn, Bloom, and Freeman, the column labeled "Ratio 1987/1973" suggests that the degree of wage erosion is monotonically related to the level of schooling completed. By 1987 the real average wage for workers who did not complete high school had dropped to 82 percent of its 1973 value, and for those with a high school degree, to 94 percent. Essentially, only those whose education went beyond the high school diploma were able to maintain their real mean earnings—at 103 percent of the 1973 value.

These results strongly endorse the authors' conclusion that the U-turn toward higher overall wage inequality is directly related to the increasing rewards for college education and the increasing penalties attached to not completing high school. The indexed values in the right-hand part of table 15 show that in 1963 those with a college degree earned about 2.1 times as much as those who did not complete high school. By 1979 this ratio was still below 2.4. By 1987, however, the ratio was more than 2.9 and presumably growing. Overall, between 1963 and 1987 the size of the earnings differential had grown by 38 percent.

But table 15 demonstrates an additional factor underlying the growing significance of education, a factor that hearkens back to the deindustrialization hypothesis. When the trend in earnings by education group is disaggregated by industry category, it becomes clear that the growing education differential is confined mainly to the service sector. Note that in 1963 the earnings ratio between people with a college degree and those who did not complete high school was roughly equivalent in the goods-producing and service sectors of the economy. The relevant ratios are 2.11 and 2.20, respectively. By 1987 the ratios have diverged substantially. In goods production the ratio has increased by less than 15 percent, to 2.42. In services, the ratio has mushroomed to 3.52, an increase of 60 percent.

Apparently, the growth in overall wage dispersion in the 1980s is due to a complex of factors that begins within individual industries and

Table 15. Mean Real Annual Earnings, by Education and Industry, 1963, 1973, 1979, 1987

Work force[a]	Earnings (dollars)[b]				Ratio, 1987/1973	Indexed values (H.S. degree = 1.000)				Percent change, 1963-87
	1963	1973	1979	1987		1963	1973	1979	1987	
Total	13,554	17,007	16,794	18,063	...	...	...	...	...	...
By industry										
Goods producing	17,015	20,344	20,652	19,864	...	...	...	...	...	...
Services	12,253	15,088	14,873	16,615	...	...	...	...	...	...
By education group										
Less than H.S. degree	10,675	12,190	11,081	10,039	0.824	1.000	1.000	1.000	1.000	...
High School degree	14,292	17,145	16,292	16,191	0.944	1.339	1.406	1.470	1.613	...
Some college	14,574	16,427	16,236	16,939	1.031	1.360	1.348	1.465	1.687	...
College degree or more	22,519	28,140	26,469	29,213	1.038	2.110	2.309	2.389	2.910	37.94
By education and industry										
Goods producing										
Less than high school degree	14,563	16,637	15,685	13,768	0.828	1.000	1.000	1.000	1.000	...
High school degree	17,621	20,527	20,366	19,087	0.930	1.210	1.234	1.298	1.386	...
Some college	19,567	20,779	21,592	20,718	0.997	1.344	1.249	1.377	1.505	...
College degree or more	30,791	36,075	34,652	33,367	0.925	2.114	2.168	2.209	2.424	14.62
Services										
Less than high school degree	9,163	9,470	8,417	7,798	0.823	1.000	1.000	1.000	1.000	...
High school degree	12,649	14,845	13,876	14,365	0.968	1.380	1.568	1.648	1.842	...
Some college	12,356	14,198	13,926	15,167	1.068	1.348	1.499	1.654	1.945	...
College degree or more	20,157	25,530	24,232	27,446	1.075	2.200	2.696	2.879	3.520	60.00

Source: Calculations from the Annual Demographic Files, *Current Population Surveys*, March 1964–March 1988.
a. Goods producing: mining, construction, durable manufacturing, and nondurable manufacturing. Services: transportation, communications, utilities, wholesale and retail trade, finance, insurance, and real estate, business and repair services, entertainment and recreation services, and professional services.
b. All dollar values are in 1987 prices as adjusted by the personal consumption expenditures (PCE) deflator.

interindustrial shifts in employment and is then ratified by the sharp educational differentials in the service sector. As the economy transfers workers from goods production, where schooling-related wage differentials are relatively low, to the service industries, where such differentials are high and rising, the degree of wage inequality is destined to increase.

Implications for Future
Trends in Wage
Differentials

What chance is there that schooling-related wage inequality will decrease in the future? Blackburn, Bloom, and Freeman place some faith in two factors that might reverse the trend toward larger earnings gaps. The first is tighter labor markets that conceivably could benefit less educated workers more than those with a college degree. The second is the market signal provided by the wage gap itself. With the return to college education growing, the authors expect the supply of college graduates to expand, ultimately driving down the wage differential between workers with more and those with less formal schooling.

At least two caveats must be applied to this optimistic scenario. One is that labor markets have already been relatively tight for a number of years, yet the wage gap has, if anything, increased not declined. The second has to do with a growing mismatch between the skills demanded and the skills offered in the U.S. economy. The supply of college graduates may increase in the future, but not necessarily fast enough to offset increasing demand. Some evidence for a growing labor market mismatch favoring skilled workers is provided in a new study that correlates data on job skill requirements with data on students' educational achievement. Using the Labor Department's scale for on-the-job verbal skill requirements, William Johnson and Arnold Packer calculate that "the 104 million nonmilitary jobs existing in 1984 required an average language proficiency of 3.0, typical of retail salespeople or skilled construction workers. By contrast, the 26 million jobs expected to be created between 1984 and 2000 will require an average level of 3.6. . . . [Today, however,] the average young adult in this country is reading only at a 2.6 level."[53] Hence, if the Johnson and Packer numbers are to be trusted,

---

53. The results of the Johnson and Packer study are reported in Edward B. Fiske, "Impending U.S. Jobs 'Disaster': Work Force Unqualified to Work," *New York Times*, September 25, 1989, pp. A1 and B6 (quotation from p. B6).

there is now an undersupply of verbally skilled workers relative to demand, and future demand shifts will likely exacerbate the mismatch.

Given this more pessimistic analysis, one can identify three factors that might reverse the wage dispersion trend. One would be a "reindustrialization" of the economy—a significant resurgence of employment in the goods-producing industries. This would move workers into industries where the mean annual wage is higher, particularly for those with less schooling, and where wage variance due to education is relatively small. The second factor would be a large increase in educational opportunity for those workers who would otherwise not go beyond high school. Reducing the variance in education by greatly increasing college attendance would reduce wage variance in the service sector and thus contribute to overall wage equality. Finally, the greater wage dispersion in service industries could be reduced by altering the institutional structure of those industries. Insofar as unionization tends to provide for greater wage equalization within an industry, as Blackburn, Bloom, and Freeman demonstrate, a larger union presence in the service sector could lead to somewhat smaller wage differentials.

It seems doubtful, however, that any of these changes will occur in the near future. The trend away from manufacturing employment, though temporarily slowed because of an increased export market, does not show any evidence of reversing. Union-organizing drives in the service economy are gaining some momentum, but the growth in union membership is well below the growth in total employment. As for expanding education and pinning our hopes on the supply side, the obstacle seems to be not so much a lack of political rhetoric as a lack of real funds, or at least the political will to spend them. To prepare more students for higher education will require better primary and secondary schools, and this will in turn inevitably require greater public spending. Moreover, with the cost of a college education rising faster than overall inflation, it is becoming more difficult for those without college degrees to afford postsecondary education even as the relative return to college increases.

What seems clear is that the U-turns in real wages and in wage dispersion will not automatically reverse simply because of a more benign business cycle or a rate-of-return-induced expansion in the college-educated labor supply. I therefore believe that attempts to maintain employment in the manufacturing sector and the pursuit of unionization in the service economy will be necessary complements to any scheme to limit the growth of inequality in the U.S. labor market.

Earnings Inequality over the Business and Demographic Cycles

Gary Burtless

THE DISTRIBUTION of American incomes is a topic of enduring interest to economists and the lay public. In recent years it has also become the subject of intense political debate as overall income growth has slowed and the disparity between rich, middle-class, and poor families has risen.

The sluggish growth in family income over the past decade and a half is due largely to the anemic pace of productivity change and to gradual changes in the composition of U.S. families. Slow productivity growth has almost halted the rise in real wages, while changing family composition has increased the share of households that lack full-time, year-round breadwinners. The latter trend has also contributed to a growth in family income inequality.

Another source of income inequality is the trend toward growing inequality in labor earnings. The amount and even the existence of an increase in earnings inequality is a matter of some dispute.[1] Those who

I am grateful to Stephen Kastenberg, Paul Bergin, Maryam Dunahay, and Brian Sayer for extensive help in preparing the paper. I also wish to thank Lynn A. Karoly and participants in labor workshops at the University of North Carolina and UCLA for useful comments.

1. Analysts who have found evidence of rising inequality, either in the work force as a whole or among male wage earners, include Barry Bluestone and Bennett Harrison in a set of books and reports, including *The Great American Job Machine: The Proliferation of Low Wage Employment in the U.S. Economy,* study prepared for the Joint Economic Committee (GPO, December 1986), and *The Great U-Turn: Corporate Restructuring and the Polarizing of America* (Basic Books, 1988), especially pp. 112–38; Robert Z. Lawrence, "Sectoral Shifts and the Size of the Middle Class," *Brookings Review,* vol. 3 (Fall 1984), pp. 3–11; and Martin D. Dooley and Peter Gottschalk, "Earnings Inequality among Males in the United States: Trends and the Effect of Labor Force Growth," *Journal of Political Economy,* vol. 92 (February 1984), pp. 58–89. Among those arguing that inequality either has not risen or has grown only modestly are Neal H. Rosenthal, "The Shrinking Middle Class: Myth or Reality?" *Monthly Labor Review,* vol. 108 (March 1985), pp. 3–10; Marvin H. Kosters and Murray N. Ross, "The Distribution of Earnings and Employment Opportunities: A Re-examination of the Evidence," AEI Occasional Paper, American En-

find evidence of rising inequality advance a number of explanations to account for it. According to one interpretation, the structure of the economy has changed, giving rise to rapid growth in low-paying jobs in the service sector. A supply-side explanation emphasizes changes in the composition of the labor force following the influx of the baby boom generation into the job market.

This paper will examine the contribution of the business cycle and demographic factors to changes in earnings inequality over time. Economists have long known that the business cycle influences the distribution of income.[2] A cyclical downturn reduces the proportion of national income going to families in the bottom income quintile and raises the proportion going to families at the top.

These cyclical changes in family income inequality arise in part from the effect of the cycle on the distribution of individual labor earnings. A rise in unemployment alters the distribution of annual wage earnings by increasing the share of earners who work fewer than fifty-two weeks a year and reducing the share who work overtime hours or on full-time schedules. It would be erroneous to conclude, however, that this effect of the business cycle will apply equally to all earners in the population. Women, for example, are more likely than men to work less than fifty-two weeks a year or on part-time schedules, even during periods when labor markets are tight. Their earnings are consequently more unequally distributed than men's, and the shape of their earnings distribution may not be affected in quite the same way by a cyclical rise in unemployment.

If high unemployment increases the inequality of earnings, the trend toward rising inequality is at least partly explainable. Civilian unemployment rose from an average rate of 4.6 percent through the 1950s and 1960s to 6.2 percent in the 1970s and 7.7 percent between 1980 and

terprise Institute, Washington, D.C., 1987; and McKinley L. Blackburn and David E. Bloom, "Earnings and Income Inequality in the United States," *Population and Development Review*, vol. 13 (December 1987), pp. 575–609. For an excellent and thorough analysis of recent trends in inequality, see Lynn Annette Karoly, "A Study of the Distribution of Individual Earnings in the United States from 1967 to 1986," Ph.D. dissertation, Yale University, 1988.

2. See Charles E. Metcalf, "The Size Distribution of Personal Income during the Business Cycle," *American Economic Review*, vol. 59 (September 1969), pp. 657–68; Lester C. Thurow, "Analyzing the American Income Distribution," *American Economic Review*, vol. 60 (May 1970, *Papers and Proceedings, 1969*), pp. 261–69; and Rebecca M. Blank and Alan S. Blinder, "Macroeconomics, Income Distribution, and Poverty," in Sheldon H. Danziger and Daniel H. Weinberg, eds., *Fighting Poverty: What Works and What Doesn't* (Harvard University Press, 1986).

1987.[3] This paper will attempt to show whether the increase in unemployment can account for much of the movement in earnings inequality. In addition, it will examine the potential effect of demographic swings in work force composition. Because these swings have been so pronounced over the past two decades, many economists and journalists attribute a major share of the blame for recent wage developments to demographic factors. As shown below, these factors can account for some of the movement in inequality in the 1970s, but none of it in the 1980s.

Measuring Earnings Inequality

Part of the controversy over recent changes in the earnings distribution arises because different analysts have used different methods and research samples to examine wage developments. These methodological differences sometimes yield widely varying interpretations of the meaning and even the direction of recent trends. For this reason it is useful to devote some attention at the outset to a careful description of the data available for analysis and the measurement techniques used to analyze them.

Sources of Data

Earnings inequality in the United States can be measured using several information sources and a variety of yardsticks. The most commonly used source of earnings data, and the one that will be used here, is the Census Bureau's Current Population Survey (CPS). The CPS is a monthly survey of nationally representative households, used primarily to measure the current unemployment rate. In March of every year the survey contains questions about household members' income, including self-employment and wage earnings, and work experience in the previous calendar year. The data on income are used to compile annual statistics on poverty and the size distribution of individual and family income. Most recent studies of the earnings distribution have been based on the March CPS files.

3. The unemployment rate of 25–54-year-old males is generally believed to be a better long-term measure of labor market tightness than the overall unemployment rate, because it excludes most of the effects of changing labor force composition. The prime-age male unemployment rate averaged 3.4 percent during the 1950s, 3.0 percent in the 1960s, 3.7 percent in the 1970s, and 6.1 percent in the 1980s through 1987.

The CPS data have important advantages over similar information that can be obtained from alternative data sets, such as the Panel Survey of Income Dynamics or the National Longitudinal Surveys. The income and earnings statistics compiled from the CPS extend back almost to World War II. The statistics derived from the survey and regularly published in the P-60 series of *Current Population Reports* have been compiled using fairly consistent methods over most of that period. Individual responses to the survey questionnaire are available on computer files for years back through 1967, permitting an analyst to measure the size distribution of earnings using a variety of alternative procedures. The sample drawn in the survey is several times larger than ones used in alternative surveys, allowing analysts to obtain highly reliable distribution statistics for many subgroups in the population.

The CPS data do present problems, which should be borne in mind when interpreting the findings reported in this paper. Information reported to Census interviewers is subject to an unknown amount of misreporting bias. Some respondents fail to answer all questions, so responses are frequently imputed using methods that have been developed over the years by Census Bureau statisticians.[4] These procedures produce a size distribution of wage and salary earnings that appears to mimic closely the data reported on income tax returns. However, the data on work experience and weekly hours of work, which must be used to infer the distribution of weekly and hourly wages, may be far less reliable.[5]

For certain indexes of earnings inequality, an especially serious reporting problem is caused by respondents' tendency to round off their annual earnings to the nearest $1,000 or even $10,000. While this phenomenon creates no bias in respondents' income reports, it produces a substantial amount of clustering in reported wages at particular earnings levels, such as $10,000 or $15,000 per year. If these earnings levels

4. For a discussion and critique of these methods see Lee Lillard, James P. Smith, and Finis Welch, "What Do We Really Know about Wages? The Importance of Nonreporting and Census Imputation," *Journal of Political Economy*, vol. 94, pt. 1 (June 1985), pp. 489–506; and Martin David and others, "Alternative Methods for CPS Income Imputation," *Journal of the American Statistical Association*, vol. 81 (March 1986), pp. 29–41.

5. On the accuracy of CPS earnings reports, see John Bound and others, "Measurement Error in Cross-Sectional and Longitudinal Labor Market Surveys: Results from Two Validation Studies," Working Paper 2884 (Cambridge, Mass.: National Bureau of Economic Research, March 1989). On the problems with retrospective unemployment reports, see George Akerlof and Janet Yellen, "Unemployment through the Filter of Memory," *Quarterly Journal of Economics*, vol. 100 (August 1985), pp. 747–73.

happen to fall just below or just above critical thresholds in the overall distribution—such as 50 percent of median earnings or twice median earnings—the fraction of all earners found to have "low," "middle-class," or "high-income" earnings will be found to be quite sensitive to the critical thresholds selected.[6]

A different kind of problem arises from the truncation of earnings reported to Census interviewers and a subsequent, more severe truncation imposed by the Census Bureau before it releases CPS files to the public. In order to preserve the confidentiality of respondents, the Bureau truncates reported earnings at a particular top-code level, currently $99,999 per year. Respondents with higher earnings than this are coded as receiving $99,999. Obviously, this procedure precludes analysis of inequality trends in the top tail of the distribution. Moreover, because the Census Bureau has not raised the top-code value in line with earnings inflation, a rising share of workers has had earnings in the top-code category. Distributional measures that are sensitive to inequality in the extreme tails of the distribution will be affected by this shortcoming. In particular, analysts who naively ignore truncation may show declining inequality or more slowly rising inequality than is actually the case.

The issue of income truncation is far from a trivial one, for the share of men with earnings in the top-code category has risen from just 0.1 percent in the late 1960s to over 2 percent by 1980. (In 1987 slightly more than 1 percent of working men were in the top-code category.) Among particular subgroups of the population, such as full-time, year-round earners or men aged 35 to 54, the problem is even more severe. To deal with income truncation in this paper, I have essentially excluded from my analysis men and women in the extreme upper tail of the distribution. For men, this means that I exclude the top 2 percent of earners each year; for women, I exclude the top 1 percent. The trends described in this paper should therefore be understood to cover only the bottom 98 percent of men and the bottom 99 percent of women. If trends in the top one or two percentiles have mirrored those in the bottom 98 or 99 percent of the distribution, many of the distributional measures I consider will have varied much more widely than my statistics reveal.

One last and significant limitation of the CPS data is the exclusion of information about many forms of compensation, including employer

6. For a good discussion of these issues, see Kosters and Ross, "Distribution of Earnings," especially notes 8 and 13.

contributions for insurance and pensions. The survey collects reliable information only about money wages. Nonwage benefits, including health and pension benefits and contributions for social security, have increased much more rapidly than money wages in recent years. From 1972 through 1985, nonwage benefits rose from 12 percent of total compensation to 17 percent.[7] The trend in average compensation is thus substantially understated by the trend in money wages shown in the CPS.

Presumably, total compensation, rather than money wages alone, provides a better index of the standard of living workers can expect to derive from their jobs. It is unclear, however, whether the discrepancy between wages and compensation should affect the interpretation of the distributional statistics described below. If nonwage benefits in every year are a constant proportion of money earnings for each wage earner, the inequality of total compensation would correspond exactly to the inequality in the same year's distribution of money wages. Fringe benefits are not a constant proportion of money wages across different earnings classes, however. Many low-wage workers are provided with no nonwage compensation beyond their employer's mandatory contribution for social security and unemployment compensation. Their nonwage compensation is a small proportion of their money wages. Fringe benefits are more important and more likely to be provided for workers further up the earnings scale.[8] Whether this means that inequality in total compensation is likely to grow faster than inequality in money wages is highly uncertain, however, and the question must be left to later study.

Groups to Be Considered

In measuring trends in the distribution of job quality or earnings, it is necessary to define a population to be examined. Some researchers examine all workers with earnings, while others exclude self-employed workers and restrict their analysis to wage and salary workers. In this paper I follow the latter procedure. Self-employment income is noto-

---

7. Kosters and Ross, "Distribution of Earnings," p. 4.

8. However, some fringe benefits are capped, either by law or by normal employer practice. Employer-provided life insurance, for example, is limited by tax law. Health benefits are typically the same for every worker covered by an employer's health plan. High-wage workers under a given plan thus receive a smaller share of their total compensation in health benefits than do low-wage workers.

riously misreported. Even if it were accurately reported, it is impossible to apportion accurately which part of self-employment income is due to the proprietor's labor and which is derived from previous investment in capital or property. For these reasons, the sample analyzed here includes only workers whose wage and salary earnings are positive and exceed their income from self-employment.

Even among wage and salary earners, the choice of an analysis sample is not straightforward. Some analysts examine all earners, while others restrict their samples to full-time, year-round workers. A few examine both these populations. In this paper I examine all workers, irrespective of whether they work year round or full time. It would be simple, of course, to extend the analysis to a more restricted sample. In some cases I will report results from a more restrictive analysis.

The usual motivation behind analyzing full-time, full-year workers is that the distribution of earnings within this group could provide a better indication of the distribution of job quality or individual earnings potential in the labor market. Distributional measures obtained with this sample exclude the influence of voluntary nonemployment, involuntary unemployment, and both voluntary and involuntary short-time hours, and thus provide a purer measure of job quality than do measures that cover part-year and part-time workers.

While this distinction is accurate as far as it goes, it ignores the possibility that many jobs may be low in quality precisely because they are associated with greater unemployment or shorter weekly hours. For example, if low wage rates are associated with greater risk of unemployment and lower weekly hours, a sampling criterion that excludes workers who suffer unemployment or involuntary short hours would leave a sample that has above-average wage rates. In a study of the influence of the business cycle on the earnings distribution it seems essential to measure the effect of cycles on workers who would be excluded under a sampling rule requiring workers to have full-time hours and at least fifty weeks of employment. The distributional statistics I report below will show the share of inequality that is due to fluctuations in annual weeks of work and weekly hours.

Measures of Inequality

Most of the recent literature on earnings inequality and job quality has been based on very simple distributional statistics that can be interpreted quite easily. The typical procedure is to establish a set of earnings thresholds that define jobs or workers of different classes. In their study for the Joint Economic Committee, Barry Bluestone and Bennett Harrison defined a low-wage worker as one whose annual earnings, measured in constant 1973 dollars, falls below $3,000—50 percent of median earnings in 1973. A high-wage worker was defined as one earning at least $12,000 per year—twice the level of median earnings in 1973. People with earnings in between these two thresholds were defined as middle-stratum workers.[9] Similarly, Robert Lawrence defined low, medium, and high weekly earnings relative to median male weekly earnings in each calendar year.[10] Since his measure excludes the effect of changing median earnings over time, it is closer to a pure distributional statistic than the one defined by Bluestone and Harrison. Nonetheless, it is based on simple population counts of workers above and below certain critical thresholds.

While this kind of statistic is easily explained and has broad intuitive appeal, it is subject to severe limitations when used to draw inferences about the size distribution of income or its trend over time. As noted earlier, the clustering of income responses in the Current Population Survey implies that the count of respondents above or below critical thresholds will be sensitive to whether the threshold is just above or just below a number that is divisible by $1,000.[11] In addition, a statistic giving population counts cannot show the degree of earnings inequality below the bottom threshold and above the top one. For example, the percentage of earners in the bottom class might remain unchanged even though each earner in that class received a proportionately smaller share of average or median income. Most people would agree that inequality has risen under these circumstances, but a count statistic would show no change.

In order to circumvent these kinds of problems, I rely on distributional statistics that show the share of income in different classes or the variance of incomes across individuals. All of these statistics, like Lawrence's, attempt to measure pure inequality; they do not measure the effects of year-to-year movements in average or median earnings.

The full distribution of earnings can be mapped using the Lorenz

9. Bluestone and Harrison, *Great American Job Machine*, p. 9.

10. Lawrence, "Sectoral Shifts and the Size of the Middle Class."

11. These problems have been carefully described in Kosters and Ross, "Distribution of Earnings"; and Michael W. Horrigan and Steven E. Haugen, "The Declining Middle-Class Thesis: A Sensitivity Analysis," *Monthly Labor Review*, vol. 111 (May 1988), pp. 3–13.

Figure 1. Lorenz Curves for Male Wage Earners, 1967 and 1987

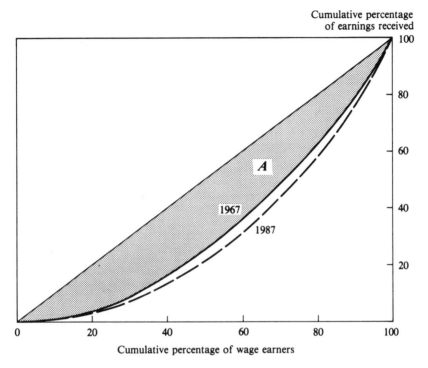

Source: Author's tabulations using March 1968 and March 1988 CPS tapes.

curve. To derive this curve, persons in the population are sorted in percentiles according to income, from lowest to highest. Points along the Lorenz curve show the cumulative share of all income that is received by people with incomes below successive percentile rankings. For example, the Lorenz curve for annual earnings of men in the bottom 98 percent of the earnings distribution is shown in figure 1. In 1967 men with earnings below the fiftieth percentile received 25 percent of all earnings received by men in this population. The Lorenz curve can be used to compare inequality over time. Because the 1987 curve, also shown in figure 1, lies everywhere below and to the right of the 1967 curve, one can infer that male earnings in 1987 were less equally distributed than they were in 1967. Men with earnings below the fiftieth percentile, for example, received only 21 percent of earnings in 1987, compared with 25 percent in 1967.

The most widely used distributional statistic, cited frequently in this paper, is the Gini coefficient, which is derived from the Lorenz curve.

The Gini coefficient measures the difference between the actual distribution and a perfectly egalitarian distribution of income. If all incomes were identical, the Lorenz curve would be a straight 45-degree line emanating from the origin. The Gini coefficient is the ratio of the area between the 45-degree line and the Lorenz curve to the total area under the 45-degree line. (In figure 1, the Gini coefficient for 1967 is the area A divided by the area below and to the right of the 45-degree line.) If all incomes were equal, the Gini coefficient would be equal to zero; if all income was received by one member of the population, the Gini coefficient would be one. The Gini coefficient for male earnings in 1967 was 0.351. By 1987 it had risen to 0.405, indicating a substantial growth in earnings inequality.

Although the Gini coefficient is the most commonly cited index of inequality, it suffers from some well-known limitations. Unlike the count statistics described earlier, it is very difficult to interpret. It is more sensitive to movements in the middle of the distribution than it is to movements at either end. More fundamentally, the index does not distinguish between inequality caused by very high incomes in the extreme upper tail of the distribution and inequality arising from very low incomes in the bottom tail. An increase in inequality at either end might cause equal movements in the Gini coefficient, but the movements would have very different implications for interpreting the trend in job quality.

As a supplement to the Gini coefficient, I therefore use two measures of inequality of income in the tails of the distribution. The first is the ratio of average earnings in the bottom quintile of the earnings distribution to average earnings in the middle quintile. The second is the ratio of earnings in the top tail of the distribution to average earnings in the middle quintile. For males, the top tail is defined as the eighty-first through the ninety-eighth annual earnings percentiles; for women, the top tail includes earnings in the eighty-first through the ninety-ninth percentiles. (Recall that I exclude the top two percentiles of men and the top percentile of women from my distributional statistics.) If both these indexes are rising simultaneously or falling simultaneously, the implications for overall inequality are ambiguous. But if the first index rises while the second remains constant or falls, a trend toward greater equality is strongly indicated. (The opposite pattern would of course indicate rising inequality.)

In addition to the statistics just mentioned, several additional indexes are useful in examining earnings inequality. One is the share of all earnings received by earners in different segments of the earnings distribution. Another is the variance of the logarithm of annual earnings, whose change over time can be easily decomposed into shares that are due to changes in the distribution of weeks worked, usual weekly hours of work, and hourly wage rates. This decomposition shows that virtually all of the secular rise in earnings inequality among men is due to the rising variance of hourly wage rates, not to changes in the distribution of weeks at work or weekly hours of work. Hence rising inequality is apparently due to increasing variance in the price of labor across different classes rather than to increasing variance in the voluntary choices of laborers.

Finally, I examine the earnings distribution with an index proposed by Henri Theil.[12] This index has the convenient property that inequality can be decomposed into the share that is due to inequality *within* designated classes of the population and the part that is due to inequality *between* classes. Analysis using this statistic shows, for example, that rising inequality among male earners is due as much to growing inequality within population groups defined by age and education as it is to growing inequality between age and education classes.

Long Trends

Some recent writing has given rise to the impression that growing earnings inequality is a recent phenomenon in the labor market. For example, the papers and books by Barry Bluestone and Bennett Harrison appear to suggest that changes in the industrial structure and economic climate have contributed to a growing incidence of low-wage employment in recent years. This was said to have occurred after a long period in which benign economic trends contributed to greater earnings equality and a rising share of middle-income jobs.

Long-term trends in the Gini coefficients for male and female earnings do not bear out this impression. As far back as 1972, Peter Henle of the U.S. Department of Labor showed that much of the postwar era has been characterized by "a slow but persistent trend toward greater inequality," both for all male earners and for those working full time and year round.[13] This finding was confirmed in a subsequent study by

12. Henri Theil, *Economics and Information Theory* (Amsterdam: North-Holland, 1967), pp. 91–134. This index is sometimes designated "Theil-I" to distinguish it from a related index that Theil later proposed.

13. Peter Henle, "Exploring the Distribution of Earned Income," *Monthly Labor Review*, vol. 95 (December 1972), pp. 16–27 (quotation on p. 16).

Henle and Paul Ryscavage, based on grouped data from the CPS, which showed that earnings inequality among men rose over the twenty-year period from 1958 to 1977. A similar trend was found among all men with earnings, men with wage and salary earnings, and men with year-round, full-time jobs. The earnings distribution among women, although more unequal than that of men, was found to have little trend over the same period.[14] Inequality among women working year round on a full-time schedule probably declined.

Using the basic procedures followed by Henle and Ryscavage, it is possible to extend their series back to 1947 and bring it forward to 1986. With the exception of three years in the 1970s, the Census Bureau has published annual tabulations of wage and salary earnings among male and female workers.[15] The tabulations, broken into as many as twenty-two earnings categories, show the number or percentage of workers with annual wage and salary earnings between specified limits.

I have used these tabulations to derive an estimate of the approximate size distribution of male and female earnings from 1947 through 1986.[16] My estimates for 1947–48 and 1950 may be suspect because of the wide range of some of the income categories used in the P-60 report for those years. Excluding these years still leaves thirty-seven years in which an estimate of the Gini coefficient can be derived using consistent methods and more or less consistent information. The full series of estimated Gini coefficients is displayed in appendix table A-1.

Trends in the Gini coefficients for male and female earners over the period 1951–86 are shown in figure 2. Although my estimates do not correspond exactly to those obtained by Henle and Ryscavage, both

14. Peter Henle and Paul Ryscavage, "The Distribution of Earned Income among Men and Women, 1958–77," *Monthly Labor Review*, vol. 103 (April 1980), pp. 3–10.

15. Data from the actual CPS files can be used to replicate the tabulations of annual earnings the Census Bureau would have produced had they maintained a consistent wage and salary distribution series throughout the 1970s.

16. In deriving my estimate of the size distribution of earnings, I used a method suggested by Emmett Spiers, "Estimation of Summary Measures of Income Size Distribution from Grouped Data," *American Statistical Association: Proceedings of the Social Statistics Section* (1977), pt. 1, pp. 252–57. The method uses linear interpolation to estimate income quantiles in lower income classes and Pareto interpolation to estimate quantiles in the higher classes where the estimator of the Pareto distribution statistic exceeds one. For a few years, notably in the mid-1970s, it is necessary to use Pareto extrapolation for males to estimate quantiles in the top-code category. However, to minimize extrapolation errors, the size distribution is only estimated up through the ninety-eighth percentile of men and the ninety-ninth percentile for women. In spite of this precaution, the estimates of the Gini coefficient are sensitive to the interpolation and extrapolation methods used, and hence they should be regarded as highly approximate.

Figure 2. Trend in Earnings Inequality among Wage Earners, by Sex, 1951–86[a]

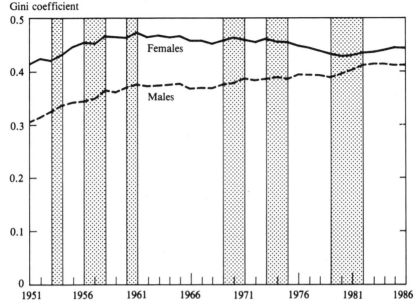

Gini coefficient

Source: Author's tabulations from U.S. Bureau of the Census, *Current Population Reports,* series P-60, various years.
a. Shaded areas indicate recession years.

sets of estimates follow a very similar pattern in the case of men. There is little correlation, however, in the case of women.[17] Earnings inequality rose for both men and women over the 1950s, reaching a peak in 1961 before declining slightly and then stabilizing in the 1960s. From the late 1960s through the early 1980s, inequality rose among male earners while remaining relatively stable among women.

17. Some difference between our two estimates is to be expected, for my estimate excludes the extreme upper tail of the distribution, whereas that of Henle and Ryscavage includes it. Moreover, the two Labor Department economists had access to unpublished Census information on the size distribution of earnings, whereas I do not. The correlation between my estimate of the Gini coefficient for males and that of Henle and Ryscavage is 0.932. The correlation for women is far lower, in part because the trend in inequality is so much weaker among women than among men after 1961. Hence the variability in both the Henle-Ryscavage and my own estimate of the Gini coefficient for women may be dominated more by measurement error than by true movement in the series. However, my estimate of the Gini coefficient for women is also well above the estimate obtained by Henle and Ryscavage. I can discover no reason for the discrepancy, since my estimates of the Gini coefficient for three other groups (male wage and salary workers and male and female full-time, year-round wage and salary workers) otherwise appear quite close to Henle and Ryscavage's estimates. Moreover, my estimate of female inequality corresponds very closely to the estimate I obtain when using individual-level data from the 1968–87 March CPS files.

Table 1. Effects of Unemployment on Male and Female Earnings Inequality, 1954–86[a]

Independent variable	Men		Women	
	Excluding T80	Including T80	Excluding T80	Including T80
	Gini coefficient			
Constant	0.2765	0.2704	0.3695	0.3661
	(26.380)	(36.845)	(20.765)	(21.365)
UR[b]	0.0025	0.0025	0.0010	0.0009
	(3.935)	(5.165)	(1.215)	(1.115)
T[c]	0.0057	0.0064	0.0074	0.0079
	(6.942)	(10.959)	(4.986)	(5.469)
$T60$[d]	−0.0043	−0.0053	−0.0088	−0.0097
	(4.786)	(8.087)	(5.384)	(5.866)
$T80$[e]	. . .	0.0016	. . .	0.0020
		(3.496)		(1.531)
$\bar{R}^2$	0.967	0.973	0.867	0.872
ρ	0.356	0.037	0.681	0.657
	Top/middle (T/M)[f]			
Constant	165.661	157.530	193.572	188.533
	(16.014)	(30.298)	(9.125)	(10.833)
UR	1.273	1.576	1.273	1.072
	(2.677)	(4.624)	(1.242)	(1.141)
T	1.231	1.964	6.356	7.189
	(1.429)	(4.722)	(3.623)	(5.023)
$T60$	0.483	−0.678	−7.467	−8.956
	(0.509)	(1.461)	(3.874)	(5.524)
$T80$	. . .	2.003	. . .	3.238
		(6.055)		(2.672)
$\bar{R}^2$	0.977	0.984	0.748	0.787
ρ	0.696	0.130	0.652	0.520
	Bottom/middle (B/M)[f]			
Constant	27.145	27.048	17.320	17.380
	(18.544)	(17.994)	(11.180)	(11.279)
UR	−0.090	−0.094	−0.071	−0.071
	(0.974)	(1.005)	(1.326)	(1.288)
T	−1.087	−1.073	−0.449	−0.452
	(9.405)	(8.851)	(3.453)	(3.448)
$T60$	1.140	1.119	0.484	0.475
	(9.064)	(8.234)	(3.324)	(3.113)
$T80$	. . .	0.043	. . .	0.057
		(0.442)		(0.441)
$\bar{R}^2$	0.817	0.812	0.881	0.877
ρ	0.280	0.281	0.894	0.878

Source: See text.

a. First-order autocorrelation estimation results. Numbers in parentheses are absolute values of *t*-statistics. ρ is estimate of autocorrelation coefficient.

b. Civilian unemployment rate.

c. Time trend (1947 = 1).

d. Time trend after 1959 (1960 = 1).

e. Time trend after 1979 (1980 = 1).

f. Ratio of average earnings in top (bottom) tail of distribution to those in middle quintile, measured in percent.

The shaded areas in figure 2 indicate years with rising average unemployment. There is clearly a tendency for male inequality to rise faster than its underlying trend rate during periods with high cyclical unemployment, but this tendency is much less evident among female earners.

In order to measure the relative contributions of secular trends and cyclical unemployment to earnings inequality, I have estimated annual time-series regressions of time trends and civilian unemployment on the estimated Gini coefficient for 1954–86.[18] The specification of the basic regression is parsimonious. It includes a time trend variable (labeled T) that rises over the entire period and a second trend variable ($T60$) that rises in years after 1959. To see whether earnings inequality has risen at a faster trend rate during the 1980s than during earlier periods, I also include in one of the specifications a separate trend variable for years after 1979 ($T80$). To capture the effects of the business cycle on earnings inequality, the specification includes the civilian unemployment rate (UR). I also experimented with alternative cyclical measures, such as the unemployment rate of men aged 25–54 and the percentage gap between actual and potential GNP as estimated by the Congressional Budget Office. Since these alternative specifications produced virtually identical results to those shown here, they will not be discussed further. All regression equations include first-order autocorrelation error correction.

The coefficient estimates for the equations are shown in the top panel of table 1. Estimates in the first and third columns were obtained with the specification that excludes a separate time trend for the 1980s; estimates in the second and fourth columns are from the specification that includes $T80$. For both men and women the results show a strong secular trend in the Gini coefficient during the 1950s, but a sharp slowdown in the trend after 1960. Among women, trend growth in inequality reversed after 1960, although there is evidence it may have resumed during the 1980s (see fourth column). For men, earnings inequality as measured by the Gini coefficient rose at a trend rate of 4 percent per decade after 1960. The coefficient on $T80$ (in second column) suggests that this trend has accelerated during the 1980s.

18. Data before 1954 were excluded from the regression because of the aforementioned problem with P-60 earnings classifications in 1947–48 and 1950 and because one of the independent variables used to control for business cycle effects—the GNP gap—was not available for years before 1954. The results shown in table 1 are not appreciably affected by including the entire time series, however.

The hypothesis that high cyclical unemployment contributes to earnings inequality is borne out by the results for men but is not supported by the results for women. A one-point rise in the civilian unemployment rate is associated with a 0.7 percent rise in the Gini coefficient for men; it is associated with a 0.2 percent rise in the Gini coefficient for women, although the latter effect is not statistically significant.[19] In one respect the difference between men and women can hardly be surprising. One reason that earnings inequality is so high among women is that a high percentage of them work relatively short weekly hours and fewer than fifty-two weeks a year, even during business cycle peaks. Consequently, the extra variability in earnings produced by cyclical fluctuations might be relatively small. Men are far more likely to work full time for fifty-two weeks a year. When cyclical unemployment is high, many male workers who suffer unemployment or involuntary short hours would otherwise have been working on full-time, year-round schedules. Their unemployment thus contributes to greater variance in male earnings.

To see the effects of cyclical unemployment on male earnings inequality, it is useful to calculate the rise in inequality that is due solely to cyclical factors. From 1967 to 1969 the Gini coefficient for men averaged 0.371 (see table A-1). By 1984–86 it had risen to 0.412, an increase of 11.1 percent. Over the same period unemployment rose from 3.6 percent to 7.2 percent. Using the coefficients reported in table 1, this should have led to a rise in the Gini coefficient for men of 2.4 percent—but the actual rise was almost five times larger. In the case of women, cyclical trends over the same period explain very little of the change in earnings inequality as measured by the Gini coefficient.

Alternative Measures of Inequality

Given estimates of the size distribution of earnings, it is possible to derive alternative measures of male and female earnings inequality. Two of these are the ratio of earnings in the top tail of the distribution to earnings in the middle (*T/M*) and the ratio of earnings in the bottom quintile to earnings in the middle (*B/M*). In some ways these measures are more revealing than the Gini coefficient, particularly when they are

---

19. The average 1954–86 value of the male Gini coefficient is 0.380 (see table A-1). Hence the coefficient on *UR* of 0.0025 implies that a one-point rise in unemployment will raise the male Gini by 0.7 percent. The average value of the female Gini coefficient over the same period is 0.452.

examined together. (Estimates of these two ratios for 1947–86 are displayed in appendix table A-1.)

As one would expect, trends in the two variables largely account for the time-series pattern of Gini coefficients. During the 1950s, the ratio of top to middle earnings rose, while the ratio of bottom to middle earnings fell, leading to a substantial increase in the Gini coefficient. Since 1960, however, the ratio of low to middle earnings has stabilized and even risen slightly; the ratio of top to middle earnings has continued to grow, rising quite sharply over the past decade. Among women, the pattern of these variables was similar to that among men during the 1950s, but has diverged since 1960, when the Gini coefficient for women stabilized.

In order to measure the impact of business cycle fluctuations on these variables, I estimated regressions with the same specifications used to analyze movements in the Gini coefficient. Results of these regressions are shown in the bottom two panels of table 1. For men the regressions are more successful at explaining variation in the ratio of top to middle incomes, T/M, than they are in explaining the pattern of bottom to middle incomes, B/M. The coefficients for men in column 1 show that earnings in the top category rose relative to those in the middle by 1.2 percentage points per year over the late 1950s; since 1960 they have risen over 1.7 percentage points per year $(T + T60)$. There is strong evidence that this trend has accelerated during the 1980s, when the rate of rise of T/M has gone above 3 percentage points a year $(T + T60 + T80)$. The unemployment rate has a sizable and statistically significant effect on T/M, causing the earnings ratio of males in the top tail to rise by 1.3 to 1.6 percentage points for every 1 percent rise in the unemployment rate.

By contrast, since 1960 there has been virtually no secular trend in male earnings at the bottom relative to average earnings in the middle (B/M). Some movement in this variable is attributable to fluctuations in the unemployment rate. As unemployment rises one point, the average earnings of males at the bottom fall about one-tenth of a percentage point relative to earnings of men in the middle quintile. Of course, if earnings of men at the bottom fall relative to those in the middle, they fall even more sharply compared with those of earners at the top, who enjoy relative gains in wage and salary income during a cyclical downturn.

Among women, earnings in the top tail of the distribution have fallen relative to those in the middle since 1960, though there appears to have been a reversal of this trend in the 1980s. Rises in unemployment are associated with gains in the earnings of women at the top relative to women in the middle. The reason may be that women in the top tail—like men in the same earnings class—are comparatively immune to the effects of cyclical fluctuations. Women on the bottom may experience modest earnings losses relative to women in the middle, although the apparent cyclical effect is not statistically significant.

Trends among Full-Time, Year-Round Workers

The data published by the Census Bureau show distributional trends among all men and women with wage and salary earnings, but they do not show trends among subgroups in this population, such as earners who work full time and year round. To examine trends among subpopulations it is necessary to examine data in the annual CPS tapes. These tapes are available back through 1967, so detailed tabulations of the earnings distribution are possible for only about half the number of years analyzed above. The shorter time series affects only slightly the interpretation of recent distributional trends.

In order to calculate inequality statistics over the 1967–87 period, I used a somewhat different population than the one described in the Census Bureau's P-60 reports. The bureau provides tabulations on the size distribution of earnings among people aged 14 and over who report positive wage and salary income. (Starting in the late 1970s, the sample was restricted to earners aged 15 and older.) The sample used in the remainder of this paper consists of men and women aged 16 and over who report positive wage and salary income that exceeds their earnings from self-employment.

Given the differences in sampling criteria, there should be differences in the resulting estimates of size distribution statistics, even if the statistics were calculated using identical procedures. Of course, the procedures are not identical, because the Census Bureau's definition of income classes has changed from time to time, whereas the estimates of size distribution statistics described here rely on the actual earnings reports of CPS respondents.[20]

20. To conserve on computation time, the estimates of Gini coefficients were obtained by dividing respondents into narrow income classes and then using linear and Pareto interpolation in order to obtain exact estimates of the size distribution of earnings. Because of the tendency of respondents to report their earnings in multiples of $1,000, this method

Estimates of the effect of unemployment and secular trends on the Gini coefficients among all earners are shown in the first and third columns of table 2. Like the estimates shown in table 1, the coefficients in table 2 show little influence of unemployment on the Gini coefficient for women but a significant effect on that for men. All of the movement in the women's Gini coefficient is explained by the time-trend variables. For men, about one-seventh of the rise in the Gini coefficient between 1967–69 and 1985–87 can be explained by the rise in average unemployment.[21] Significantly, the time-trend coefficient for years after 1979 shows an acceleration toward inequality among men and a reversal of the previous trend toward equality among women. The coefficients in the lower two panels show the influence of unemployment and secular trends on the incomes of earners in the top and bottom quintiles relative to those in the middle. The effect of unemployment is similar to that found for the longer period, 1954–86. A rise in unemployment increases the earnings of men in the top quintile relative to those in the middle, while depressing earnings among men at the bottom. Both effects are statistically significant at conventional levels. Among women there is a similar pattern, although the effects of the unemployment rate are much smaller and are not statistically significant. It is notable that both among men and women there has been a trend in the 1980s toward rising relative earnings in the top quintile and declining relative earnings at the bottom, controlling for the effects of the business cycle. Most of the rise in inequality during the 1980s is accounted for by this trend factor; the contribution of higher unemployment has been relatively modest.

The second and fourth columns in table 2 contain coefficients for an identically specified model estimated on men and women who work full time and year round. Not surprisingly, the influence of cyclical unemployment is much weaker for this group than it is for all earners. In no case is the coefficient on unemployment statistically significant at conventional significance levels. If one excludes the effects of cyclical un-

---

probably produces more accurate estimates of certain distributional statistics than would reliance on actual earnings responses. See Sandra A. West, "Standard Measures of Central Tendency for Censored Earnings Data from the Current Population Survey," BLS Statistical Notes, no. 26 (March 1987), and the related discussion in Kosters and Ross, "The Distribution of Earnings," note 13.

21. Based on my tabulations of the CPS files, I estimate that the Gini coefficient for males rose from 0.354 in 1967–69 to 0.404 in 1985–87. Over the same period, unemployment rose from 3.63 percent to 6.80 percent. Thus the rise in unemployment explains only $(6.80 - 3.63) \times 0.0022$ of the rise in the male Gini—or roughly one-seventh of the actual rise, which was 0.050.

Table 2. Effects of Unemployment on Male and Female Earnings Inequality for All Workers and Full-Time, Year-Round Workers, 1967–87[a]

Independent variable[b]	Men		Women	
	All workers	Full-time year-round	All workers	Full-time year-round
	Gini coefficient			
Constant	0.3020	0.2138	0.4968	0.2897
	(36.983)	(25.344)	(37.860)	(23.548)
UR	0.0022	−0.0006	0.0005	−0.0008
	(3.486)	(0.715)	(0.672)	(0.686)
T	0.0020	0.0015	−0.0018	−0.0014
	(5.824)	(3.923)	(3.513)	(−2.451)
T80	0.0010	0.0031	0.0020	0.0061
	(1.399)	(4.241)	(1.867)	(5.771)
$\bar{R}^2$	0.977	0.954	0.841	0.803
ρ	0.444	0.200	0.648	0.250
	Top/middle (T/M)			
Constant	156.950	166.397	286.832	171.435
	(33.445)	(36.634)	(17.123)	(50.448)
UR	1.385	0.036	0.594	−0.194
	(3.072)	(0.085)	(0.602)	(0.590)
T	1.477	0.560	−0.955	0.380
	(6.698)	(2.644)	(1.424)	(2.372)
T80	1.561	1.730	1.765	1.575
	(3.819)	(4.381)	(1.295)	(5.315)
$\bar{R}^2$	0.980	0.940	0.452	0.942
ρ	0.173	0.201	0.625	0.160
	Bottom/middle (B/M)			
Constant	16.644	50.231	6.127	23.874
	(17.903)	(18.762)	(10.116)	(4.402)
UR	−0.246	0.259	−0.058	0.342
	(3.130)	(1.124)	(1.059)	(0.798)
T	0.006	−0.195	0.196	0.823
	(0.154)	(1.623)	(7.070)	(3.484)
T80	−0.068	−0.490	−0.188	−1.757
	(0.849)	(2.128)	(3.587)	(3.809)
$\bar{R}^2$	0.684	0.828	0.906	0.704
ρ	0.345	0.323	0.259	0.412

Source: See text.

a. First-order autocorrelation estimation results. Numbers in parentheses are absolute values of *t*-statistics. ρ is estimate of autocorrelation coefficient.

b. See table 1 for definitions of variables.

employment on annual weeks of work and eliminates some of its impact on weekly hours, it is hardly surprising that the influence of business cycles on earnings inequality should almost disappear. The results for full-time, year-round workers show a trend toward accelerated inequality during the 1980s. In fact, the trend toward inequality is usually faster among these workers than it is among all workers with wage and salary earnings, particularly at the bottom of the earnings distribution. This finding strongly suggests that inequality may be rising because of growing inequality in weekly earnings.

Quintile Shares

One way to understand recent changes in the earnings distribution is to examine trends in the share of earnings received by workers in different parts of the distribution. A customary division of the income distribution ranks earners according to income level and then allocates them into quintiles. Because of top-coding in the CPS public use files, it is not possible to directly measure wage and salary earnings in the top quintile of the distribution. Consequently, I determine total earnings among the bottom 98 percent of male earners and the bottom 99 percent of female earners and then calculate the share of earnings received by men and women in each of the bottom four quintiles and by men and women in the top quintile, excluding men in the top 2 percent and women in the top 1 percent of earners.

Women in the bottom three quintiles receive a smaller proportion of female earnings than men in the corresponding quintiles receive of male earnings (see the means of dependent variables reported in table 3). Women in the top quintile receive a larger proportion of earnings than men at the top. However, earnings among women in the bottom quintiles have been rising faster than earnings of women in the middle and near the top of the distribution. Consequently, female earnings have become somewhat more equal over time, although this pattern has been reversed during the 1980s.

Among men, earnings in the bottom three quintiles have shrunk relative to earnings at the top. Men in the top income category received 35.7 percent of earnings in 1967 and 1968. By 1987 their share had risen to 40.0 percent. All of the gain was at the expense of earners in the bottom three quintiles. The share of men in the bottom quintile shrank from 3.4 percent in 1967 to 2.8 in 1987; the share of men in the second

Table 3. Effects of Unemployment on Male and Female Quintile Earnings Shares, 1967–87[a]

Independent variable[b]	Earnings received (percent)				
	Bottom quintile	Second quintile	Middle quintile	Fourth quintile	Top quintile
			Men		
Constant	3.777	15.557	22.230	25.722	32.714
	(27.96)	(64.05)	(156.57)	(135.00)	(70.21)
UR	−0.068	−0.125	−0.037	0.048	0.182
	(4.83)	(4.95)	(2.52)	(2.44)	(3.75)
T	−0.009	−0.098	−0.072	0.057	0.121
	(1.38)	(8.24)	(10.35)	(6.19)	(5.32)
T80	−0.025	−0.018	−0.052	−0.067	0.162
	(2.08)	(0.86)	(4.20)	(3.98)	(3.96)
$\bar{R}^2$	0.900	0.977	0.986	0.904	0.970
Durbin-Watson	1.477	1.598	1.523	1.827	1.299
Mean of dependent variable (percent)	3.02	11.70	19.68	27.70	37.90
			Women		
Constant	1.260	5.919	16.473	30.049	46.298
	(11.54)	(16.01)	(40.96)	(183.43)	(60.15)
UR	−0.018	−0.036	−0.025	−0.001	0.080
	(1.55)	(0.94)	(0.60)	(0.05)	(0.99)
T	0.034	0.095	0.048	−0.063	−0.113
	(6.30)	(5.26)	(2.43)	(7.90)	(3.01)
T80	−0.041	−0.067	−0.080	0.009	0.179
	(4.30)	(2.07)	(2.27)	(0.64)	(2.65)
$\bar{R}^2$	0.785	0.816	0.229	0.951	0.319
Durbin-Watson	0.957	0.649	0.787	1.343	0.700
Mean of dependent variable (percent)	2.11	8.51	17.65	28.10	43.62

Source: See text.
a. Ordinary-least-squares estimates. Numbers in parentheses are absolute values of t-statistics.
b. See table 1 for definition of variables.

quintile fell from 13.2 percent to 10.7 percent; and the share received by men in the middle quintile fell from 20.5 percent to 18.7 percent.

Changes in the share of income received by each quintile can be analyzed using methods similar to those used above to analyze movements in the Gini coefficient.[22] Regression equations showing the effect of the unemployment rate and time-trend variables are displayed in table 3. Even though the error terms are correlated across the five

22. The first analysts using this procedure to examine the overall income distribution were Alan S. Blinder and Howard Y. Esaki, "Macroeconomic Activity and Income Distribution in the Postwar United States," *Review of Economics and Statistics*, vol. 60 (November 1978), pp. 604–09.

equations, the most efficient method of analysis is separate ordinary least squares on each regression equation, which is the method used in table 3. The results shown in table 3 are consistent with those shown in tables 1 and 2. Among males, movement in the unemployment rate has a statistically significant, though modest, effect on the distribution of male earnings. If unemployment rises by one percentage point, the share of earnings received by the bottom, second, and middle quintiles drops by 0.07 percent, 0.12 percent, and 0.04 percent, respectively. These changes are 2.3 percent, 1.1 percent, and 0.2 percent, respectively, of the typical share of income received by the three categories of workers. By contrast, the earnings share of the fourth quintile rises by 0.05 percentage points and the share of the top quintile rises by 0.18 percentage points with every one-point rise in the unemployment rate. Fluctuations in the unemployment rate have a much smaller effect, if any, on the distribution of wage and salary earnings among women.

Coefficients on the time-trend variables confirm the previous finding that inequality among males has risen substantially since 1967. During the late 1960s and 1970s, earners in the top two quintiles gained primarily at the expense of earners in the second and middle quintiles. During the 1980s the trend toward lower relative earnings in the bottom three quintiles has accelerated, while the share of earnings received by workers in the fourth quintile has begun to shrink. Controlling for business cycle effects, the share received by earners in the top category has grown at a trend rate of 0.3 percentage points per year over the 1980s.

The trend of inequality among women has followed a less consistent pattern. From 1967 through 1979, inequality fell as earnings in the bottom three quintiles grew in comparison with earnings in the top two categories. During the 1980s, however, relative earnings in the lowest and third quintiles began to fall and the share of earnings received by earners in the second quintile grew at a much slower pace than it had in the 1960s and 1970s. The share of earnings received by women in the top category began to rise in the 1980s, reversing the pattern of the 1960s and 1970s.

Summary

The contribution of economic fluctuations to earnings inequality using several different measures can be summarized briefly. Average unemployment has fluctuated widely over the past two decades, and civilian unemployment during the middle 1980s was double the level of the late

1960s. According to regressions covering the years from 1954 through 1986, this change in unemployment accounts for roughly one-fifth of the rise in the Gini coefficient for men from the late 1960s to the mid-1980s, but almost none of the fluctuation in the Gini for women. Regression results covering only the period since 1967 suggest that about a seventh of the fluctuation in the Gini coefficient for men has been due to cyclical factors.

Results from 1954–86 and 1967–87 are also reasonably consistent in what they show about the impact of unemployment on the ratio of earnings at the top and bottom of the distribution in comparison with earnings in the middle. As the unemployment rate rises, the relative gap between high and moderate earners rises, as does the gap between moderate and low earners. For female earners, the effect of the business cycle on inequality appears to be substantially smaller than it is for men. For both men and women, the effect of the business cycle on a sample restricted to full-time, year-round workers is negligible.

All of the results derived so far show a persistent trend toward inequality among men, especially those who are full-time, year-round workers. This trend has occurred because earnings in the top portion of the distribution have risen relative to earnings in the middle and at the bottom. More recently, earnings in the bottom quintile have fallen relative to earnings received by workers both at the top and in the middle of the distribution. The trend toward inequality among men has almost certainly accelerated since 1979. Distributional trends among women have been quite different, at least until recent years. After 1960, there was little measurable change in female inequality, although statistics for the 1980s show a break in this pattern. For women, as for men, the decade of the 1980s has seen growing inequality, caused both by relative gains among workers in the top tail of the distribution and by relative losses among workers at the bottom.

Inequality within Regions and Demographic Groups

Thus far I have considered national-level statistics for earnings inequality and unemployment. The effect of cyclical unemployment on inequality appeared to be modest, but this conclusion might have to be modified if inequality were found to differ substantially among geographic regions depending on their average unemployment rates. Tightness in local labor markets varies widely in the United States. Regions such as New England and the mid-Atlantic states have enjoyed below-average unemployment for a decade, while areas such as the upper Midwest and the mid-South have suffered persistently high unemployment over the same period. These conditions will tend to raise inequality between regions, even though they may reduce inequality within regions experiencing tight labor markets.

To examine this hypothesis I have calculated distributional statistics for the nine census regions of the United States. Gini coefficients for males in the nine regions are shown in appendix table A-2. Because the samples for the regions are far smaller than those for the nation as a whole, regional distributional statistics will be subject to a greater amount of sampling variability. The Gini coefficients reported in table A-2 reflect this problem; they show greater year-to-year fluctuation than the corresponding national-level statistics. Much of this movement presumably reflects measurement error.

The Gini coefficients shown in table A-2 provide no obvious indication that low regional unemployment leads to low earnings inequality among males. New England, which has enjoyed the lowest regional unemployment in recent years, experienced a relatively large proportional rise in male earnings inequality. The West North Central region, which experienced rising unemployment over the two decades after 1967, saw a comparatively modest rise in earnings inequality. Inequality among men has risen within all nine regions. The opposite pattern was found for women (not shown here). Inequality has fallen within eight of the nine geographic regions and has risen in only the mid-Atlantic states.

To see whether regional unemployment patterns can explain much of variation in regional inequality, I pooled the time-series data from the nine regions and estimated two statistical models appropriate to panel data: a fixed-effects model and a one-way variance components model. The two specifications yielded similar results, so only those from the random-effects model will be described here. In addition to the regional unemployment rate, the specification of independent variables includes the fraction of earners in a region aged 16–24 (*Fraction* < *25*) and the fraction aged 45 and older (*Fraction* ≥ *45*).[23] These variables were included under the assumption that differing demographic compositions across regions might affect regional earnings inequality.

Coefficient estimates for the random-effects model are reported in

23. Because the models were estimated separately for male and female earners, these fractions were separately calculated for men and women as well.

Table 4.   Effects of Unemployment and Demographic Factors on Regional Earnings Inequality, by Sex, 1967–87[a]

Independent variable	Men	Women
	Gini coefficient	
Constant	0.5165	0.3753
	(41.198)	(38.131)
UR	0.0028	0.0004
	(6.848)	(1.088)
Fraction < 25[b]	−0.0008	0.0016
	(2.273)	(6.203)
Fraction ≥ 45[c]	−0.0043	0.0007
	(15.721)	(2.586)
	Top/middle (T/M)	
Constant	359.204	216.514
	(36.976)	(17.909)
UR	1.214	0.284
	(4.047)	(0.562)
Fraction < 25[b]	−1.758	1.861
	(6.622)	(5.982)
Fraction ≥ 45[c]	−3.544	−0.243
	(17.436)	(0.870)
	Bottom/middle (B/M)	
Constant	17.193	16.274
	(12.358)	(20.378)
UR	−0.316	−0.029
	(6.828)	(0.871)
Fraction < 25[b]	−0.137	−0.046
	(3.424)	(2.198)
Fraction ≥ 45[c]	0.109	−0.092
	(3.621)	(4.356)

a. Random-effects model estimates of time-series, cross-sectional panel data on nine regions and twenty-one time periods. Numbers in parentheses are absolute values of *t*-statistics.
b. Percentage of male or female earners under age 25.
c. Percentage aged 45 or older.

table 4. As was true of earlier statistical results, the explanatory power of the equation is much better for men than for women. Estimates of the effect of the regional unemployment rate on inequality are generally consistent with those shown in table 1. A one-point rise in the unemployment rate is associated with about a 0.7 percent rise in the Gini coefficient for men and a much smaller and less reliably measured rise for women. The same one-point change in unemployment yields a 1.2 percentage point rise in the ratio of earnings in the top male class to earnings in the middle; it yields a 0.3 percentage point drop in the ratio of earnings in the bottom quintile compared with earnings in the middle.

Among women, the effect on earners in the top class relative to those in the middle is somewhat smaller, while the effect on women in the bottom quintile relative to those in the middle is negligible.

These estimates correspond to those presented above in showing that rising unemployment is a statistically significant though modest part of the explanation for rising male inequality in recent years. Among women, the effect of unemployment on these measures of inequality is small or negligible, though the actual change in inequality has been scanty as well.

Another plausible explanation for movements in earnings inequality is the changing composition of the labor force. It should be obvious that the demographic composition of the population may influence inequality.[24] The entry of a large cohort of young, inexperienced workers can affect the distribution of earnings in at least two ways. First, a growing proportion of the labor force will work at entry-level wage rates for fewer than fifty-two weeks a year. This will raise the share of workers receiving relatively low annual earnings. In addition, the influx of a large number of workers with approximately equal education and experience may tend to drive down the wages that entering workers can expect to earn.[25] This will change the relative earnings of entering workers in comparison with experienced workers.

To see whether this hypothesis explains the recent pattern of male and female earnings inequality, I have separately calculated Gini coefficients for different age and sex groups. The results of these tabulations are displayed in figure 3. As with the regional Gini coefficients described earlier, the estimates shown in figure 3 contain a great deal more variation due to measurement error than do estimates for the population as a whole. Nonetheless, both panels show familiar patterns. Earnings inequality is generally higher among women than men, except in the oldest age group. But inequality has grown in every age category for males while remaining essentially unchanged among women. Only among women past age 54 has there been some tendency toward greater inequality, and that trend has been modest in comparison with similar trends for men.

24. For example, the reported coefficients on the demographic variables in table 4 suggest that a rising share of 25-to-44-year-old workers in the population contributes to growing inequality. Note that earnings inequality *falls* with increases in the share of younger and older workers in the population.

25. See Finis Welch, "Effects of Cohort Size on Earnings: The Baby Boom Babies' Financial Bust," *Journal of Political Economy,* vol. 87, pt. 2 (October 1979), pp. S65–97.

Figure 3. Trend in Earnings Inequality within Sex and Age Groups, 1967–87

Gini coefficient

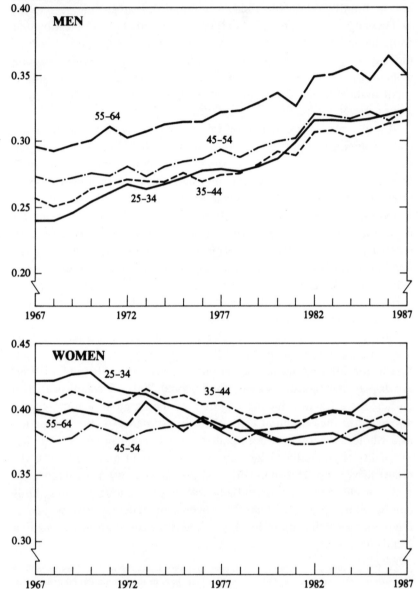

Source: Author's tabulations using March CPS tapes.

The numbers displayed for males in figure 3 provide some evidence in support of the hypothesis that generational crowding has affected income disparities *within* birth cohorts. Inequality has risen most among the youngest age groups. Yet generational crowding by itself cannot provide a complete explanation of growing inequality among men, for the trend is apparent even in the oldest age groups, where no effect would be anticipated.

In its purest form, the hypothesis of generational crowding refers to two separate phenomena. The first is the change in *weights* of different classes in the wage-earning population, and the second is the change in *relative earnings* among those classes. If the size of the baby boom generation has contributed to inequality, it is primarily because it has increased the proportion of workers in certain low earnings categories—part-time, part-year, or low-wage workers, for example—or because its sheer size has increased the earnings differential between younger and older workers. Both of these phenomena can be examined using the individual-level data from the CPS.

In order to examine the effect of changing population composition on earnings inequality, I have calculated the Gini coefficient and other distributional measures under the assumption that population composition remained unchanged after 1967. This calculation is straightforward. If the population is divided into a particular number of categories, or cells, the weight of each cell will correspond to its proportion in the overall population. By weighting each observation in the CPS by an appropriate adjustment factor, it is possible to duplicate the distribution of 1967 cell weights for each year after 1967.[26] This procedure can be followed for an arbitrarily large number of cells, although there are of course practical limits arising from the size of the CPS sample.

An adjustment of this kind eliminates the influence on the Gini coefficient of changes in the relative size of each population category. It does not eliminate the effect of changing inequality *between* different cells, nor does it eliminate the effect of trends in inequality *within* given cells.

The effects of this adjustment for inequality, calculated with the Gini coefficient, are shown in table 5. (Similar calculations were performed for other distributional measures; they showed similar results.) The

---

26. If the cell weight in 1967 is W_{67} and the weight of the corresponding cell in a succeeding year is W_t, then each observation in that cell should be weighted using the adjustment factor W_{67}/W_t in the subsequent year.

Table 5. Actual and Hypothetical Gini Coefficients under a Fixed Population Distribution, by Sex, Alternate Years, 1967–87

Year	Actual Gini coefficient	Age distribution constant[a]	Education distribution constant[b]	Age and education distribution constant[c]	Age and work experience distribution constant[d]
			Men		
1967	0.351	0.351	0.351	0.351	0.351
1969	0.359	0.355	0.359	0.355	0.352
1971	0.370	0.366	0.370	0.366	0.360
1973	0.370	0.364	0.372	0.365	0.364
1975	0.374	0.372	0.378	0.373	0.365
1977	0.380	0.379	0.386	0.378	0.373
1979	0.380	0.379	0.389	0.378	0.377
1981	0.392	0.395	0.401	0.393	0.386
1983	0.405	0.416	0.417	0.414	0.404
1985	0.403	0.416	0.419	0.416	0.409
1987	0.405	0.420	0.419	0.417	0.414
			Women		
1967	0.458	0.458	0.458	0.458	0.458
1969	0.455	0.454	0.448	0.449	0.453
1971	0.457	0.458	0.451	0.452	0.456
1973	0.459	0.458	0.455	0.455	0.458
1975	0.451	0.452	0.449	0.450	0.451
1977	0.446	0.449	0.446	0.446	0.447
1979	0.437	0.442	0.438	0.436	0.443
1981	0.434	0.445	0.438	0.439	0.447
1983	0.441	0.457	0.447	0.451	0.462
1985	0.443	0.461	0.455	0.458	0.469
1987	0.440	0.459	0.452	0.455	0.471

Source: Author's tabulations of March CPS tapes, 1968–88.

a. Men and women divided into seven age groups: 16–19, 20–24, 25–34, 35–44, 45–54, 55–64, and 65 and older.

b. Six educational categories were defined: less than a high school education; some high school, but less than 12 years of schooling; 12 years of schooling; some college; college graduate; and two or more years of schooling beyond college.

c. In order to eliminate cells with zero weight, the bottom two age categories were combined for this tabulation.

d. Four categories of work experience were used: full-year and part-year workers on full-time schedules, and full-year and part-year workers on part-time schedules. These categories were further divided into seven age categories.

numbers shown in table 5 make plain what was already evident in figure 3. The changing weights of different population categories have not been large enough to explain growing inequality among men. The trend toward inequality would have been somewhat more gradual through the middle 1970s if the population structure had remained unchanged, but only a small proportion of the trend through the end of the 1970s can be explained by the growing size of population cells in the extreme tails of the male earnings distribution. Over the 1980s, demographic and work experience trends should have *reduced* the trend toward inequality. Instead, inequality jumped very sharply between 1979 and 1982.

For women the numbers shown in table 5 tell a similar story. Changes in the composition of the working population have actually moderated the trend toward inequality that would have occurred if the female population structure had remained stable. Notice that the 1987 estimate of the Gini coefficient is lower in column 1, which shows the actual Gini coefficient, than it is in any of the columns to the right. In one case the hypothetical Gini coefficient is 7 percent above the actual Gini in 1987. The changing composition of the female working population has evidently offset the effects of growing inequality within or between different categories of female workers.

The Theil index of inequality provides a convenient way to divide earnings inequality into the part that is due to inequality within population classes and the part arising from systematic differences between classes. If the Theil index is designated R, then

$$(1) \qquad R = \frac{1}{n} \sum_i \frac{Y_i}{\overline{Y}} \, \log \frac{Y_i}{\overline{Y}},$$

where Y_i is the earnings of individual i, $\overline{Y}$ is average earnings in the population, and n is population size. This is equivalent to

$$(2) \qquad R = \sum_i \frac{n_g}{n} \frac{\overline{Y}_g}{\overline{Y}} R_g + \frac{1}{n} \sum_g n_g \frac{\overline{Y}_g}{\overline{Y}} \log \frac{\overline{Y}_g}{\overline{Y}},$$

where R_g is the Theil index within category g, $\overline{Y}_g$ is average income within category g, and n_g is the number of people in category g. The first term in equation 2 represents the sum of inequality within groups in the population, weighted by the share of income received by each group; the second term reflects differences in average income between groups.

Table 6 shows the trend in earnings inequality as measured by the Theil index, as well as a decomposition of inequality in each year into the two components just mentioned. As expected, the index shows a pattern of rising inequality among men but no strong trend among women (column 1). Column 2 shows the fraction of inequality that is due to inequality *within* six age groups of the population; column 3 shows the fraction due to inequality *between* these same six groups.

Table 6. Proportion of Earnings Inequality due to Inequality within Groups and between Groups, by Sex, Alternate Years, 1967–87

		Age[a]		Education[b]		Age and education[c]	
Year	Theil index[d] (1)	Within groups (2)	Between groups (3)	Within groups (4)	Between groups (5)	Within groups (6)	Between groups (7)
			Men				
1967	0.2110	0.70	0.30	0.92	0.08	0.61	0.39
1969	0.2237	0.67	0.33	0.92	0.08	0.59	0.41
1971	0.2365	0.68	0.32	0.93	0.07	0.60	0.40
1973	0.2376	0.68	0.32	0.93	0.07	0.61	0.39
1975	0.2402	0.69	0.31	0.91	0.09	0.61	0.39
1977	0.2479	0.69	0.31	0.92	0.08	0.61	0.39
1979	0.2474	0.70	0.30	0.91	0.09	0.63	0.37
1981	0.2625	0.70	0.30	0.90	0.10	0.62	0.38
1983	0.2790	0.71	0.29	0.88	0.12	0.62	0.38
1985	0.2765	0.71	0.29	0.87	0.13	0.62	0.38
1987	0.2758	0.72	0.28	0.87	0.13	0.62	0.38
			Women				
1967	0.3420	0.91	0.09	0.90	0.10	0.79	0.21
1969	0.3567	0.91	0.09	0.90	0.09	0.79	0.21
1971	0.3588	0.90	0.10	0.90	0.10	0.78	0.22
1973	0.3592	0.89	0.11	0.91	0.09	0.78	0.22
1975	0.3470	0.88	0.12	0.89	0.11	0.77	0.23
1977	0.3392	0.88	0.12	0.90	0.10	0.78	0.22
1979	0.3317	0.89	0.11	0.90	0.10	0.79	0.21
1981	0.3238	0.88	0.12	0.90	0.10	0.79	0.21
1983	0.3385	0.87	0.13	0.88	0.12	0.76	0.24
1985	0.3422	0.86	0.14	0.86	0.14	0.75	0.25
1987	0.3459	0.86	0.14	0.86	0.14	0.75	0.25

Source: Author's tabulations of March CPS tapes, 1968–88.
a. Population divided into six age groups: 16–24, 25–34, 35–44, 45–54, 55–64, and 65 and older.
b. See table 5, note b.
c. Population divided into 6 × 6 categories defined by age and education.
d. Calculated by excluding the top 2 percent of male earners and the top 1 percent of female earners.

Columns 4 and 5 show the decomposition of inequality within and between six educational categories, while the last two columns show the decomposition within and between the 6 × 6 categories defined by age and education.

Inequality between population groups has increased over time, among both men and women. This rise has been offset among women by declining inequality within population classes, as weighted by their share of all women's earnings. This is consistent with the results shown in table 5, which indicate that changes in the composition of female workers have held down the growth in earnings inequality that would otherwise have occurred.

The findings for men are quite different. Inequality between age and education groups has risen, but inequality *within* these groups has risen about as fast. For example, columns 3 and 7 show that the percentage of all inequality attributable to differences between age groups, on the one hand, and between age-education groups, on the other, has remained fairly stable over the past two decades.[27] The rise in the Theil index over that period is thus attributable to equal proportional gains in within-group and between-group inequality.

This set of findings has important implications for explanations of recent inequality that emphasize the relative size of entering worker cohorts during the 1970s and early 1980s. While some of the trends described in this section are consistent with that explanation, the tabulations show that generational crowding, by itself, cannot explain most of the long-term trend. As I have shown, changing weights of population groups in the upper and lower tails of the earnings distributions have been too small to account for much of the trend in inequality among men. Since 1979 these changes have actually tended to depress the growth of inequality among women. Average earnings differences between age groups have risen, as predicted by the generational crowding hypothesis. But the results shown in table 6 indicate that this effect can explain less than a quarter of the recent change in male earnings inequality. Most of the rise has been due to growing disparities in earnings among men within population groups, including groups that stood to gain from the influx of new, inexperienced workers in the 1970s.

Inequality in Weeks, Hours, and Wages

If cyclical unemployment has an effect on earnings inequality, it should arise primarily through its influence on the distribution of annual weeks worked and, to a lesser degree, weekly hours. The distribution of hourly wage rates of people who work at least one week during the year should be largely unaffected, at least in the short run, by macroeconomic fluctuations.[28] In the long run, aggregate demand in the econ-

27. The numbers in column 5 indicate, however, that the differences between educational groups have grown rapidly over the late 1970s and 1980s. In fact, between-group inequality as measured by the Theil index has more than doubled since 1975, indicating that the payoff to higher education has risen dramatically since that year.

28. Even if workers earning low wages are the ones most likely to become unemployed during a downturn, they will still show up as wage earners in the CPS unless their unemployment lasts an entire calendar year. This occurs infrequently, even in severe recessions. Of course, if workers with limited job experience are induced to enter the market

omy might affect the distribution of hourly earnings through its effect on the relative demand for different classes of workers.

With appropriate data, it would be straightforward to decompose the inequality in annual earnings into the proportions that are due to inequality in weeks worked, in hours worked per week, and in hourly wages. The best measure of inequality for this purpose is the variance of the logarithm of annual earnings, or var(e) (lowercase letters will be used to designate logarithms). If K denotes weeks worked per year, H average hours of work per week while working, and W the hourly wage rate, then

$$(3) \quad \text{var}(e) = \text{var}(k) + \text{var}(h) + \text{var}(w) + 2 \, \text{cov}(k,h)$$

$$+ \, 2 \, \text{cov}(h,w) + 2 \, \text{cov}(k,w).$$

If good information were available about individual weeks, hours, and wage rates, equation 3 would provide a simple way to decompose earnings inequality into its component parts. To be sure, var(e) is not without problems as a measure of earnings inequality.[29] But these are relatively minor compared with its advantages for present purposes.

A major problem with equation 3 is that individual-level data about K and H from the CPS extend back only to 1975. Starting in that year, information about wage rates must be inferred from responses about annual earnings, weeks, and usual weekly hours, for respondents are not directly asked to report hourly wages.[30] This shortcoming of the data may cause serious errors in estimating the variance of wage rates. Respondents are asked to report usual weekly hours, so their answers will not reflect variations in hours over the course of the year. As a result, some of the variability in annual earnings that ought properly to be attributed to hours will be attributed to wage rates instead.

The trend in var(e) for men and women, as well as the trend in the Gini coefficient and Theil inequality index over the same period, is shown in figure 4. All three measures show broadly similar movements

when unemployment rates are low, there will be some cyclical fluctuation in the wage rates of people who are wage earners at some point during a calendar year.

29. See John Creedy, *Dynamics of Income Distribution* (Oxford: Basil Blackwell, 1985), esp. pp. 12–21.

30. Until 1975, annual weeks spent working were only reported in broad categories—categories too broad to be used in calculating weekly earnings, except for year-round workers. Usual weekly hours were not reported at all on the public use version of the CPS, although workers on full-time and part-time schedules were identified.

Figure 4. Trends in Earnings Inequality under Alternative Measures, by Sex, 1967–87[a]

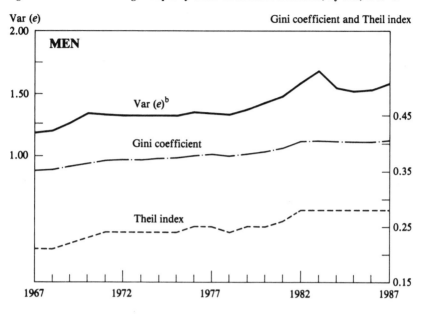

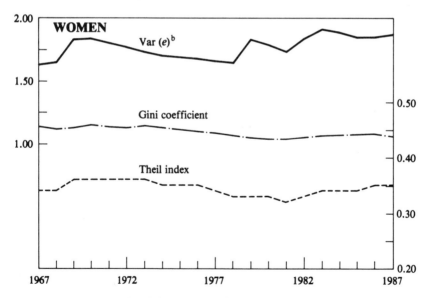

a. Excluding earnings reports of men in the top 2 percent of the earnings distribution and women in the top 1 percent.
b. Var (e) is the variance of the natural logarithm of annual earnings.

in income inequality over the past two decades, though var(e) appears more sensitive to business cycle fluctuations. (Note, for example, that var(e) reaches a peak both for men and women in 1983.) This is probably explained by a major difference among the three inequality measures. Unlike the other two indexes, var(e) places greater weight on negative than on positive deviations from average earnings.

A decomposition of the change in var(e) since 1975, the first year in which the decomposition can be made, is shown in table 7. The first column shows the average value of var(e) in 1986–87 measured as a percentage of var(e) in 1975. The variance of log earnings has risen about 10 percent among women and nearly twice that among men. Columns 2 through 7 show the contribution to the growth in var(e) that has occurred as a result of the six factors indicated in equation 3 above. Among both men and women, by far the most important contribution has come from the increase in the variance of log wage rates (column 4). The next most important factors are the changes that have occurred in the covariance of log wages and log weekly hours and in the covariance of log wages and log annual weeks of work (columns 6 and 7). That is, workers with abnormally low wage rates are now more likely to work short hours and few weeks per year, and vice versa. Changes in the variance of log weeks worked per year and of log hours of work per week have played little role in changing var(e) among men; among women, particularly younger women, they have tended to reduce earnings inequality.[31]

It would be useful to estimate the effect of the business cycle on each of the components of var(e) represented in equation 3. Unfortunately, the very short time series available for analysis—thirteen years—means that estimates from ordinary statistical procedures would be quite unreliable. Simple regressions of the var(e) components on unemployment and a time trend yield results that are strongly consistent with patterns described earlier. The effect of unemployment on inequality among men has the expected sign and is usually statistically different from zero,

---

31. As noted earlier, the inferences in this paragraph are based on potentially unreliable calculations of the distribution of hourly wage rates in the entire March CPS sample, separately for men and women. However, these inferences seem to me to be much more convincing than ones based on trends in a combined sample of men and women that is restricted to workers who are paid by the hour. This is the sample used to derive the figure shown in Marvin Kosters' comment below. Much of the rise in the variance of wages is no doubt due to the growing gap between workers who are paid by the hour and salaried workers who are paid on a weekly or monthly basis.

Table 7. Source of Change in the Variance of Log Earnings, by Age and Sex, 1975–87[a]
Percent

Age group	Change in variance of log earnings[b] (1)	Var(k) (2)	Var(h) (3)	Var(w) (4)	Cov(k,h) (5)	Cov(h,w) (6)	Cov(k,w) (7)
			Men				
25–34	51	−3	3	59	6	13	23
35–44	51	5	4	42	6	16	27
45–54	45	−11	2	88	5	7	8
55–64	38	12	14	63	11	−1	2
All men 16 and over	18	−10	−1	75	10	13	13
			Women				
25–34	5	−370	−72	385	−42	119	81
35–44	5	−327	−141	375	−52	151	94
45–54	13	−96	−40	205	−24	40	15
55–64	55	3	5	76	7	6	4
All women 16 and over	10	−92	−28	143	8	43	26

Source: Author's tabulations of March CPS tapes, 1968–88.
a. Figures in columns 2–7 do not necessarily sum to 100 percent because of rounding. See text for definition of variables in columns 2–7.
b. The change in the variance of log earnings is the ratio of var(e) in 1986–87 to var(e) in 1975, converted to percent, minus 100 percent.

while the effect on women is much smaller than for men and is usually statistically insignificant.

These results are undoubtedly quite sensitive to the time interval used for estimation. For example, an equation for males estimated over 1975–87 yielded the following results:

$$(4) \qquad \text{var}(e) = \underset{(11.12)}{0.749} + \underset{(6.21)}{0.047\ UR} + \underset{(11.10)}{0.026\ T.}$$
$$\bar{R}^2 = 0.928$$

An identically specified equation estimated over the twenty-one-year period 1967–87 yielded a much smaller estimate of the effect of the unemployment rate (UR) on var(e):

$$(5) \qquad \text{var}(e) = \underset{(22.26)}{1.120} + \underset{(1.92)}{0.019\ UR} + \underset{(5.45)}{0.015\ T.}$$
$$\bar{R}^2 = 0.825$$

If the coefficient estimate in equation 4 is accepted, about 45 percent of the rise in var(e) between the late 1960s and late 1980s can be attributed to the effect of higher unemployment. If the estimate in equation 5 is valid, less than 20 percent of the growth in inequality is due to higher unemployment. Given this broad range, it is probably unwise to analyze the components of var(e) using regression techniques.

The results obtained in this section are nonetheless suggestive and are also consistent with findings of earlier sections. The recent rise in the variability of earnings among men and women cannot be attributed to rising inequality in weeks worked per year or usual hours of work per week. Among women, trends in the latter two variables should have contributed to a *reduction* in earnings inequality. Virtually all of the increased earnings inequality has been due to rising inequality in hourly wages and a growing correlation between low wages, on the one hand, and low weekly hours and annual weeks of work, on the other. Although the time series available for analysis is too short for reliable inference, it appears that fluctuations in the variance of earnings and many of its components are positively correlated with the unemployment rate, especially among men.

Prospects for the Earnings Distribution

Earnings inequality has risen in the past decade, moderately in the case of women and far more significantly among men. Some part of the rise among men is due to slack conditions in the labor market. Analysis of historical time-series data shows that inequality among men is moderately sensitive to the rate of unemployment, while most indexes of inequality among women are relatively unaffected. Even among men, however, the changing level of unemployment over the 1970s and 1980s cannot explain a large share of the change in earnings inequality. If inequality is measured using the Gini coefficient, the change in unemployment can explain no more than a fifth of the rise in inequality that has occurred since the late 1960s.

Rising unemployment clearly cannot explain developments in inequality since the early 1980s. Unemployment has fallen substantially since 1983, yet inequality has failed to fall among men and has begun to rise among women. The demographic explanation for these trends is also becoming less credible over time. Since the beginning of the decade the influx of new labor market entrants has slowed. The composition of the labor force is no longer changing in a way that should increase the share of wage earners at the extreme lower tail of the distribution. Controlling for the effects of business cycle fluctuations, earners in the lower tail are nonetheless receiving a smaller share of earnings, while the share received by earners at the top continues to grow.

Some of the rise in inequality is due to growing disparities in the incomes of men and women in different age or education groups. Among men, the gap between younger and older workers has risen, as has the gap between well-educated earners and workers with limited educational attainment. Both these trends suggest that the payoff to greater skill and longer work experience is growing. Most of the rise in male inequality, however, is due to growing inequality within narrow population groups, defined by age, educational attainment, geographic location, and work experience.

This pattern is hardly consistent with an explanation of recent inequality that emphasizes the role of demographic structure. It may be consistent, however, with an explanation that emphasizes growing returns to skill and experience in the labor market. For reasons that are not entirely clear, employers now offer proportionately greater rewards to workers who bring more skills, experience, and educational attainment to their jobs. The sharp rise in inequality *within* homogeneous groups defined by age, education, geographic region, and work experience may reflect as yet unmeasurable dimensions of worker skill or ability that enter into the determination of individual wages. If these dimensions of worker skill could be measured, I suspect that one would find that inequality across skill categories has risen in recent years.

In view of the persistent historical trend toward greater inequality among males, it seems doubtful that any explanation relying solely on cyclical factors—such as the rate of unemployment or the share of wage earners aged 16–34—will end up accounting for a large share of the movement in inequality since the 1950s. While a steep drop in unemployment or a sharp fall in the share of workers under age 30 might halt the trend toward greater male inequality, the halt would be only temporary unless this long-term pattern is reversed. I find no evidence to suggest that the trend toward inequality is slowing. It has almost certainly accelerated during the 1980s.

GARY BURTLESS

Table A-1. Gini Coefficients and Other Distributional Statistics for Male and Female Earners, 1947–86

	Male earners			Female earners		
Year	Gini coefficient	T/Mᵃ	B/Mᵇ	Gini coefficient	T/Mᵃ	B/Mᵇ
1947	0.327	186.8	22.3	0.403	219.8	14.3
1948	0.328	183.7	20.6	0.403	220.3	15.2
1949	0.333	183.4	19.4	0.410	226.7	14.7
1950	0.335	183.5	18.3	0.432	234.7	10.5
1951	0.307	174.1	22.6	0.415	228.1	13.9
1952	0.315	177.1	21.6	0.424	235.6	13.3
1953	0.325	180.5	19.6	0.421	237.8	13.9
1954	0.336	183.5	18.4	0.431	248.0	13.7
1955	0.341	181.1	16.3	0.446	264.7	13.1
1956	0.343	182.7	15.9	0.453	271.4	12.8
1957	0.350	185.2	15.1	0.452	267.2	12.5
1958	0.365	190.7	13.2	0.467	281.6	11.6
1959	0.361	191.3	14.1	0.466	281.8	11.7
1960	0.370	195.1	13.2	0.465	280.7	11.6
1961	0.376	198.5	12.5	0.473	291.2	11.3
1962	0.372	194.8	12.7	0.467	285.4	11.5
1963	0.373	195.9	12.5	0.468	283.1	11.1
1964	0.376	199.8	12.5	0.465	278.8	11.1
1965	0.378	199.1	12.0	0.467	279.6	10.7
1966	0.368	196.3	13.3	0.458	268.9	10.8
1967	0.369	199.9	13.4	0.458	266.3	10.6
1968	0.369	197.3	13.0	0.452	259.9	10.5
1969	0.376	201.5	12.9	0.458	268.5	10.5
1970	0.379	204.7	12.6	0.462	272.6	10.1
1971	0.386	208.4	12.4	0.459	268.4	10.0
1972	0.383	210.8	13.2	0.456	267.4	10.2
1973	0.386	210.0	12.6	0.461	276.6	10.5
1974	0.389	213.3	12.9	0.456	268.9	10.5
1975	0.386	209.8	13.2	0.454	270.6	11.0
1976	0.393	214.5	12.6	0.448	263.0	10.7
1977	0.393	217.4	13.4	0.444	261.7	11.2
1978	0.392	217.4	13.7	0.439	256.3	12.1
1979	0.389	218.9	14.5	0.432	247.5	12.2
1980	0.394	223.0	14.4	0.429	247.8	12.3
1981	0.401	228.2	13.8	0.430	250.1	12.5
1982	0.411	238.4	13.5	0.435	254.1	12.1
1983	0.413	237.8	13.0	0.437	256.4	12.0
1984	0.413	237.5	13.2	0.440	260.0	11.8
1985	0.411	239.0	13.9	0.442	264.7	12.1
1986	0.411	241.0	14.3	0.442	268.0	12.3

Source: Author's tabulation using statistics published in Census Bureau P-60 reports (various years).
a. Ratio of average earnings in top tail of distribution to average earnings in middle quintile.
b. Ratio of average earnings in bottom quintile of distribution to average earnings in middle quintile.

Table A-2. Gini Coefficients for Men within Nine Census Regions, 1967–87

Year	New England	Mid-Atlantic	East North Central	West North Central	South Atlantic	East South Central	West South Central	Mountain	Pacific
1967	0.324	0.328	0.318	0.373	0.378	0.403	0.382	0.343	0.344
1968	0.324	0.327	0.329	0.354	0.375	0.386	0.381	0.349	0.352
1969	0.330	0.341	0.331	0.360	0.382	0.392	0.379	0.360	0.361
1970	0.349	0.350	0.336	0.370	0.383	0.386	0.382	0.371	0.361
1971	0.355	0.352	0.344	0.379	0.381	0.388	0.393	0.387	0.372
1972	0.368	0.355	0.346	0.382	0.380	0.383	0.394	0.375	0.370
1973	0.366	0.352	0.346	0.383	0.386	0.383	0.399	0.375	0.363
1974	0.366	0.354	0.343	0.387	0.392	0.394	0.383	0.375	0.382
1975	0.377	0.354	0.358	0.381	0.388	0.380	0.389	0.371	0.376
1976	0.376	0.362	0.361	0.385	0.392	0.389	0.385	0.380	0.382
1977	0.371	0.366	0.358	0.398	0.393	0.384	0.387	0.392	0.384
1978	0.381	0.366	0.353	0.378	0.393	0.387	0.389	0.395	0.381
1979	0.385	0.365	0.356	0.387	0.391	0.387	0.399	0.390	0.383
1980	0.371	0.371	0.371	0.392	0.400	0.391	0.389	0.387	0.393
1981	0.376	0.380	0.377	0.393	0.405	0.405	0.395	0.392	0.399
1982	0.393	0.387	0.391	0.414	0.419	0.401	0.411	0.410	0.410
1983	0.392	0.390	0.396	0.406	0.410	0.419	0.422	0.414	0.402
1984	0.399	0.389	0.395	0.407	0.405	0.421	0.424	0.411	0.401
1985	0.388	0.390	0.399	0.414	0.403	0.409	0.418	0.400	0.400
1986	0.390	0.383	0.394	0.401	0.403	0.416	0.436	0.417	0.399
1987	0.389	0.388	0.396	0.396	0.401	0.408	0.430	0.422	0.412

Source: Author's tabulation of March CPS tapes, 1968–88.

Comment by Marvin H. Kosters

Earnings dispersion and unemployment rates were both higher in the 1980s than previously. Major changes also took place in the demographic composition of the work force. To what extent can changes in earnings dispersion be traced to cyclical sources, and to what extent to changes in demographic composition? These questions deserve the careful and thorough examination they receive in Gary Burtless's paper.

The answers, in brief, are that cyclical conditions account for only a small share of changes in earnings dispersion for men and even less for women, and that higher dispersion in the 1980s cannot be accounted for simply by compositional change. As is often the case in research, these answers give rise to further questions about forces that have contributed to changes in earnings dispersion.

To examine cyclical effects on earnings dispersion, reliance is mainly placed on the unemployment rate. Most of the emphasis in the analysis of inequality over the cycle is placed on how hours and weeks of work—and therefore annual earnings—might be influenced by cyclical conditions. The unemployment rate is conceptually closely related to changing labor force utilization and time worked, but dispersion over the cycle might also be influenced by differences in the cyclical sensitivity of wages in different parts of the distribution. This raises a question as to whether other cyclically related measures, in particular inflation, might also play a role.

Although unemployment serves as an indicator of demand pressures on wages, it seems possible that some measure of inflation might reflect such pressures more directly. This is because changes in inflation may serve as an indicator of the ability of firms to pass on labor cost increases or the degree to which firms expect increases in costs to be validated through rising prices.

To explore the possibility that inflation can provide additional information on the cyclical responsiveness of earnings dispersion, I used the data reported in table A-1 in regressions covering the same time period and using the same specification as those reported in table 1. Annual changes in CPI-X1 were used as the inflation measure, both as an alternative and as a supplement to the unemployment rate. In all of these regressions, the signs of inflation coefficients point to a more sluggish response to inflation in the upper part of the earnings distribution. That is, higher inflation is associated with a reduction in the Gini coefficient and a narrowing of the ratio of the top quintile of the distribution to the middle quintile. As in the case of unemployment, however, the tendency for high inflation to reduce dispersion is more apparent and consistent for the top quintile than for the bottom. Despite the consistency of the signs for inflation coefficients, however, they generally fall short of conventional levels of statistical significance.

The inclusion of the inflation variable in regressions similar to those reported in table 1 has little influence on the size or significance of most of the other coefficients. There is, however, one interesting exception: the trend variable for the 1980s. In almost all cases, substituting the inflation variable for unemployment or adding it reduces the size and sharply reduces the statistical significance of the 1980s trend variable. Adding the 1980s trend variable when inflation is already included tends to reduce the statistical significance of the inflation variable. These regression results suggest that the lower inflation of the 1980s may ac-

Table 8. Effects of Unemployment and Inflation on Male and Female Earnings Inequality, 1954–86[a]

Dependent variable[b]	Men	Women
	Gini coefficient	
Unemployment rate	0.0028	0.0008
	(5.92)	(1.03)
Inflation	− 0.00093	− 0.00079
	(3.69)	(1.68)
	Top/middle (T/M)	
Unemployment rate	1.252	0.882
	(2.79)	(0.96)
Inflation	− 0.508	− 1.255
	(1.80)	(2.19)
	Bottom/middle (B/M)	
Unemployment rate	− 0.082	− 0.046
	(0.88)	(0.95)
Inflation	0.027	0.032
	(0.51)	(0.90)

a. Regressions also include a constant term and two time trends (*T* and *T60*). They also include an estimate of ρ, the first-order autocorrelation coefficient. Numbers in parentheses are *t*-statistics.
b. See table 1 for definition of variables.

count for at least part of the higher earnings dispersion that prevailed then.

Comparison of the results of these exploratory regressions has persuaded me that there is considerable interplay between the 1980s trend variable and the inflation variable. Since presentation of these comparisons is somewhat cumbersome, I present in table 8 comparisons of the coefficients and *t*-statistics for unemployment and inflation only when they are both included in the same regressions but the 1980s trend variable is excluded. These regressions were estimated in the same form as those reported in columns 1 and 3 of table 1, with year-to-year price changes included as an additional variable.

As shown in table 8, unemployment does not appear to perform markedly better than inflation in terms of the statistical significance of the coefficients. The order of magnitude of their effects also appears to be roughly comparable. Although the mean for the inflation variable is only about two-thirds that for unemployment, its variance is about three times as large, which compensates to some extent for the typically smaller absolute size of the inflation coefficients.

The simple measure of inflation that I have used is not necessarily the most appropriate measure of the effects of changes in inflation. Moreover, the effects of inflation on the earnings distribution may not have been stable across cycles. Nevertheless, the case for including an inflation variable seems at least as strong as that for a 1980s trend variable, and the effects of its inclusion raise some question about whether the higher earnings dispersion of the 1980s represents the beginning of a new trend.

The analysis in Burtless's paper of the effects of the changing demographic composition of the work force demonstrates convincingly in my view that the changes in inequality are not attributable simply to changes in relative numbers of workers in different age and schooling classes. It seems apparent that changes in relative earnings within and between these classes have contributed to changing overall dispersion. Some of these relative earnings changes may be attributable to changes in relative supply represented by a changing demographic composition, and some may be attributable to demand changes. It is important to recognize, of course, that changes in dispersion within broad demographic groups are not necessarily related in any simple way to relative supply changes. For example, an increase in the mean relative earnings of groups whose relative supply was reduced could be associated with either an increase or a reduction in their earnings dispersion.

As noted in Burtless's paper, it is important to keep in mind the fact that age and schooling are measures of only two broad dimensions of labor quality. According to the Theil index reported in table 6, for example, more than 60 percent of male earnings inequality consists of dispersion within, instead of between, the broad age and schooling classes used in the analysis. Although within-group dispersion might be reduced somewhat further by narrower classes, the more important point is that within-group dispersion would still probably account for half the total dispersion. The remaining within-group dispersion would presumably be accounted for by factors such as unique abilities, differences in the quality of schooling and of skills acquired through work experience, differences in individual ability and effort, differences in geographic location, and luck. Changes in overall inequality can consequently be importantly affected by changes in supply or demand within age and schooling classes for these other dimensions of labor quality.

It seems clear that changes in earnings inequality cannot be entirely explained by relative quantities, such as those represented by demographic composition and cyclical changes in working time. That is, as the paper concludes, changes in relative wages—particularly among age and schooling classes but also perhaps among other indicators of labor quality—have apparently contributed to changes in earnings dispersion.

Figure 5. Coefficients of Variation in Hourly Wages of Workers Paid by the Hour, 1973–87[a]

Coefficient of variation

Source: Author's calculations from May (1973–78) and Second Quarter (1979–87) CPS Microdata files.
a. All wage and salary workers 16 years and older who work for a private or government employer and who are paid by the hour and report an hourly wage rate. The coefficient of variation is the quotient of the standard deviation and the mean of the hourly wage distribution.

Nevertheless, there is reason to believe that the extent to which increased earnings dispersion can be traced to increased dispersion in hourly wage rates may be exaggerated by the results reported in table 7 and discussed in the section on inequality in weeks, hours, and wages.

The decomposition of the change in the measure of earnings variance into factors that contributed to the change suggests that dispersion in hourly wages has increased a great deal. Other measures of hourly wage dispersion, however, show a very different pattern. The hourly wage measure analyzed in table 7 is computed from annual earnings, weeks of work, and usual weekly hours during the preceding year. Usual hourly earnings are reported directly for workers paid by the hour in other monthly surveys, however. As shown in figure 5, a simple measure of dispersion, the coefficient of variation, of reported hourly wages for these workers shows virtually no trend since the mid-1970s. Workers paid by the hour, of course, account for only part of the work force. Hourly earnings are not reported directly for workers not paid by the hour, and although a computed measure of their hourly wage dispersion shows a marked decline over the period, this is largely a consequence of the growing importance of the top-code for weekly earnings, which remained fixed in nominal terms throughout the period.

One puzzle that is presented by these very different indicators of hourly wage dispersion is how to account for these different trends derived from different monthly surveys. A second, more substantive puzzle is how the relatively stable dispersion for directly reported measures of hourly earnings can be reconciled with the results reported in this paper suggesting that changes in dispersion for hourly wages may be responsible for much of the change in annual earnings dispersion. It is possible that covariance patterns, which were also found to be important, may provide the key to reconciling these divergent trends.

Are Part-Time Jobs Bad Jobs?

Rebecca M. Blank

BY THE early 1980s, 17 percent of the U.S. labor force, a historic high, was employed part time. Much of this surge in part-time employment was due to an increase in the percentage of workers involuntarily employed part time. As a result of this trend, there has been increased concern about the nature of part-time jobs. A common perception is that in comparison with an equivalent full-time job a part-time job pays lower hourly wages, provides lower fringe benefits, and may provide less opportunity for career advancement. At its worst, part-time work may be considered a form of disguised unemployment. However, there are alternative views of part-time work. Many part-time workers voluntarily choose part-time jobs. For most of these workers part-time work provides an opportunity for flexible work hours, additional income, and continued labor market involvement while still permitting pursuit of significant activities outside the labor market. According to this perspective, part-time work is superior to full-time work for those workers who choose to work part time.[1] A second perspective is that those workers who work part time may be less skilled or less productive. Workers unable or unwilling to find full-time jobs may be signaling that they are "bad workers" along some dimension. If part-time jobs provide worse compensation than full-time jobs, this may merely reflect the nature of the part-time work force. This paper investigates differences in part-time and full-time compensation, asking whether these differences can be explained by the behavior and skills of the part-time work force, or whether part-time jobs are simply "bad jobs" for those who fill them.

The author wishes to acknowledge the financial support of the Brookings Institution and National Science Foundation grant RII-8800091, and to thank Peter Perales for research assistance.

1. For a discussion of the potential advantages of part-time work, see Hilda Kahne, *Reconceiving Part-Time Work: New Perspectives for Older Workers and Women* (Rowman & Allanheld, 1985).

Part-Time Work, 1968–87

Trends in part-time work over the past twenty years are shown in table 1, using data from the Current Population Survey (CPS).[2] The percentage of adult workers in nonagricultural civilian employment who work part time grew from 12 percent in 1968 to over 15 percent in 1987, with the peak of over 17 percent occurring in 1982.[3] Not surprisingly, a much higher percentage of women than men regularly work part time. The percentage of women working part time has remained roughly constant at around 25 percent over the past twenty years. Given the growing size of the female work force, however, this implies that the number of part-time jobs has expanded significantly over this same period. Among men, the percentage of part-time workers has increased from 5 percent to over 8 percent. The overall increase in part-time work is thus due to an increase in part-time work among men as well as to the rise in female employment.

The CPS categorizes part-time workers as "voluntary" and "involuntary."[4] Voluntary part-timers are those who, when asked why they are working part time, respond that they wanted part-time work. Involuntary part-timers are those who respond that they can find only part-time work or that they are constrained from working more hours because of slack economic conditions. It is clear from table 1 that the percentage of workers involuntarily working part time has risen significantly over

2. For other discussions of the trends in part-time work, see Ronald G. Ehrenberg, Pamela Rosenberg, and Jeanne Li, "Part-Time Employment in the United States," in Robert A. Hart, ed., *Employment, Unemployment, and Labor Utilization* (Boston: Unwin Hyman, 1988); Bernard E. Ichniowski and Anne E. Preston, "New Trends in Part-Time Employment," in *Proceedings of the 38th Annual Meeting, December 28–30, 1985* (Industrial Relations Research Association, 1986), pp. 60–67; and Eileen Applebaum, "Restructuring Work: Temporary, Part-Time and At-Home Employment," in Heidi I. Hartmann, ed., *Computer Chips and Paper Clips: Technology and Women's Employment*, vol. 2 (National Academy Press, 1987), pp. 268–310.

3. Part-time work is officially defined as fewer than thirty-five hours per week. Because few people work between thirty-one and thirty-four hours, variations in this definition do not create major changes in results. Analysis of the jobs held by workers who work thirty to thirty-four hours indicates that they are more similar to the jobs held by those who work twenty-five to twenty-nine hours than to the jobs held by those who work thirty-five to thirty-nine hours. See Janice Neipert Hedges and Stephen J. Gallogly, "Full and Part-time: A Review of Definitions," *Monthly Labor Review*, vol. 100 (March 1977), pp. 21–28.

4. For a discussion of the CPS definitions of voluntary and involuntary part-time workers, see Thomas J. Nardone, "Part-Time Workers: Who Are They?" *Monthly Labor Review*, vol. 109 (February 1986), pp. 13–19.

Are Part-Time Jobs Bad Jobs?   125

Table 1. Part-Time Work among Male and Female Workers, 1968–87[a]
Percent

	All Workers	Women			Men		
			Part-time workers			Part-time workers	
Year	Working part time	Working part time	Voluntary	Involuntary	Working part time	Voluntary	Involuntary
1968	11.9	23.4	86.1	13.9	5.3	68.8	31.2
1969	12.3	23.5	86.4	13.6	5.6	69.0	31.0
1970	13.2	24.6	84.8	15.2	6.3	64.7	35.3
1971	13.5	25.0	83.4	16.6	6.5	63.5	36.5
1972	13.3	24.7	84.1	15.9	6.4	66.8	33.2
1973	13.2	24.6	85.0	15.0	6.2	68.3	31.7
1974	13.8	25.0	83.1	16.9	6.7	63.9	36.1
1975	14.9	25.9	79.9	20.1	7.8	56.8	43.2
1976	14.5	25.3	81.4	18.6	7.3	60.0	40.0
1977	14.5	25.1	81.1	18.9	7.3	62.8	37.2
1978	14.2	24.7	81.6	18.4	6.9	65.0	35.0
1979	14.2	24.5	81.4	18.6	6.9	64.5	35.5
1980	15.1	24.8	79.5	20.5	8.0	58.7	41.3
1981	15.5	25.3	77.7	22.3	8.1	56.2	43.8
1982	17.1	26.8	73.2	26.8	9.7	48.9	51.1
1983	17.0	26.4	72.1	27.9	9.6	50.1	49.9
1984	16.0	25.2	73.7	26.3	8.8	52.9	47.1
1985	15.8	25.0	74.6	25.4	8.6	54.8	45.2
1986	15.8	24.6	75.2	24.8	8.7	55.1	44.9
1987	15.4	24.1	76.4	23.6	8.5	56.6	43.4

Source: U.S. Department of Labor, Bureau of Labor Statistics, *Labor Force Statistics Derived from the Current Population Survey, 1948–1987* (August 1988), table B-19.
a. Persons at work in nonagricultural industries, aged 20 or older.

the past twenty years, from 14 percent to 24 percent among women, and from 31 percent to 43 percent among men, peaking near 50 percent in the early 1980s. However, while involuntary part-time work has increased, it is still important to observe that over three-fourths of all women part-timers and over half of all men part-timers indicated they were working part time by their own choice in 1987.

Figure 1 provides a graphical representation of the trends in part-time employment among women and men, respectively. The upper line in each panel shows the total percentage of workers on part-time schedules, and the lower line shows the percentage of workers who indicate they work part time voluntarily. The area between these two lines represents involuntary part-time employment. These figures show the cyclical nature of involuntary part-time work.

One way to investigate these changes in part-time work is to see how fully they can be explained by movements in the aggregate unemploy-

Figure 1. Part-Time Work among Male and Female Workers, 1968–87

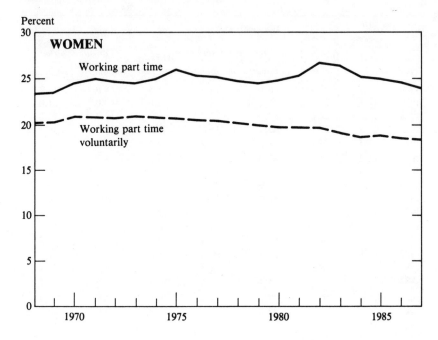

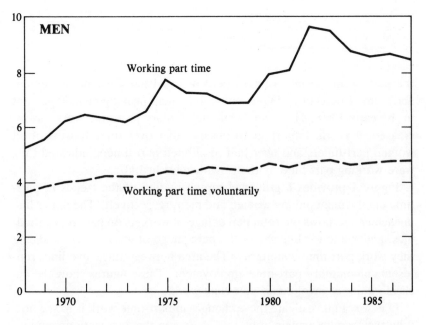

Table 2. **Responsiveness of Part-Time Work to Changes in Unemployment, 1968–87**[a]

	Women			Men		
	Percent	Part-time workers		Percent	Part-time workers	
Independent variable	working part time	Percent involuntary	Percent voluntary	working part time	Percent involuntary	Percent voluntary
Constant	21.746	1.259	20.487	3.634	0.005	3.627
	(0.218)	(0.353)	(0.343)	(0.265)	(0.303)	(0.088)
Time trend	−0.053	0.109	−0.162	0.116	0.075	0.041
	(0.012)	(0.019)	(0.019)	(0.014)	(0.016)	(0.005)
Unemployment rate[b]	0.569	0.396	0.173	0.398	0.341	0.057
	(0.042)	(0.067)	(0.066)	(0.051)	(0.058)	(0.017)
R^2	0.929	0.921	0.845	0.956	0.905	0.928

a. Numbers in parentheses are standard errors.
b. Total civilian unemployment rate for all workers.

ment rate. If changes in the percentage of part-time workers are highly correlated with movements in unemployment, this would be evidence that increases in part-time work reflect slack labor market demand and are thus an indication of underemployment. Table 2 contains results of a regression of the percentage of all male and female workers in part-time employment on a time trend and the aggregate civilian unemployment rate. The table shows results for three dependent variables: the percentage of all workers in part-time jobs, which is then broken into the percentages of those working part time voluntarily and involuntarily.

The coefficients suggest that both involuntary and voluntary part-time employment increase with the unemployment rate, although the response of involuntary part-time work is much larger. A 1 point increase in unemployment increases the percentage of women working part time by 0.6 percentage points, 70 percent of which is an increase in involuntary unemployment. A 1 point increase in unemployment increases the percentage of men working part time by 0.4 percentage points, 86 percent of which is an increase in involuntary unemployment. However, even with the unemployment rate accounted for, there are still significant underlying time trends in part-time employment. With unemployment held constant, part-time work among women actually declines, although this decline is the result of a negative time trend in voluntary part-time employment, offset somewhat by a smaller positive time trend in involuntary part-time employment. For men, both involuntary and voluntary part-time employment show a significant increasing trend.

Thus, while table 2 indicates that changes in part-time work (and especially involuntary part-time work) are indeed correlated with the

unemployment rate, movements in unemployment do not fully explain
the overall trends in part-time work over the past twenty years. In
addition, the magnitude of the unemployment coefficients are quite
small. Even if unemployment were to double from 5 to 10 percent, a
very large increase, the percentage of women working part time would
rise by only 2.5 percentage points, and the percentage of men working
part time would rise by only 2 percentage points.

Differences in Compensation

The usual way to distinguish "good" from "bad" jobs is to compare
their compensation. Jobs with high wages and high fringe benefits are
typically considered "good jobs." An examination of CPS data for 1987
will allow a comparison of wages and benefits for full- and part-time
jobs.[5]

The occupational distribution of part-time work among female and
male workers, and the simple wage differentials between part-time and
full-time workers by occupation, are shown in table 3. The first row
indicates that the 26 percent of employed women in the sample who
held part-time jobs in 1987 earned on average $0.67 less per hour than
full-time earners. Less than 5 percent of the men in the sample worked
part time, and they earned $0.80 per hour less on average than full-time
workers.

However, these aggregate patterns obscure occupational differences
among workers.[6] Compared with all workers, both male and female
part-time workers are disproportionately likely to be in service occu-

5. The data used throughout the remainder of this paper are drawn from the March
1988 Current Population Survey (CPS). I use responses to questions asking about workers'
employment during 1987. The sample includes all persons between the ages of 18 and 65
who were not in school, retired, disabled, or self-employed in 1987. This provides a sample
of 25,143 women, 17,441 of whom are wives and 7,702 of whom are single household
heads, and 26,384 men. Wages are defined as annual earned income divided by the product
of usual work hours per week times weeks of work during the year. Part-time work status
is based on the usual hours of work per week and ignores differences in weeks of work
over the year, focusing solely on hours worked in periods when work occurs. Note that
this definition undercounts part-time jobs and focuses instead on part-time workers since
it does not identify those individuals whose full-time hours are the result of several part-
time jobs; however, the number of workers holding multiple part-time jobs is small.

6. For a discussion of trends in the occupational location of part-time and full-time
workers, see Karen C. Holden and W. Lee Hansen, "Part-Time Work, Full-Time Work,
and Occupational Segregation," in Clair Brown and Joseph A. Pechman, eds., *Gender
in the Workplace* (Brookings, 1987), pp. 217–46.

Table 3. Differences in Wages for Full-Time and Part-Time Workers, by Sex and Occupation, 1987

Sex and occupation	Percent of all workers	Percent of all part-time workers	Percent working part time	Average wage (dollars) Part time	Average wage (dollars) Full time	Number of observations
Women						
All workers	100.0	100.0	26.0	8.03	8.70	25,143
Professional, manage-rial, and technical	30.5	22.4	19.1	11.32	11.23	7,680
Sales	11.0	16.2	38.4	7.73	8.11	2,754
Clerical	29.7	25.6	22.4	7.70	8.19	7,466
Service	16.5	28.8	45.2	6.27	5.49	4,160
Craft, operative, and labor	12.3	7.0	14.9	6.71	7.01	3,083
Men						
All workers	100.0	100.0	4.7	12.46	13.26	26,384
Professional, manage-rial, and technical	32.2	23.9	3.5	19.29	16.91	8,503
Sales	10.6	9.9	4.4	13.34	13.49	2,808
Clerical	5.7	8.2	6.8	8.60	12.08	1,494
Service	8.2	22.2	12.8	8.78	9.20	2,163
Craft, operative, and labor	43.3	35.8	3.9	10.84	11.34	11,416

Source: Current Population Survey, files data March 1988. Data include all persons aged 20 to 65 in nonagricultural industries who report any work during 1987.

pations and less likely to be in professional or craft occupations. The percentages of workers in sales and clerical occupations are largely similar for part-time and full-time workers, although women part-timers are somewhat more likely to be in sales and male part-timers are somewhat more likely to be in clerical occupations. For both men and women, service occupations employ the highest share of part-timers. A high percentage of female sales workers is also part time.

The aggregate negative wage differential between part-time and full-time work is less evident within occupation-specific data. For women, average part-time wages are lower only in sales, clerical, and craft jobs. Women in part-time service jobs actually appear to earn higher average wages than full-time workers, while there is little such difference among female workers in professional jobs. Among men, part-time workers earn consistently less in every occupational category except professionals, where there is a large positive differential in favor of part-time workers. Thus, particularly among women, the lower average wage earned among all part-time workers appears to disguise significant differences between part-time and full-time wages in different occupations.

130   REBECCA M. BLANK

**Table 4.   Differences in Fringe Benefits for Full-Time and Part-Time Workers,
by Sex or Marital Status and Occupation, 1987**
Percent

Sex or marital status and occupation	Included in pension plan		Included in health plan	
	Part time	Full time	Part time	Full time
Female heads				
All workers	14.2	50.2	25.6	74.1
Professional, managerial, and technical	23.0	62.4	41.3	85.9
Sales	11.8	31.9	20.5	60.3
Clerical	20.6	55.9	36.8	82.1
Service	8.1	28.3	17.2	46.4
Craft, operative, and labor	18.8	45.2	22.8	69.1
Wives				
All workers	17.9	50.9	17.8	59.7
Professional, managerial, and technical	26.2	64.0	23.5	68.0
Sales	12.0	29.7	16.4	44.7
Clerical	18.6	55.0	18.4	63.1
Service	13.4	27.6	12.1	37.2
Craft, operative, and labor	18.3	41.7	20.8	58.8
Men				
All workers	18.3	58.5	37.1	79.0
Professional, managerial, and technical	24.5	67.6	43.6	86.1
Sales	18.5	44.2	38.7	75.3
Clerical	17.6	70.0	44.1	84.8
Service	12.9	55.6	27.8	71.8
Craft, operative, and labor	17.7	54.5	36.5	75.2

Source: See table 3.

However, the data shown in table 3 make no adjustments for the worker skills or job characteristics of the part-time work force.

Differentials in the availability of pension and health plans for part-time and full-time workers are shown in table 4. The CPS explicitly asks whether individuals were included in a pension plan or provided with health insurance through their employers in 1987. Data are shown for female household heads, wives, and men, since significant differences occur between female heads and wives. Among all workers only 14 to 18 percent of part-time employees are included in a pension plan, while 50 to 58 percent of full-time employees are covered by a plan. Pension coverage differences between part-time and full-time workers generally appear quite similar for all three groups of workers, although men are somewhat more likely to be covered by pensions on average. Of course, these differences may merely reflect differences in experience and age, which determine pension vesting procedures.

Health insurance coverage is more common than pension coverage. Wives are far less likely than either female heads or men to be covered by a health plan, in either part-time or full-time work. This is not surprising since wives are more likely to have access to health coverage as a result of their spouses' employment.

The occupation-specific data indicate significant differences in the likelihood of workers' receiving fringe benefits. These occupational patterns are similar across all three groups of workers. Service workers, whether full time or part time, are least likely to receive either pensions or health coverage while professional and managerial workers are most likely to receive these benefits. In general, across all occupations part-time workers are one-third to one-half as likely as full-time workers to receive benefits. A comparison of tables 3 and 4 indicates that greater differences occur between part-time and full-time workers in fringe benefits than in wages.

The Effect of Part-Time Work on Wages

While tables 3 and 4 show that on average part-time workers receive lower compensation than full-time workers in most occupations, these data ignore all differences in worker skills and in industry and regional characteristics. It may be that part-time workers are less educated, are less experienced, work in nonunion jobs, or work in other situations where their lower wage reflects characteristics not related to part-time work per se. I now undertake to control more carefully for these other factors.

Single-Equation Estimates

A common assumption in most empirical labor market analysis is that wages are unaffected by hours of work.[7] To the extent that part-time work is considered, it is typically represented by a dummy variable

7. Surprisingly little research exists on wage differentials between part-time and full-time workers in the United States. Recent exceptions include Ehrenberg and others, "Part-Time Employment"; and James E. Jones and Ethel B. Long, "Married Women in Part-Time Employment," *Industrial and Labor Relations Review*, vol. 34 (April 1981), pp. 413–25. The returns to part-time work over a woman's career have been studied by Mary Corcoran, Greg J. Duncan, and Michael Ponza, "A Longitudinal Analysis of White Women's Wages," *Journal of Human Resources*, vol. 18 (Fall 1983), pp. 497–520.

in the wage equation, allowing for an additive shift effect on the regression constant. Thus the following equation is estimated,

$$(1) \qquad\qquad w = X\beta + \alpha PT + e,$$

where w is the logarithm of the wage rate, X is a vector of personal and job characteristics, including a constant, PT is a dummy variable equal to 1 if an individual works part time, and e is a random error term. It is typically found that α, the effect of part-time work on wages, is negative and significant.

Estimates of the effects of part-time work from a variety of ordinary-least-squares wage regressions on female and male workers are shown in the first and third columns of table 5. All the typical human capital variables are included in these regressions, as well as a variety of industry and region-specific characteristics. The part-time dummy variable has a significant and negative coefficient of -0.214 among all women workers, controlling for all other variables, and a coefficient of -0.297 among all men workers. These coefficients imply that hourly wages for part-time workers are about one-fifth lower than full-time wages among women and one-quarter lower than full-time wages among men. When the same regression specification is run separately for workers in each of the five occupational categories, negative part-time effects are found in all five regressions, although the magnitude of the part-time effect differs across the occupations. For women and men, the largest negative wage effect occurs among clerical and sales workers and the smallest effect among service workers. The pattern of occupational wage effects is different from that visible among occupations in the raw data in table 3. For instance, professional part-time workers actually showed slightly higher average wages than full-time workers in the data in table 3, but when other wage-determining variables are held constant, there is a significant negative effect associated with part-time work in professional occupations. Interestingly, service occupations, which employ the largest share of part-time workers, appear to show no significant part-time wage differential for women and only a small differential for men. In general, however, the results shown in table 5 duplicate the standard wisdom regarding part-time work: part-time workers receive significantly lower hourly wages than full-time workers, although the wage-rate penalty varies across occupations.

In view of the trend toward increasing involuntary part-time employment, it would also seem useful to enter an additional dummy vari-

Table 5.   Effects of Part-Time Work on Wages, by Occupation and Sex, 1987[a]

	Women		Men	
Occupation	Part-time dummy variable	Instrumental part-time variable[b]	Part-time dummy variable	Instrumental part-time variable[b]
All workers	−0.214 (0.008)	−0.622 (0.066)	−0.297 (0.017)	0.823 (0.115)
Professional, managerial, and technical	−0.191 (0.017)	−0.387 (0.117)	−0.138 (0.035)	0.937 (0.158)
Sales	−0.192 (0.028)	−1.161 (0.221)	−0.431 (0.063)	0.805 (0.301)
Clerical	−0.203 (0.140)	−0.385 (0.108)	−0.399 (0.052)	−0.782 (0.482)
Service	−0.024 (0.020)	−0.448 (0.165)	−0.124 (0.037)	−0.707 (0.443)
Craft, operative, and labor	−0.118 (0.026)	−0.559 (0.162)	−0.278 (0.026)	0.742 (0.266)

a. Dependent variable is logarithm of wages. Numbers in parentheses are standard errors. All specifications include variables for race, marital status, age, age squared, years of education, state unemployment rates, industry unionization rates, female percentage by industry, and a constant. Industry-specific data vary with two-digit industrial classifications. Industry unionization rates are calculated from the subsample within the March 1988 CPS who were questioned about labor union coverage on their current job. The female percentage is derived from annual BLS statistics for 1987 published in *Employment and Earnings*, January 1988. State unemployment rates come from the 1987 annual averages published in *Employment and Earnings*, May 1980.

b. Instruments for part-time work are number of children under age 6, total household size, nonlabor market household income, and a constant.

able into the wage regressions to indicate whether a part-time job is involuntary. When such a term is included in wage estimates similar to those reported in the first and third columns of table 5, it has a significant and negative effect in the aggregate regression and in three of the five occupation-specific regressions for women. (These results are not shown in the table.) For men, an additional involuntary part-time dummy variable is insignificant in the aggregate regression and significant in only two of the five occupation-specific regressions. In other words, some involuntary part-time workers (particularly women) experience not only the standard negative wage differential associated with part-time work but also an additional negative wage effect, even controlling for human capital and industry effects.

Since the data set includes information on compensation beyond wages, it would seem useful to include this information in the estimations. If I knew the dollar value of individual pension and health plans, I could compute a measure of "full compensation" by summing the value of wage and fringe benefits to the workers. However, since I do not have this information, I can presumably control for the effect of fringe benefits on wages by entering dummy variables that indicate the presence of fringe benefits on the right-hand side of the wage equation. This is the equation

(2) $w = X\beta + \alpha PT + \delta_1 F_1 + \delta_2 F_2 + e,$

where F_1 is a dummy variable equal to 1 if a worker is included in a pension plan on the job, and F_2 is a dummy variable equal to 1 if a worker is included in a health plan. In a simple compensating wage differential story, one would expect wages and fringes to substitute for each other, resulting in negative values for δ_1 and δ_2.

As others have found, this prediction is strongly rejected.[8] Both δ_1 and δ_2 are strongly positive and significant when equation 2 is estimated. Jobs that provide fringe benefits also pay higher wages. In addition, the inclusion of fringe benefits in the regressions significantly increases the explanatory power of the equations. Inclusion of the dummy variables representing pension and health coverage dramatically boosts the R^2 statistics on these regressions.

However, the estimation of equation 2 raises an even more critical concern for this analysis. The part-time coefficient (α) in equation 2 is dramatically different from that in equation 1. In contrast to the results shown in table 5, when fringe benefits are included among the right-hand-side variables the effect of part-time work becomes insignificant or (in some cases) significant and positive.

Capturing the Effects of Unmeasured Characteristics

These surprising results would be correct if equation 2 described a reasonable model of how wages, fringe benefits, and part-time work are related.[9] However, given the dramatic change in the results caused by adding two additional variables describing fringe benefits, it is reasonable to worry about statistical and specification problems. In particular,

8. For a discussion of the evidence and theories regarding compensating wage differentials, see Charles Brown, "Equalizing Differences in the Labor Market," *Quarterly Journal of Economics,* vol. 94 (February 1980), pp. 113–34.

9. For instance, one could argue equation 2 was the appropriate model if fringe benefits were set institutionally and attached to jobs, while wages were more dependent on particular worker characteristics. In this case, the instrumental estimation procedure described below should produce similar results to those that result from estimating equation 2, which it does not.

there may be unmeasured variables that are simultaneously correlated
with wage rates and fringe benefits and with the propensity to work part
time. For instance, it seems plausible to assume that wages, fringe benefits, and part-time jobs are all simultaneously affected by unobservable
job-specific effects. Both high wages and the availability of fringe benefits provide information on whether a job is a "good job" that is not
readily available by simply controlling for worker characteristics. These
unobserved variables may include the extent to which the employer
invests in workers on this job or the extent to which the worker and
the employer have implicit contracts with each other to ensure more
stable employment patterns. Whether a job is part time may also be
correlated with these same underlying factors. One can model this "good
job" story by assuming that there is some unmeasurable fixed effect that
characterizes a job. Let the wages and fringe benefits available to worker
i in job j be described as

(3a) $$w_{ij} = X_{ij}\beta + \alpha_1 PT_{ij} + \pi_j + e_{ij};$$

(3b) $$F_{ij} = Z_{ij}\tau + \alpha_2 PT_{ij} + \theta_1\pi_j + u_{ij};$$

(3c) $$PT_{ij} = T_{ij}\mu + \theta_2\pi_j + v_{ij},$$

where π is a fixed effect unique to job j. In this situation, the error in
the part-time variable PT $(\theta_2\pi_j + v_{ij})$ is clearly correlated with the error
in equation 3a $(\pi_j + e_{ij})$, and estimates in which this correlation is not
accounted for (such as columns 1 or 3 of table 5) are incorrect. Inclusion
of fringe benefits in equation 3a may proxy for the unmeasurable error
term π_j, and significantly change the measured effect of part-time work
on wages.

   An alternative story might focus on unmeasured differences between
workers rather than between jobs. Part-time jobs might not be bad jobs;
they might simply be filled with poor workers. There may be unmeasured
characteristics determining worker productivity that cannot be measured
in this data set but that employers observe, such as effort or motivation.
More motivated workers may earn better wages, receive more fringe
benefits, and be more likely to choose full-time work. If these effects
are not controlled for, the result is a model similar to equation 3 in
which the fixed effects that refer to jobs (π_j) should now be written as
unmeasured worker fixed effects (π_i). As before, if these effects exist

and are not controlled for, the ordinary-least-squares estimates will be wrong.

With suitable longitudinal information it would be possible to choose between the two models just described. Lacking this type of data, an alternative approach is to create an instrumental variable representing a worker's part-time status. This variable could be created using a set of independent variables that are correlated with the choice of part-time work but uncorrelated with wage determination, thus purging the part-time variable of any correlations with unmeasured effects that may also be correlated to wages. The estimated coefficient on such an instrumental variable should provide an unbiased estimate of the true α_1. I created an instrumental variable representing part-time status using family size, number of children under age 6, and household unearned income. The estimated probability of working part time, based on a probit estimate of the choice between part-time and full-time work using these instruments as independent variables, is entered into equation 3a in place of the actual part-time dummy variable. While these instruments may safely be assumed to be independent of any job-specific effects, they are less persuasively independent of worker-specific effects, a point to which I shall return below.

The estimated coefficients on the instrumental variable for part-time status from wage equations for females and males are shown in the second and fourth columns of table 5. These coefficients are quite different from those in columns 1 and 3. For women, they are uniformly negative, significant, and somewhat larger than the initial part-time work effects shown in column 1. For men, the instrumental part-time variable shows a significant and positive wage effect for all part-time workers, which is mirrored in positive effects in three of the five occupations.[10]

If the instrumental-variable procedure appropriate for estimating equation 3a is taken as the correct model, then the unambiguous conclusion is that part-time work has a uniformly negative effect on wages among women, although this effect varies in magnitude and significance across occupations. The answer to the question "Do part-time female

10. Further inclusion of fringe benefit variables in these equations has little impact on the coefficient on the instrumental part-time variable. Proper estimation requires instrumenting the fringe benefit variables as well, but instruments for fringe benefits are not readily available. (No reasonable variables in the data set that are correlated with fringes would not also be correlated with wages.) I estimate both pension and health availability with a probit equation using all variables in the wage regression, including occupational dummies, and then include the estimated probabilities from these two probits as instruments for fringes in the wage regression.

workers earn less, controlling for their different human capital, occupational, and industry characteristics?" is clearly "Yes." Among men, the results are more ambiguous. Part-time male workers in clerical and service occupations appear to earn less after controlling for personal and industry characteristics. But part-time men in professional, sales, and craft occupations actually appear to be better paid than equivalent full-time workers.

However, there are reasons to believe that the instrumental-estimation results shown in table 5 are still not completely satisfactory. First, all results so far have been based on samples of labor force participants. Especially among women, adjusting for the composition of individuals who actually choose to join the labor force can significantly change the coefficients in regression equations that predict wage rates. This might be particularly important when the focus is on the effect of part-time work on wages, since the choice of part-time work is essentially a choice of how many hours to work. By ignoring all individuals who have chosen not to work (that is, have chosen to work zero hours), one may seriously misestimate the effect of observed choices of hours among workers. Since virtually all nondisabled adult men work, the adjustment for labor force participation rarely has much impact on male wage equation coefficients.

Second, existing research indicates that the observed distributions of wage rates among part-time workers, on the one hand, and among full-time workers, on the other, are affected by differences between the two kinds of workers.[11] Differences in who selects part-time versus full-time work can influence the statistical estimate of the difference in wages caused by part-time versus full-time work, a process referred to as "selection bias." In particular, if the resulting differences are due to unmeasurable factors, such as ambition or general intelligence, the observed wage difference might also be attributable to these unmeasurable factors rather than to the part-time nature of some jobs. Under these circumstances, a special procedure must be used to account for the correlation between low wages and part-time work that arises because of the special character of workers who choose to work part time.

The usual procedure to account for the problem of selection bias is to include a variable (the "Heckman selectivity term") in the wage

11. Wayne Simpson, "Analysis of Part-Time Pay in Canada," *Canadian Journal of Economics*, vol. 19 (November 1986), pp. 798–807; and Brian G. M. Main, "Hourly Earnings of Female Part-Time versus Full-Time Employees," University of St. Andrews, Department of Economics, August 1987.

equation that accounts for self-selection into part-time work. The procedure is not applicable in this case, because both wage rates and the choice of part-time work are both in turn conditioned upon a person's decision to work. But one cannot adjust for selection into the labor market by including a selectivity variable in a probit equation that predicts the choice of part-time work.[12] A more complicated estimation method is needed.

Even if the labor force participation choice is ignored, the instrumental-variable procedure used above still does not adequately account for the compositional differences between part-time and full-time workers. In the instrumental-variable procedure, a variable representing the "probability of working part time" is included in a single equation that predicts the wages of all workers, whether part time or full time. In contrast, in a procedure that accounts for compositional differences, or selection effects, two wage equations would be estimated. One would show the determinants of wages among part-time workers and would include a variable to capture the effects of selectivity into part-time work. The other would show the determinants of wages among full-time workers and would include a selectivity term for full-time work. The results obtained by estimating two separate wage equations with sample selection variables are not typically equivalent to those obtained by estimating one equation with instrumental variables.

A third problem with the estimates shown in table 5 is that they allow the effect of part-time work to operate only through the constant term in the wage equation. In practice, part-time workers may face an entirely different wage determination process from the one faced by full-time workers. This can be represented in a regression context by permitting variables in the regression equation to take different coefficients for part-time workers than they take for full-time workers.[13] Alternatively, it can be represented by estimating separate wage equations for the two kinds of workers as the selectivity correction described above would do.

---

12. The problem is essentially that the errors become heteroskedastic when a selectivity term is entered into a probit.

13. Of course, one can interact the instrumental part-time dummy variable with all the other variables in the wage regression in the instrumental variable estimates shown above; however, if there are biases in these estimates due to selection effects, this will merely compound them.

Modeling Women's Wages and Work Choices Together

I want to estimate the determinants of women's wages, accounting for two types of choices. First, there is the choice to participate or not participate in the labor market (desired hours are positive or not). Second, depending upon the choice to participate, an individual chooses to work part time or full time. Past research indicates that workers' choices of hours are separately determined from the decision to work or not work. Thus I will separate these two choices into different equations.[14] I will test the assumption that workers who have selected part-time employment face a different wage determination process than workers who have selected full-time employment.

The model I intend to estimate is based upon three equations. The first is a participation equation:

$$(4) \qquad P^* = U_w - U_{nw} = Z_1 \tau_1 + v.$$

P^* is a continuous variable that measures the utility comparison between working (U_w) and not working (U_{nw}). P^* is unobservable, but I do observe the dichotomous variable P, where $P = 1$ when $P^* > 0$ and $P = 0$ when $P^* \leq 0$. Thus I can estimate the determinants of the probit equation

$$(4') \qquad P = 0 \text{ if } P^* \leq 0 \ (v \leq -Z\tau_1);$$

$$P = 1 \text{ if } P^* > 0 \ (v > -Z\tau_1).$$

The second equation is based upon hours choices among workers:

$$(5) \qquad H = 0 \text{ if } P^* \leq 0;$$

$$H = Z_2 \tau_2 + u \text{ if } P^* > 0.$$

I assume that the particular value of hours is not relevant. The only important characteristic of the hours choice is whether $0 < H < 35$ or

---

14. The most typical explanation for this is the presence of fixed costs of work. See Rebecca M. Blank, "Simultaneously Modelling the Supply of Weeks and Hours of Work among Female Household Heads," *Journal of Labor Economics*, vol. 6 (April 1988), pp. 177–204.

$H \geq 35$. I define a dichotomous variable FT (for full time), where $FT = 1$ if $H \geq 35$, and $FT = 0$ if $0 < H < 35$. Thus I can estimate the determinants of a probit equation on full-time versus part-time work:

$$(5') \qquad\qquad FT = 0 \text{ if } H = 0;$$

$$FT = 0 \text{ if } 35 > Z_2\tau_2 + u;$$

$$FT = 1 \text{ if } 35 \leq Z_2\tau_2 + u.$$

Finally, the wage equation is conditional upon the values of both FT and P:

$$(6) \qquad\qquad w = X\beta + e \text{ if } P = 1 \text{ and } FT = 1;$$

$$w = X(\beta + \alpha) + e \text{ if } P = 1 \text{ and } FT = 0.$$

Equations 4', 5', and 6 can be jointly estimated. There are three possible states for any individual. One cannot work, one can work part time, or one can work full time. These three possible situations can be represented by a three-part likelihood function for a single individual i:

$$(7) \qquad L_i = Pr\,(v_i \leq -Z_{1i}\tau_1) + Pr\,(e_i = [w_i - X_i(\beta + \alpha)]/\sigma,$$

$$-Z_{2i}\tau_2 < u_i < 35 - Z_{2i}\tau_2, v_i > -Z_{1i}\tau_2)$$

$$+ Pr\,(e_1 = (w_i - X_i\beta)/\sigma, u_i \geq 35 - Z_{2i}\tau_2, v_i > -Z_{1i}\tau_1).$$

Summing the logarithm of this likelihood function across all individuals and applying standard maximum-likelihood techniques will result in appropriate estimates for the coefficient vectors β, α, τ_1 and τ_2, the standard error of $e(\sigma)$, as well as the correlation coefficients between e and u (Γ_{eu}), between e and v (Γ_{ev}), and between u and v (Γ_{uv}).

Note that this model assumes that the selection of part-time work can be characterized by the variables in the vector Z_2. For involuntary part-time workers this may be inaccurate; a better model would estimate desired part-time or full-time status separately from actual part-time or full-time status.[15] I do not do this largely because of the econometric problems of adding an additional constraint to the model. However,

---

15. For an estimate of the choice of part-time work that separates desired and actual hours, see Leslie A. Sundt, "'Involuntary' Employment and Labor Market Constraints upon Women," University of Arizona, Department of Economics, October 1988.

one should view the coefficients on the part-time versus full-time equation as reduced-form coefficients that imbed the effects of both choice and labor market constraints. (For instance, I included state unemployment rates in the vector of part-time versus full-time choice determinants. This variable is missing from the specification reported below only because it was insignificant in all estimates.) In addition, I allow the effects of being involuntarily unemployed to enter the wage equation through an additional dummy variable term, as discussed below.

If the only element of the wage coefficient vector β that is allowed to differ with part-time work is the constant, maximum-likelihood estimates from this procedure should provide a set of wage parameters comparable to those estimated in table 5, but with the labor force participation and part-time work decisions explicitly taken into account. Such a set of estimates is provided in column 1 of table 6. Columns 2 and 3 present the respective estimates of the coefficients τ_2 (choice of full-time work) and τ_1 (choice of labor market participation). Several facts should be noted about the coefficients in these three columns.

First, the wage coefficients are significantly different in these estimates from those in the earlier ordinary-least-squares and instrumental-variable estimates. The effects of age, age squared, education, and marital status are uniformly smaller in these estimates. This is the typical pattern when selection corrections make a difference. The pattern is not surprising, given that the correlation coefficients between labor market participation and wages and those between labor market participation and part-time work are both clearly significant.

Second, it is clear from columns 2 and 3 that labor market participation is a distinguishably different choice than the choice of full-time or part-time work. Labor market participation is more strongly affected by age, education, marital status, children under 6, and unearned income than is the choice of full-time or part-time work.[16]

Third and most significant, once this full accounting of labor market choices has been made, the effect of part-time work becomes *positive* and significant, with a coefficient of 0.168. This fuller maximization procedure appears to indicate that the negative effects of part-time work found in table 5 were reflecting the effect of selection into part-time jobs; they did not measure the true effect of part-time work on wages.

16. A likelihood ratio test of this model against a model that includes only a wage equation and an ordered probit in hours (combining the labor market participation decision and the part-time work decision and forcing them to share a single set of coefficients) indicates that the three-equation model provides a significantly better fit.

Table 6. Effects of Part-Time Work on Wages, Controlling for Choice of Part-Time Work and Labor Market Participation, for Women, 1987[a]

| | | | | Wages[b] | |
Independent variable	Wages (1)	Choice of full-time work (2)	Choice of labor market participation (3)	Full-time effects (4)	Additive part-time effects (5)
Age	0.026* (0.007)	−0.003 (0.003)	−0.020* (0.002)	0.028* (0.010)	−0.010 (0.015)
Age squared	−0.0002* (0.0001)	...	...	−0.0002* (0.00001)	0.0001 (0.0002)
Education	0.041* (0.005)	−0.004 (0.011)	0.074* (0.008)	0.042* (0.007)	0.002 (0.010)
Marital status	0.118* (0.034)	−0.225* (0.068)	−0.317* (0.058)	0.093* (0.039)	0.007 (0.007)
State unemployment rate	−0.021* (0.006)	...	...	−0.027* (0.008)	0.050* (0.015)
Industry unionization rate	0.004* (0.001)	...	...	0.004* (0.001)	−0.002 (0.002)
Industry percent female	−0.003* (0.001)	...	...	−0.004* (0.001)	0.006* (0.001)
Constant	1.031* (0.172)	1.393* (0.192)	0.879* (0.152)	1.091* (0.220)	−0.370 (0.379)
Number of children under 6	...	−0.149* (0.049)	−0.313* (0.030)	...	...
Family size	...	−0.055* (0.020)	−0.033* (0.013)	...	...
Nonearned household income/1,000	...	−0.029 (0.029)	−0.070* (0.016)	...	...
Part-time dummy	0.168* (0.072)	...	...	...	...
Involuntary part-time	...	...	...	...	−0.200* (0.039)
Correlation of errors Wages and full-time work (equations 1 and 2)	−0.501* (0.051)				−0.490* (0.060)
Wages and labor market participation (equations 1 and 3)	0.871* (0.011)				0.812* (0.019)
Full-time work and labor market participation (equations 2 and 3)	−0.775* (0.128)				0.978* (0.132)
Likelihood value	−5,526				−5,497

*Significant at 5 percent level or better.
a. Estimation results from a three-equation simultaneous model. Numbers in parentheses are standard errors.
b. Coefficients on the full-time versus part-time equation and labor market participation equation not shown. (They are not distinguishable from the results in columns 2 and 3.) A complete set of estimated coefficients is available from the author.

This may be due to unmeasurable personal factors that make part-time workers lower in productivity, or to unmeasurable job factors that make part-time jobs lower in productivity. The finding implies that those who work part time would also receive lower wages if they held the same jobs but worked full time. Unmeasured correlations between women who choose to work and to work part time and the wage determination process prevent the ordinary-least-squares and instrumental-variable procedures from measuring this accurately.[17]

However, even this conclusion needs more elaboration. The earlier estimation procedures indicated the importance of accounting for occupational differences in the effect of part-time work. Rather than estimating a single part-time effect, I have estimated separate part-time effects for workers in each occupation (results not shown). The results are similar to the aggregate effect shown in column 1 of table 6. Part-time work has a positive effect on wages in every occupation, although the effect is insignificant in sales and craft jobs. Part-time workers in professional and managerial positions show particularly large and positive wage differentials, holding all other variables constant. Allowing for these occupational differences results in a significantly higher likelihood value, as determined by a likelihood ratio test.

The estimates in the first column of table 6 restrict the part-time effect to only a shift effect on the constant. The fourth and fifth columns relax this restriction and allow all the coefficients of the wage (β) to differ by a factor α, as described in equation 6. The resulting estimates of β and α are presented in columns 4 and 5, respectively. The estimated coefficients in column 5 are *additive* effects to the full-time coefficients in column 4; thus the question of whether part-time wages are determined differently from full-time wages becomes a question of whether the coefficients in the fifth column are significantly different from zero.

Returns to age, education, and marriage are not significantly different among part-time workers. This contradicts the belief that part-time workers receive a lower return on their investment in human capital. A study by Jones and Long found lower returns to education for part-time workers using 1970 U.S. data, but Simpson's study of 1981 Canadian

---

17. The reason why the ordinary-least-squares estimates in table 5 differ is clear, but the reason why the instrumental-variable estimates do not show positive part-time effects may be more puzzling. There are two factors: First, the instrumental-variable procedure does not account for the labor market participation choice, which has a major effect on the wage regression. Second, as noted above, this procedure is not an adequate method of accounting for selection of part-time work.

data did not.[18] I have estimated models similar to those in table 6 using identical 1983 data from the CPS. These estimates do indicate significantly lower returns to education for U.S. part-time workers in the data for 1983. One hypothesis is that there was some change in the mid-1980s in the wage determination process for part-time workers and that the effect of human capital characteristics is converging between part-time and full-time workers. Alternatively, the relation between part-time work and the returns to human capital may vary between years, particularly as the macroeconomic environment varies (although the estimates in table 6 control for differences in unemployment rates). Any definite statement about this requires further research using data from a variety of years.

While personal characteristics do not affect the wages of part-time workers differently from the wages of full-time workers, the regional and industry environment does have a differential effect. The effect of industry unionization rates is insignificantly different, but the negative wage effect of being in a highly feminized industry is completely absent for part-time workers, and there is even a small positive differential. Similarly, the negative effect of state unemployment rates on full-time wages is not present at all for part-time workers. Thus for part-time female workers the effect of the job environment on wages is different than for their full-time colleagues. Once all of these other factors have been accounted for, the additional effect of part-time work on the constant is insignificant.[19]

The estimates shown in table 6 also include a dummy variable that measures whether a part time worker is working part time involuntarily. As was found in ordinary-least-squares wage regressions without selection adjustments, wages are significantly lower among involuntary female part-time workers. This may reflect both the quality of those workers who are unable to find full-time jobs and the fact that a worker who plans to move into full-time work as soon as it is available may not seek a good part-time job.

The results shown in table 6 imply that there is no simple way to characterize the effects of part-time work on women's wages. All else

18. Jones and Long, "Married Women"; and Simpson, "Analysis of Part-Time Pay."
19. The estimates in columns 4 and 5 of table 6 have also been expanded to include occupational constants interacted with a part-time dummy variable. When all variables are fully interacted with part-time work, the occupational constants, like the additive constant term in table 6, are insignificant, with the exception of a weakly significant positive effect on professional wages.

equal, part-time work in unionized or traditionally female occupations may pay as well as or better than full-time work. These differences in the effect of job environment on part-time wages are highly correlated with occupation-specific effects on part-time work; occupation-specific differences between the wages of part-time and full-time workers exist, but a full interaction of all variables with a part-time dummy makes these occupation-specific effects insignificant.

The overall conclusions from these estimates are threefold. First, in order to fully measure the effect of part-time work on wages, one needs to account for the decision to enter the labor market as well as to seek part-time work. These selection adjustments result in an estimate of the part-time versus full-time wage differential that is positive for workers in all occupations, although there are differences in its magnitude across occupations. Women in professional, managerial, and technical occupations who work part time receive particularly significant positive repayments. Second, characterizing the effect of part-time work as a simple shift effect on wages is not an adequate specification, since the wages of part-time workers are determined by a different set of regression coefficients. While their returns to human capital characteristics are largely similar to those of full-time workers in the 1987 data, part-time workers do not appear to suffer as much from working in highly feminized industries, and they are not strongly affected by regional unemployment rates. Third, the effect of being involuntarily unemployed remains negative and significant, even when all other differences are accounted for. This implies that, all other variables held constant, involuntary part-time workers earn lower wages from part-time work than do voluntary part-timers.

Modeling Men's Wages and Work Choices Together

In view of the findings above about the effect of choosing to work and to work part time on women's wages, it is interesting to compare the equivalent results for men. As noted above, virtually all adult men (over 90 percent of the sample) work during the year. This makes the adjustment for labor market participation less significant among men.[20]

20. Virtually no previous studies have found selection adjustments significant among male populations. I have duplicated the results presented here for men with the full three-equation model including a selection adjustment for labor force participation, and it makes little difference in the estimates.

Table 7. Effects of Part-Time Work on Wages, Controlling for Choice of Part-Time Work, for Men, 1987[a]

Independent variable	Wages (1)	Choice of full-time work (2)	Full-time effects (3)	Additive part-time effects (4)	Choice of full-time work (5)
			Wages		
Age	0.058* (0.005)	0.003 (0.002)	0.061* (0.005)	−0.034* (0.013)	0.003 (0.002)
Age squared	−0.00056* (0.00006)	...	−0.0006* (0.0001)	0.0004* (0.0001)	...
Education	0.075* (0.002)	0.033* (0.009)	0.073* (0.003)	−0.009 (0.007)	0.033* (0.009)
Marital status	0.133* (0.018)	0.200* (0.081)	0.130* (0.019)	−0.077 (0.053)	0.200* (0.082)
State unemployment rate	−0.015* (0.004)	...	−0.014* (0.004)	−0.009 (0.011)	...
Industry unionization rate	0.002* (0.0005)	...	0.002* (0.0005)	0.004* (0.002)	...
Industry percent female	−0.004* (0.0004)	...	−0.004* (0.0004)	−0.002 (0.001)	...
Constant	0.142 (0.105)	0.751* (0.180)	0.140 (0.112)	0.670* (0.310)	0.752* (0.184)
Number of children under 6	...	−0.514* (0.058)	...	...	−0.499 (0.581)
Family size	...	0.130* (0.028)	...	...	0.129* (0.029)
Nonearned household income/1,000	...	−0.027* (0.003)	...	...	−0.027* (0.003)
Part-time dummy	−0.181* (0.096)	...	...	...	...
Involuntary part time	...	...	...	−0.254* (0.024)	...
Correlation coefficient	−0.094 (0.078)			−0.075 (0.086)	
Likelihood value	−6,917			−6,876	

*Significant at 5 percent level or better.
a. Estimation results from a two-equation simultaneous model. Numbers in parentheses are standard errors.

Therefore I estimate a two-equation model for men, using a sample solely of workers to estimate wages simultaneously with a part-time versus full-time choice equation. Using the notation defined above, this yields the joint model:

(8) $$w = X\beta + e \text{ if } FT = 1;$$
$$w = X(\beta + \alpha) + e \text{ if } FT = 0$$

For any individual i, the likelihood function is a two-part equation:

(9) $$L_i = Pr[e_i = (w_i - X_i\beta)/\sigma, u_i \geq 35 - Z_{2i}\tau_2]$$
$$+ Pr\{e_i = [w_i - X_i(\beta + \alpha)]/\sigma,$$
$$- Z_{2i}\tau_2 < u < 35 - Z_{2i}\tau_2\}.$$

Summing the logarithm of this likelihood function across all individuals and applying standard maximum-likelihood techniques results in estimates for the coefficient vectors β, α, τ_2, the standard error of e, and the correlation between e and u.

The results of such estimations for men, allowing only the constant to vary with part-time work, are shown in columns 1 and 2 of table 7. Column 1 presents the coefficients (β) on the wage equation, plus a part-time dummy variable, and column 2 presents the coefficients (τ_2) that determine the choice between part-time and full-time work. Two primary observations should be made about these results. First, the choice of full-time versus part-time work among men is significantly different from that among women. Education, marriage, and family size all have significant and positive effects on the probability a man will work full time, while they have negative effects for women.

Second, accounting for the selection of part-time work in the wage estimates for men has little effect, particularly on the estimated overall influence of part-time work on wages. The effect of part-time work is negative and significant in the wage equation, as it is in the ordinary-least-squares estimates shown in table 5.[21] The correlation coefficient

21. The instrumental-variable estimates in table 5 are significantly different. I believe this reflects the problems with these measures when selection occurs. These estimates enter "probability of working part time" into all wage equations, while the selection adjustment accounts for part-time work only among part-time workers. Given that very few men work part time, and that the probability of part-time work is much less accurately estimated for men, the instrumental-variable estimates result in strange coefficients.

between the wage and the choice equations is insignificant, implying that the joint estimation has little effect on either equation. In other words, there are few unmeasured correlations between wage rates and choice of work hours among men; estimating either of these equations separately provides unbiased coefficient estimates. When the single part-time dummy variable is replaced with occupation-specific part-time dummy variables, all of these are negative, although the professional and the clerical coefficients are insignificant.

These estimates constrain any part-time difference to occur solely through a shift effect in the constant. Following the same process as for women, the next estimates free up the part-time effect and allow each wage coefficient to vary between part-time and full-time workers. Columns 3 and 4 of table 7 show the respective estimates of β and α in equation 8. As before, column 4 presents the additive effect of part-time work on the full-time coefficient in column 3; thus only if the estimate in column 4 is significantly different from zero is a differential effect of the part-time versus full-time choice implied. Column 5 shows the part-time versus full-time choice equation. The coefficients here are quite similar to those in the previous estimation, and as before there is no significant correlation between these estimates and the wage estimates, implying that the simultaneous-equation estimation has little effect on the coefficients.

In comparison with the results for women shown in table 6, the fully interactive set of part-time effects shown in column 4 of table 7 indicates that part-time male workers receive significantly lower returns to both age and education than do their full-time male colleagues. They also benefit more from unionization when it occurs. Similar to women, involuntary male part-timers continue to earn significantly lower wages, even after all wage coefficients are allowed to vary between part-time and full-time workers.

The results of these estimates indicate that the effect of part-time work is quite different for men than for women. There are few unobserved correlations for men between selection of part-time work and their wages. As a result, the conclusions from the simple ordinary-least-squares estimations shown in table 5 are mirrored in the more complex simultaneous estimates shown in table 7. Male part-timers with education and experience equivalent to that of male full-timers are paid less in part-time jobs, even after choice of this work is accounted for. In contrast, women's wages are much more affected by their decision to enter the labor force as well as to take part-time work. There are clearly unobserved correlations between the wage rates received by part-time women and the choice to work part time. These differences may reflect both differences among women in terms of who chooses to work part time and the nature of the part-time jobs women receive.

The Effect of Part-Time Work on Fringe Benefits

While wages are the major component of compensation, the share of fringe benefits in total compensation has increased steadily over time.[22] The lack of fringe benefits in many part-time jobs, as seen in table 4, is often cited as clear evidence that part-time work is not as well compensated as full-time work. However, if most part-time workers are less skilled or have fewer years of experience, they might not be eligible for many of these benefits even if they were in full-time work. This is especially true with respect to pensions, where employees typically must work a minimum number of years before they are vested in a pension. The laws governing pensions explicitly exclude workers in very low-hour part-time jobs.[23] From the employer's perspective, fringe benefits often involve fixed costs that do not vary with a worker's hours. Thus paying fringe benefits to part-time workers results in a higher cost per employee than for full-time workers. Particularly if part-time workers are viewed as more temporary workers in whom a firm is less willing to invest training or resources, employers would want to avoid paying them large fixed fringe benefits.[24]

The same techniques I have used to investigate the effect of part-time work on wages can be used to study the effect of part-time work on fringe benefits. As noted above, I cannot observe the value of fringe benefits received by a worker; I have information only on whether or not an individual receives pension payments or some form of health

22. For a discussion of the growing share of fringe benefits in compensation, see Stephen A. Woodbury, "Substitution Between Wages and Nonwage Benefits," *American Economic Review*, vol. 73 (March 1983), pp. 166–82.

23. The Employee Retirement Income Security Act (ERISA) does not require that pensions be available, but if a firm chooses to offer them, it must follow ERISA provisions for all workers employed more than 1,000 hours annually (20.8 hours per week for full-year workers).

24. For a discussion of the employer's decision on whether to provide fringe benefits to part-time workers, see Mark Montgomery, "On the Determinants of Employer Demand for Part-Time Workers," *Review of Economics and Statistics*, vol. 70 (February 1988), pp. 112–17.

insurance. Thus I can only estimate the determinants of the dichotomous dummy variable that reflects receipt of pension and health insurance and cannot estimate the determinants of the amount of fringe benefits provided.

Probit estimates of the probability that a worker is included in a pension plan or a health plan are shown in table 8, using the same specification used for wages in tables 6 and 7. The coefficients estimating the determinants of pension plans for women and men appear very similar to wage estimates. Greater age, higher education, and higher unionization rates increase the probability of receiving a pension. Marital status and state unemployment rates appear insignificant. However, quite unlike wages, the female percentage in the industry increases the probability of receiving a pension—for both sexes. The determinants of pension plans for women are quite similar to those for men.

The effect of part-time work in the pension probit equation is negative and strongly significant, even after all other variables have been accounted for. In addition, a term representing involuntary part-time work has a further negative effect on the probability of receiving a pension. At the mean values for a married woman, the probability of receiving a pension falls from 55 percent for a full-time worker to 21 percent for a voluntary part-time worker and to 11 percent for an involuntary part-timer. For a similar married man, it falls from 56 percent for a full-time worker to 17 percent for a voluntary part-timer and to 7 percent for an involuntary part-timer. Clearly, part-time workers are far less likely to receive pensions, even if their skills and industry characteristics are held constant. Involuntary part-timers are even worse off.

Equivalent coefficients for the probability of receiving a health plan are quite different from those of pension plans, indicating that eligibility for these two forms of fringe benefits is differently determined. There are also significant differences between the male and female coefficients, implying that a woman's probability of receiving health insurance through her employer is determined differently from a man's. For both sexes, the probability of being included in a health plan is positively affected by education levels, but only for men is it positively affected by age. Being married has a strong negative effect on the probability of getting health coverage among women, consistent with the raw data shown in table 4. Higher industry unionization rates increase the probability of health coverage, and higher state unemployment rates decrease it.

However, while the other determinants of health and pension plans

Table 8. Estimates of Effects of Part-Time Work on Receipt of Fringe Benefits, by Sex, 1987[a]

Independent variable	Female workers		Male workers	
	Included in pension plan	Included in health plan	Included in pension plan	Included in health plan
Age	0.064*	-0.002	0.095*	0.065*
	(0.018)	(0.018)	(0.018)	(0.018)
Age squared	-0.0007*	0.0001	-0.0009*	-0.0006*
	(0.0002)	(0.0002)	(0.0002)	(0.0002)
Education	0.052*	0.047*	0.062*	0.057*
	(0.011)	(0.011)	(0.009)	(0.010)
Marital status	-0.015	-0.474*	0.066	0.047
	(0.060)	(0.062)	(0.066)	(0.071)
State unemployment rate	-0.015	-0.042*	-0.008	-0.012
	(0.015)	(0.015)	(0.014)	(0.014)
Industry unionization rate	0.025*	0.011*	0.023*	0.008*
	(0.002)	(0.002)	(0.002)	(0.002)
Industry percent female	0.004*	-0.001	0.005*	0.002
	(0.002)	(0.002)	(0.001)	(0.002)
Constant	-2.702*	0.149	-3.609*	-1.689*
	(0.388)	(0.372)	(0.382)	(0.387)
Part-time dummy	-0.946*	-1.131*	-1.084*	-1.013*
	(0.071)	(0.066)	(0.142)	(0.129)
Involuntary part time	-0.379*	-0.210*	-0.532*	-0.536*
	(0.110)	(0.094)	(0.113)	(0.105)
Likelihood value	-1,413	-1,448	-1,590	-1,312

*Significant at 5 percent level or better.
a. Numbers in parentheses are standard errors.

may vary, health plans also are far less likely to be received by part-time workers. The health plan equations, like the pension equations, show a strong and significant negative coefficient on the part-time dummy variable and a further significant negative effect for involuntary part-timers. At the mean values, a married full-time female worker has a 59 percent probability of being included in a health plan, while a full-time male worker has a 79 percent probability. An equivalent female part-timer has only an 18 percent probability of receiving health benefits, while an equivalent male part-timer has a 42 percent probability. Part-time workers appear unambiguously worse off with regard to fringe benefit coverage.

When the effect of part-time work on these two fringe benefits is allowed to vary by occupation, there is little difference between the coefficients for each occupation. Unlike the effect on wages, the effect of part-time work on the receipt of health and pension plans does not appear to vary across occupations. In a similar manner, one can interact the part-time dummy with all other variables in the regression. The effect on the estimates for both pensions and health plans is relatively small. While a few of the interactive terms have significant coefficients, the simple shift effect on the constant for part-time workers remains at about the same level as shown in table 8, and the additive negative effect for involuntary part-timers is also largely unaffected. In short, allowing the determinants of fringe benefits to vary completely between part-time and full-time workers does little to explain the much lower recipiency rates of part-timers.

Finally, just as the corrections for deciding to enter the labor market and choose part-time work showed strong effects on the wage estimates for women, probit equations of pension and health recipiency can be estimated jointly with labor market and part-time versus full-time choices. I do not present these results here, largely because they do not provide new information. While the selection adjustments do make minor differences in the coefficients determining eligibility for pension and health benefits, the effect of working part time remains strongly significant and negative even after such adjustments are made, for both men and women.

The conclusion here is simple and unambiguous: part-time workers, especially involuntary part-timers, are far less likely to receive either health or pension benefits on their job, even after all other factors are accounted for.

Are Part-Time Jobs Bad Jobs?

The answer that emerges to the question "Are part-time jobs bad jobs?" is more complex than a simple "yes" or "no." It is true that most part-time workers appear to earn lower wages than equally skilled full-time workers in the same industry and region, although these differences are small or insignificant for certain occupations. And part-time workers are unambiguously less likely to receive fringe benefits. In addition, workers who are involuntarily in the part-time labor force receive lower wages and are even less likely to receive fringe benefits than equivalent voluntary part-time workers.

However, these apparent negative aspects of part-time work need to be considered in conjunction with several other issues. The data available in this study do not allow investigation of many of the nonwage aspects of part-time work, particularly the interaction of part-time jobs with workers' household time constraints. Part-time jobs may allow variations in work hours that could be critically important to both women and men with family and home responsibilities. The great majority of part-time workers are voluntarily working part time, which implies that they must perceive advantages to part-time work that are only poorly measured here.

Reinforcing this perspective on part-time jobs are the indications that once the choices to enter the labor market and to do part-time work are accounted for, part-time female workers actually appear to earn higher wages across all occupations than equivalent full-time workers. There are several ways to interpret this result. There may be unmeasured productivity-related factors that are correlated with the determination of who works part time that would make these women less productive if they were full-time workers. This is consistent with the view that part-time workers are often focused on their activities outside the job. The fact that selection adjustments affect wages implies that the variables entering the selection equation—such as number of young children and total number of people in the household—actually affect the wage determination process for these workers. These workers choose part-time jobs that allow them to work productively and also fulfill their other responsibilities.

In addition, the importance of the selection adjustments may reflect the differences between the jobs chosen by or available to part-time versus full-time workers. The occupational distribution differs significantly between these two labor market groups. Even at a three-digit occupational level, part-time workers are disproportionately grouped in different jobs from full-time workers. Thus women who work part time have different jobs from women who work full time, and the selection adjustment indicates the effect this has on wages. The significant differences in the effect of industries and regions on wages in part-time and full-time work provide further evidence that the selection effect is closely tied to the job options of part-timers.

However, before concluding that all women who choose to work part time must be better off despite less generous wages and fringe benefits, recall that the definition of a voluntary part-timer is someone who indicates she sought only part-time work. This may or may not indicate the presence of serious constraints on choice. For instance, female household heads who cannot find adequate child care may seek only part-time work. Nonetheless, they may be dissatisfied with their inability to work full time. Thus, to judge whether a woman's part-time job is really a free choice, one needs more information than is available from the CPS interviews.

Of course, involuntary part-time workers clearly face labor market constraints. Their consistently lower compensation, even after selection adjustments, reinforces the conclusion that they are worse off in part-time jobs. Unfortunately, the data here do not allow one to determine whether this is the nature of the jobs they are forced to take in the absence of full-time work, or whether this is a reflection of some negative unmeasured productivity characteristics of these workers (which may also be the reason they are unable to find full-time work).

From a policy perspective, there are at least three important issues relating to part-time work. First, the significant use of part-time work among women and the growing number of men in part-time jobs underscore the importance of part-time employment in the labor market. The fact that the percentage of women working part time has remained largely unchanged, even during a twenty-year period in which the composition of the female labor force changed dramatically, implies that part-time jobs fill an important role for many women who desire income and labor market involvement but cannot make a full-time labor market commitment. In addition, the high percentage of part-time jobs among service workers suggests that continued growth in the service occupations will also mean future growth in part-time work.

Second, the extent to which policymakers should be concerned with part-time compensation levels depends on the nature of the choice to take part-time work. Many workers who select part-time jobs are making a preferred choice that leaves them better off than they would be in full-time employment. However, the evidence here indicates that workers of the same age and education level are paid less for part-time work and receive lower fringe benefits. Thus workers in low-income households who are the primary support of their family and whose "choice" of part-time work reflects difficult family and household constraints— such as inaccessible child care, transportation problems, or health limitations—should be a concern of policymakers. In these situations the lower wages and fringe benefits available to part-time workers may have serious negative effects on their household's health status, retirement options, and general economic well-being. In this case, the reasons behind the choice of part-time work as well as the lower compensation levels associated with it are valid policy concerns.

Third, the persistence of a rise in the number of involuntary part-time workers whose hours are limited by labor market demand indicates underemployment and should be an ongoing policy concern. The correlation of involuntary part-time employment with overall unemployment rates provides evidence of this. While part-time workers may be better off than completely unemployed workers, they still may experience significant economic problems in their households, particularly since part-time work often means not just less income, but also an interruption in badly needed fringe benefits.

The short answer to the question "Are part-time jobs bad jobs?" is "It depends." The part-time work force is composed of a heterogeneous group of workers employed in a mix of very different jobs. Men and women appear to face different determinants of part-time work and a different set of part-time jobs. Part-time professionals may encounter issues associated with their employment that are very different than those faced by part-time service or clerical workers. Similarly, the extent to which part-time work is freely chosen or is the result of a set of household and economic constraints is important in answering this question for any individual. Future research in this area would benefit from information that allows a fuller model of the household and family constraints faced by part-time workers. In addition, data that provide more explicit information on the availability of various fringe benefits and on the magnitude of nonwage compensation would allow for much more thorough exploration of the determinants of how compensation in part-time jobs differs from full-time compensation. In a similar manner, data that provide more information on the ways in which employers view part-time workers, why they offer certain part-time jobs, and how they decide on compensation schemes for part-time workers would be useful.

Finally, the importance of part-time work to women is more than just a question of how part-time workers are treated in the labor market. Many current proposals for welfare reform focus on placing women in part-time jobs on the assumption that this provides a stepping-stone for more extensive future labor market involvement. Dynamic estimates of the extent to which part-time work is an avenue to full-time jobs will be important in understanding how women are affected by their extensive use of part-time employment.

Comment by Karen Holden

The motivation behind this volume rests on the recent and curious rise in income inequality in the United States, unexpected after decades of relative stability. This rise in income inequality was concurrent with a number of other social and economic phenomena: the baby boom generation entered the work force, started forming families, and is now swelling the ranks of prime-age workers; the industrial distribution of workers shifted away from manufacturing toward services; union membership fell as a percentage of the work force; college entry among young blacks declined; female headship of families increased; and women continued to move into both full-time and part-time work. Papers in this volume look at these changes in family and population composition and ask whether and how they have contributed to the increase in earnings inequality.

Surprisingly little research has been published on the effect of paid work by women on income distribution—and the papers in this volume reflect this research gap. That issue is a large and complex one, and a single paper could hardly do justice. Indeed, though it never directly addresses the issue of income distribution, Rebecca Blank's paper is an example of the detailed analyses necessary for a full understanding of how different labor market choices by women may influence the size distribution of family incomes. Briefly, Blank discusses several alternative approaches that can be (and have been) used to analyze the effects of working part time on cash wages. She prefers on good theoretical grounds statistical models that control for selection into the labor market (in the case of women) and into part-time work (for both sexes). The wage determination process is shown to be quite different for part-time and full-time work and for women and men, but not necessarily in all occupations to the detriment of part-time workers.

The issues I address here are what is meant by "bad" jobs in a labor market in which work choices are not prescribed, problems that arise in distinguishing part-time and full-time workers in the Current Population Survey, and the relevance of Blank's conclusions to income distribution issues and their policy implications.

The Nature of "Bad" Jobs

"Bad," according to the *American Heritage Dictionary*'s first definition is a comparative term meaning inferior or poor. Whether part-time jobs are to be considered "bad" depends on the standard against which those jobs are judged and the ability to analytically distinguish deviations from that standard. Economists have used compensation as a measure of "bad" and "good" employment outcomes, most often in comparing employment outcomes for men and women and whites and blacks.[25] These studies attempt to distinguish the "true" effects of race and sex from the effect of other factors that are considered legitimate criteria in job assignment and wage setting. A finding of negative effects of sex and race with appropriate controls for demographic characteristics, hours of work, and occupation is typically interpreted as evidence of different (and illegal) treatment of women and blacks in the labor market.

Blank's study is in that same tradition, asking about the "true effect of part-time work." That is, the part-time dummy on her simultaneous estimates is presumed to capture the influence of workers' compensation merely because of fewer hours worked. The answer appears to be that this true effect is not negative. Part-time work is not bad (as measured by lower *cash* hourly wages) compared with equivalent full-time work offered by the same employers. The explanation for the overall lower hourly wages of part-time workers must then lie either (or both) in unmeasured characteristics of the women who select part-time work or in unmeasured differences between the jobs that employers designate as full and part time. These two explanations, however, have very different implications for the question of whether part-time jobs are to be considered bad jobs. If it is the case that particular kinds of women select part-time work, choosing the preferred combination of compensation and hours of work from among an array of equivalent (and equally available) part-time and full-time work opportunities, then the compensation of full-time workers in equivalent jobs is the appropriate standard. The positive part-time wage effect implies that these part-time jobs are not bad, since full-time workers are being paid even less.[26]

25. James P. Smith and Michael P. Ward, "Time-Series Growth in the Female Labor Force," *Journal of Labor Economics*, vol. 3, pt. 2 (January 1985), pp. S59–90.

26. This outcome may result if lower wages are offered to equivalent workers with full-time jobs because "all else equal" family obligations reduce their productivity at full-time hours, while part-time workers face less competition from family concerns during their fewer hours on the job.

However, if women are prevented from working part time in those occupations where they face the most favorable full-time opportunities, the full-time wage rates of women in the occupations in which they do work is not an appropriate standard; the mean higher wage of part-time workers does not reflect the cost to the *individual* of (constrained) part-time work.

The appropriate standard against which to judge the effects on wages of an individual's own part-time work is the wage she would obtain if she were able to participate full time. Controlling for the effects of job selection yields a comparison with full-time workers in equivalent jobs who may not face the same job-selection constraints, rather than a comparison with the more appropriate full-time wage the woman would otherwise receive. Distinguishing between the influence of worker-driven and employer-driven part-time job constraints has always been the key issue in research on part-time work. Blank's paper shows it remains the important issue, since the "pure" part-time effect—the effect on offered wages of redefining a given job as part time—is unimportant in determining the "bad" job status of part-time work.

Identification of Part-Time Jobs

To distinguish the influence of part-time work on wages, full-time and part-time workers must be appropriately distinguished. Blank uses CPS data on usual hours of work over a twelve-month period to distinguish those who work part time and full time, a distinction based on a cutoff at thirty-five hours a week. Unfortunately, observed variations over the year in hours of work and secular increases in the percentage of part-time workers working "intense" hours of work (thirty to thirty-four hours a week) suggest that this cutoff may inappropriately classify as part time many workers whose jobs do not fit the assumed characteristics of part-time employment. Mistakenly counting many committed, long-hour workers as part-timers could bias findings on part-time work effects, thus obscuring the true effect among workers whose hours of work and job opportunities do in fact diverge from those of full-time workers.

The March CPS provides data on hours worked during two reference periods: usual hours worked during the previous year (1986 in the data used by Blank and in this discussion) and total hours worked at all jobs in the week before the survey (March 1987). Blank uses the data on usual hours of work in 1986 in two ways: first, to define full-time workers (thirty-five or more hours) and part-time workers (less than thirty-five hours) and, second, to calculate an hourly wage rate (1986 earnings/ [weeks worked x usual hours of work per week]).[27] Because the dependent variable (wage) and the independent variable (part time versus full time) are derived from identical data items, systematic errors in reported usual hours will bias results. If total hours worked by part-time workers in the year are underestimated by "usual" weekly hours worked, wages of part-time workers will be exaggerated.

The CPS provides no direct measure of the stability of weekly work hours over the previous year. However, comparison of the two different measures of hours of work—hours worked during a usual week in 1986 and those worked during the 1987 reference week—provides a rough measure of that stability. The concern is whether there is any systematic difference in those two periods between part-time and full-time workers that leads to different biases in wage estimates for the two groups. Table 9 shows the ratio of hours worked in 1986 to reference-week hours in 1987 among part-time and full-time workers, classified by usual hours of work last year. I use the same CPS survey as did Blank, selecting the sample of women as described in her paper.

Only 78 percent of women with a job in both periods reported hours of work per week during the two periods that differ by no more than 20 percent, with roughly equal proportions reporting far fewer and far greater hours in 1986 than in 1987. Hourly wages (based on usual hours of work) are likely to be overestimated for workers who more often work longer than usual hours when hours of work change, and wages will be underestimated for workers who more often work shorter than usual hours. The data in the first column of table 9 indicate that the two biases are equally likely, and therefore that, on average, wages may be accurately estimated.

A comparison of 1986 full-time and part-time workers, however, shows that in 1987 those who had been usual part-time workers in 1986 were far more likely than full-timers to report greater than usual hours of work. In contrast, the deviation for full-time workers in either direction was small. If this pattern represents standard variations in hours of work by persons working part time throughout the year on the same job (rather than being due to a job change between January 1, 1987,

---

27. Hours worked are not tied to a single job, so full-time workers may have held multiple part-time jobs, and for all workers hours of work during the previous year may have fluctuated either on a single job or as a result of a job change.

**Table 9.   Difference between Women's Usual Hours of Work in 1986 and Hours
Worked during Reference Week in 1987**

	1986 work status		
Ratio[a]	All	Full time	Part time
Less than 0.80	11.9	9.0	22.4
0.80 to 1.20	77.5	80.2	67.9
More than 1.20	10.6	10.8	9.8
Total	100.0	100.0	100.0

Source: Calculated by author from CPS data.
a. Usual hours worked in 1986 ÷ hours worked during reference week in 1987.

and the interview date), then wages of 1986 part-time workers based on usual hours of work will be inaccurately estimated and, on average, overestimated.[28]

The greater hours that some part-timers work means that many are occasionally—and perhaps often—able to work full time. Of all workers who were classified as part time in 1986, and who also worked in 1987, 23 percent reported full-time hours during the 1987 reference week; only 7 percent of usual full-time workers reported not working full time in 1987 (table 10). The increase to full-time work occurred among all those who worked less than thirty-five hours a week in 1986, but was most likely for those who usually worked thirty to thirty-four hours.

Whether persons working close to a full-time schedule should be classified as part-time or full-time workers is an ongoing controversy. Hedges and Gallogly argue against an official change in the CPS classifications on the basis that this group has overall greater similarity to other part-time workers than to full-time workers.[29] It should be noted, however, that the comparisons supporting this conclusion did not distinguish between men and women. The preponderance of women in all part-time categories and of men in full-time work may suffice to account for their findings even if male and female "intensive" part-time workers are more similar to male and female full-time workers, respectively. Indeed, when Hedges and Gallogly looked at the distribution by sex and industry of workers working thirty to thirty-four hours, they found the distribution "resembles the group at the lower range of full time more than it does other part-time workers."[30]

Since then, Smith has noted a major increase in the percentage of

28. A change to a full-time job before January 1 will also overestimate wages if recent job changers consider "usual" hours to be those worked on the longer-held part-time job.
29. Hedges and Gallogly, "Full and Part-time."
30. Hedges and Gallogly, "Full and Part-time," p. 26.

Table 10. Women's Part-Time and Full-Time Status during Reference Week in 1987, by Usual Hours of Work in 1986

Weekly hours worked in 1986	1987 reference week status	
	Full time	Part time
Less than 35	23.1	76.9
1–24	18.5	81.5
25–29	24.6	75.4
30–34	31.0	68.9
35 or more	93.1	6.7

Source: Calculated by author from CPS data.

women working "intense part-time" schedules, implying that the classification of this group is now an even more serious issue in research on part-time work.[31] By May 1987, 34 percent of females working part time during the reference week reported thirty to thirty-four hours of work.[32] Among major occupational groups, this intensive part-time category ranged from 26 percent of service workers to 43 percent of craft workers.

It is difficult to argue that the growing numbers of women who work intense schedules are less committed to work than women who work a few more hours. These intense part-timers may be highly motivated workers willing to trade some compensation for flexibility in work schedules. The growing prevalence of their "good" part-time jobs may be obscuring the continuing cost to other women of working part time in "bad" jobs. To attribute average part-time effects to both these groups is likely to be quite misleading.

I can only call for a more careful look by researchers at the distinction between part-time and full-time workers, making sure that the criterion used to distinguish them conforms to the theoretical differences being tested. Two distinctions may be obscured by a simple separation based solely on a single-period measure of hours of work. First, part-time workers are concentrated either at thirty to thirty-four hours a week or at fewer than twenty-five. It may be that those working fewer than twenty-five hours conform to assumptions about family or job constraints better than do the intense part-timers. Second, the important—and the-

31. Shirley J. Smith, "The Growing Diversity of Work Schedules," *Monthly Labor Review,* vol. 109 (November 1986), pp. 7–13.

32. A smaller percentage of the female labor force worked part time during the 1987 reference week than in 1986 (17 percent versus 20 percent). But a larger percentage of the 1987 reference week part-timers were working thirty to thirty-four hours than the usual part-time work force (34 percent versus 30 percent). As a percentage of the total labor force, then, the percentage working relatively short and stable hours is far smaller than is implied by data on usual hours worked per week during 1986.

oretically correct—distinction might be between inflexible and flexible hours of work, with intense part-timers enjoying the best of all worlds: nearly full time but flexible hours of work.[33] The growing importance of this group would be consistent with gains in women's employment, their move into occupations previously dominated by men, and the positive part-time wage effects shown in Blank's paper.

Part-Time Work and the Earnings Distribution

What do Blank's findings have to say about the effects on the earnings distribution of women working part time? The effects must be judged against the counterfactual of full-time paid work; part-time workers will have income reduced by their shorter work week, but also perhaps by lower compensation when they do work.

Economic theory suggests that because, all else being equal, higher nonwage income dampens hours worked, women in high-income families should be more likely to work part time than women in low-income families. However, this income-equalizing effect is offset by other factors—for example, the influence of children on hours of work by single mothers, the positive influence of women's market wages on hours of work, and the correlation between the educational levels (and hence market wages) of husbands and wives. The sparse evidence available indicates that the influence of wives' earnings on the distribution of income across married couples is at most modest.[34] There is little research that looks at the income distribution effects among women in general, including those never married and formerly married.[35]

The dramatic increase in the number of families headed by women and the shift in the cause of female headship from widowhood to divorce or birth out of wedlock surely means that part-time work can no longer

33. It is interesting to note that Hedges and Gallogly find professional and technical workers—the occupational group for which a higher wage for part-timers is found in Blank's paper (table 3)—are the only occupational group for which the "intense" part-timers were reported to be more like full-timers than other part-time workers.

34. Sheldon Danziger, "Do Working Wives Increase Family Income Inequality?" *Journal of Human Resources*, vol. 15 (Summer 1980), pp. 444–51; and James A. Sweet, "The Employment of Wives and the Inequality of Family Income," *American Statistical Association: Proceedings of the Social Statistics Section* (1971), pp. 1–8.

35. Robert T. Michael, "Consequences of the Rise in Female Labor Force Participation Rates: Questions and Probes," *Journal of Labor Economics*, vol. 3, pt. 2 (January 1985), pp. S117–46.

be considered a privilege enjoyed only by relatively well-off married women. It is not just married women who work less than full time: 20 percent of unmarried women aged thirty-five to forty-four are not in the labor force, and among all unmarried women who work, 22 percent do so for fewer than thirty-five hours a week.

The key question is whether women who work part time face a dual disadvantage, caused not only by their working fewer hours but also by the different treatment they may be accorded merely because they do not work full time. If female heads are more constrained than male heads to working part time and their hourly compensation is further reduced because they work part time, income inequality will increase as the sex distribution of family heads changes. More serious is the likely persistence of this income inequality if female household heads (or women at risk of divorce) working part time are provided less financial security through fringe benefits. This is why Blank's finding that part-time workers, even after controlling for selectivity effects, are less likely to have health and pension benefits is particularly disturbing.

This is the case for other fringe benefits as well. For example, the lack of vacation and sick leave also reduces the total compensation for part-time work.[36] In the March 1987 CPS, individuals with a job but not at work during the survey week were asked if they were paid for time off. About 63 percent of those who reported usually working full time at their current job reported being paid for time off; only 26 percent of the usual part-time workers were so compensated. Thus part-time jobs appear to provide little security against interruptions to earnings caused by events such as illness and retirement and are in this sense clearly bad jobs. This difference will not be reflected in cash income distribution measures, but it does have meaning for the ability of these workers to change their position in the income distribution over time.

Summary and Policy Implications

The major challenge presented by Blank's paper is for a more complete understanding of the complexities of part-time work choices. Do part-time work opportunities severely constrain the types of jobs and wages of women who seek part-time work? Are women who work part

36. The lack of fringe benefits is partly a result of the fact that women are more likely to be paid by the hour than are men, even when they report full-time working hours. See Earl F. Mellor and Steven E. Haugen, "Hourly Paid Workers: Who They Are and What They Earn," *Monthly Labor Review,* vol. 109 (February 1986), pp. 20–26.

time less committed to work over the long run? Or are women who work part time willing to trade noncash forms of compensation for *flexible* hours? The power of selectivity effects indicates that a simple ordinary-least-squares model is not a good representation of the wage determination process. By walking through the different analytical approaches—with their sharply different conclusions about part-time work effects—Blank shows how shaky is the understanding of this process.

The major body of her paper concerns itself with cash wages. But fringe benefits now represent a major component of total compensation among all workers. Blank's conclusion that part-time workers receive substantially lower compensation in this form is disturbing since the lack of health insurance and pension coverage has implications for the health and welfare of individuals over time. The percentage of part-time workers participating in health insurance and pensions is lower than the percentage of part-time female workers working intense hours. Thus even this highly committed group apparently forgoes the security provided by fringe benefits. Current proposals for the privatization of employment-related social insurance and for increases in part-time work opportunities should consider the low coverage rates offered to part-time workers. If long-term income security is an important social goal, it is clearly not being provided to part-time workers, even those who work relatively long hours. If, in addition, part-time jobs grant smaller increases for experience (a variable that is not explicitly included in Blank's estimates), then these indeed are bad jobs in terms of the ability of their holders to provide for their long-term economic security and advancement.

Despite my reservations about the part-time versus full-time designation and the wage variable, I consider Blank's paper an important contribution to the work on part-time employment effects. Simple ordinary-least-squares models of part-time work effects aggregate selectivity and the pure effects of working part time. The folly of that aggregation is made explicit here, even though the different selectivity effects cannot be distinguished. Clearly, better data on variations in hours of work are important. Further, theoretical models need to reflect the complexities of the part-time job market. Blank's paper shows that to come to analytical conclusions or to make policy prescriptions on the basis of simple models is misguided.

Effects of Cohort Size on Postsecondary Training

Linda Datcher Loury

THE BABY boom of the 1940s and 1950s has resulted in substantial changes in the age composition of the labor force. The fraction of the labor force aged 25–34 rose from 20.7 percent in 1960 to 29.4 percent in 1986.[1] This number will decline in the future, however, as birth rates for those entering the labor market in the 1980s and 1990s were substantially lower than for the preceding generation. The number of births per 1,000 for women aged 15–44 was 19.4 in 1965, compared with 25.0 in 1955.[2] Such dramatic changes could have a significant effect on the distribution of labor earnings within and across demographic groups.

Many analysts have investigated some effects of the baby boom on relative earnings by estimating the effect of changes in the size of various age and schooling groups.[3] There is a consensus that the baby boom generation has lower earnings than older cohorts and that college-educated males have suffered the largest decline in relative earnings. However, these studies disagree on the size of the effect and how it changes as the cohort ages.

Part of the debate about the size of the effect and its variation over the life cycle hinges on the effect of cohort size on educational attainment and other training. Although large cohorts tend to have lower wages,

1. Bureau of the Census, *Statistical Abstract of the United States, 1988* (December 1987), table 609.
2. Bureau of the Census, *Historical Statistics of the United States, Colonial Times to 1970,* Bicentennial Edition (1975), pt. 1.
3. Richard B. Freeman, "The Effect of Demographic Factors on Age-Earnings Profiles," *Journal of Human Resources,* vol. 14 (Summer 1979), pp. 289–318; Finis Welch, "Effects of Cohort Size on Earnings: The Baby Boom Babies' Financial Bust," *Journal of Political Economy,* vol. 87 (October 1979), pp. S65–S97; Mark C. Berger, "Changes in Labor Force Composition and Male Earnings: A Production Approach," *Journal of Human Resources,* vol. 18 (Spring 1983), pp. 177–96; and David C. Stapleton and Douglas J. Young, "The Effects of Demographic Change on the Distribution of Wages, 1967–1990," *Journal of Human Resources,* vol. 19 (Spring 1984), pp. 175–201.

individuals born into such groups may alter their earnings prospects by adjusting their training to distinguish themselves from others in the same generation. That is, individuals may choose their training in order to move out of the most adversely affected school or training groups within their age cohort. Since past studies of the effect of the size of various cohorts usually ignore the dependence of school attainment and other training on birth cohort size, they may not adequately measure the effect on earnings of membership in a large birth cohort.

The effect of this omission is unclear. On the one hand, lower earnings due to large cohort size may persist throughout the life cycle. If individuals alter their training in order to avoid such adverse effects, then previous studies may have overestimated the negative effect of large birth cohorts on earnings. On the other hand, the effect of cohort size may be largely confined to the beginning of work life. In that case, individuals who adjust their training choices based on current relative earnings may worsen rather than improve their future relative earnings. Choices about educational attainment and postschool training have long-term effects on individual earnings and the distribution of labor earnings across demographic groups. These differences would persist after transitory relative wage losses in the early years of their careers had dissipated.

While some analysts have investigated the effect of differences in cohort size on education and other training, there is little agreement about even the direction of the effect. The purpose of this paper is to provide additional evidence about the direction and magnitude of the effect of cohort size on college attendance and other types of postsecondary training and to indicate the implications for the distribution of earnings.

Previous Literature

All previous literature about the effect of cohort size on training is based ultimately on the human capital theory of investment. The decision to invest in additional training depends on the expected rate of return and therefore on marginal costs and benefits of training. The costs of training include earnings forgone during the investment period; the benefits include the gain in earnings after training is completed. Changes in birth cohort size may affect both the marginal benefits and marginal costs of training and thus may alter the amount of training individuals wish to obtain.

While this basic theory is common to all previous work, there is no consensus about the direction of the effects of a surge in cohort size. Dooley and Gottschalk and Wachter and Kim conclude that an unusually large generation will invest more in training.[4] Wachter and Wascher suggest that the effect of a population boom depends on whether an individual is born before or after the peak of the demographic cycle.[5] Ahlburg, Crimmins, and Easterlin and Stapleton and Young provide evidence that members of the baby boom generation have acquired less training than previous generations and that members of the baby bust generation will acquire more.[6]

Differences among the studies arise largely from assumptions about the nature of the demand for labor.[7] Consider first the studies that imply that members of large cohorts will invest in additional training. Dooley and Gottschalk treat labor as a single homogeneous factor of production. They draw three conclusions about training investment that are relevant to this paper. First, they suggest that more rapid growth in the wage gain for each additional unit of training raises the amount of post-schooling investment that individuals will wish to undertake. Second, increases in the growth rate of the labor force will reduce the growth in the wage gain for each additional unit of training. This result is based on a well-known implication of the one-sector neoclassical model of economic growth. In that model, the steady-state level of real wages is negatively related to the rate of labor force growth. Finally, Dooley and Gottschalk argue that, because the baby boom generation faces declining rates of labor force growth over the remainder of the century, the wage

4. Martin D. Dooley and Peter Gottschalk, "Earnings Inequality among Males in the United States: Trends and the Effect of Labor Force Growth," *Journal of Political Economy*, vol. 92 (February 1984), pp. 59–89; and Michael L. Wachter and Choongsoo Kim, "Time Series Changes in Youth Joblessness," in Richard B. Freeman and David A. Wise, eds., *The Youth Labor Market Problem: Its Nature, Causes, and Consequences*, National Bureau of Economic Research conference report (University of Chicago Press, 1982), pp. 155–98.

5. Michael L. Wachter and William L. Wascher, "Leveling the Peaks and Troughs in the Demographic Cycle: An Application to School Enrollment Rates," *Review of Economics and Statistics*, vol. 66 (May 1984), pp. 208–15.

6. Dennis Ahlburg, Eileen M. Crimmins, and Richard A. Easterlin, "The Outlook for Higher Education: A Cohort Size Model of Enrollment of the College Age Population, 1948–2000," Working Paper 80-10 (University of Minnesota, Industrial Relations Center, 1980); and David C. Stapleton and Douglas J. Young, "Educational Attainment and Cohort Size," *Journal of Labor Economics*, vol. 6 (July 1988), pp. 330–61.

7. See Rachel Connelly, "A Framework for Analyzing the Impact of Cohort Size on Education and Labor Earnings," *Journal of Human Resources*, vol. 21 (Fall 1986), pp. 543–62.

gain from additional training will eventually grow and the boom generation will therefore invest more in postschool training. It can be inferred that workers born during the baby bust will invest less in training because the growth in the wage gain will moderate as the size of the labor force stabilizes. The Dooley and Gottschalk model focuses on the effects of labor force growth on postschool training, but the same analysis should apply to investment in formal schooling; thus the boom generation should have higher levels of education, ceteris paribus.[8]

Using data for the twelve Current Population Surveys for March 1968–79, Dooley and Gottschalk grouped out-of-school civilian males aged 16–62 into 1,960 education-experience categories. To test whether growth in the labor force raises investment in postschool training, they estimated the effect of labor force growth on the within-cohort variance in annual and weekly earnings. According to their theory, rapid labor force growth should be associated with low variance in earnings within cohorts. Declining rates of labor force growth should raise the variance in earnings during the investment period, when more able individuals undertake additional training and earn relatively less than they would in the absence of such changes in labor force growth. Declining rates of labor force growth should also raise the variance in earnings during most of the postinvestment period, when more able individuals have higher earnings than they would otherwise as they reap the benefits of their additional training.

Wachter and Kim also conclude that the baby boom generation will acquire more schooling. Although their conclusion is the same as that of Dooley and Gottschalk, their reasoning is quite different. Wachter and Kim assume that younger workers and older workers are imperfect substitutes for each other because they possess different amounts of specific training. As a result, an increase in the size of the younger generation lowers the earnings of that generation relative to older ones. This decline in earnings reduces fertility and increases labor force participation rates among the young. Institutional factors such as the minimum wage and government transfer programs raise the probability that

8. This conclusion is, however, at variance with evidence from Freeman and others that shows a decline in college attendance among male high school graduates in the boom generation. See Richard B. Freeman, "Implications of the Changing U.S. Labor Market for Higher Education," Working Paper 697 (Cambridge, Mass.: National Bureau of Economic Research, June 1981). Dooley and Gottschalk, "Earnings Inequality among Males," attribute this discrepancy to three possible causes: decline in susceptibility to the military draft, a shift from college enrollment to other types of postsecondary formal training, and higher direct costs of college education.

some of the additional workers will be unemployed as offered wages decline. According to Wachter and Kim, many of these displaced workers may now opt to receive additional schooling because the opportunity cost of training in terms of forgone earnings is low.

Wachter and Kim test this model using time-series aggregate data from 1954–78. They regress employment, unemployment, and school enrollment rates on a variety of variables, including the ratio of the population aged 16–24 to the population aged 16 and over. They find that an increase in the ratio of young people raised the fraction of individuals engaged in full-time schooling.

In contrast to the two studies just described, Wachter and Wascher argue that the effect of cohort overcrowding depends not on cohort size but on an individual's position relative to the peaks and valleys of the demographic cycle. Like Wachter and Kim, they assume that experienced and inexperienced workers are imperfect substitutes in production and that individuals select the amount of training to undertake in order to maximize lifetime income. Because larger cohorts will bid down wages, lifetime earnings are inversely related to cohort size. Wachter and Wascher also assume, however, that education is a good substitute for experience. This implies that individuals born before the peak of a large generation will acquire additional training to become more similar to workers in the smaller, more experienced cohorts born just before them. Individuals born after the peak will tend to obtain less training in order to become more similar to smaller, less experienced cohorts born after the boom.

Wachter and Wascher estimate their model using annual time-series school enrollment from 1948–80 as the dependent variable. Data were gathered for males and females aged 16–17, 18–19, and 20–24. The authors find that, for both males and females in each age group, an increase in the ratio of the size of the neighboring *older* cohort to the size of the own cohort lowers school enrollment rates. Thus workers born after the peak of a baby boom invest less in education. The authors also find that an increase in the ratio of the size of the neighboring *younger* cohort to the size of the own cohort raises school enrollment rates, implying that those individuals born before a peak fertility year make greater investments in schooling.

The third group of studies—Stapleton and Young and Ahlburg, Crimmins, and Easterlin—concludes that the boom generation will choose *less* schooling. Unlike previous analysts, these authors assume that, although all young workers and older workers are imperfect substitutes, the degree of substitutability is lower for college-educated workers than it is for workers with less schooling. This implies that growth in the size of the young cohort reduces wages of young workers relative to those of old workers and that the effect is largest for college-educated workers. As a large generation ages, the relative earnings of older workers fall compared with those of younger workers. Again the effect is largest for those with college schooling. Thus the cost of investment in schooling in terms of forgone earnings is comparatively high because earnings of less skilled workers do not fall much. Moreover, the large cohort will not obtain as much benefit from additional schooling, because the earnings of college-educated workers in a large generation are especially depressed. Both these effects reduce the level of schooling acquired by baby boomers.

In contrast to the models of Wachter and Wascher and Dooley and Gottschalk, this theory suggests that workers in a baby bust generation will acquire more schooling than workers in a boom generation. When members of a baby bust are young, the relative wages of workers with only high school diplomas are low because there are many older such workers from the previous generation and substitutability between high school–educated workers across age groups is relatively high. This implies that the opportunity cost of investing in schooling is low and the subsequent earnings of high school–educated workers relative to college-educated workers are low.

Using a model like that employed by Freeman,[9] Stapleton and Young first estimate the elasticities of substitution between workers in different age and education groups with time-series data from 1967–83. They find strong evidence for their hypothesis that substitutability between younger and older workers declines with additional years of schooling. They then simulate the effects of a baby boom using a CES production function with two careers, college and high school, based on the estimated elasticities of substitution. The results of the simulation are largely consistent with their hypotheses about the effects of the baby boom.

Ahlburg, Crimmins, and Easterlin present evidence that also supports the conclusion that the boom generation will acquire less schooling and the baby bust generation will acquire more. Using time-series data, they regress college enrollment rates (for those aged 18–19 and 20–24) on a number of variables, including cohort size as measured by the overall fertility rate during the years when the cohort was born. They find that

9. Freeman, "Effect of Demographic Factors."

cohort size has a large significant and negative effect on college enrollment rates of men and women in both age groups.

Note that the differential substitutability models of Stapleton and Young and Ahlburg, Crimmins, and Easterlin are consistent with the earlier findings of Freeman, Welch, Berger, Stapleton and Young, and Mattila.[10] The first four studies show that in the 1970s there was a decline in the relative earnings of young male workers compared with older male workers, with the largest reductions for college-educated younger workers. Combined with Mattila's evidence that male school enrollments respond strongly to changes in the expected rate of return to education, these studies imply that the baby boom generation would have less schooling and the baby bust generation would have more schooling as the decline in relative earnings moderates.

While this previous research provides some insight into the effects of cohort size on schooling and other training, there are several reasons for additional empirical work. First, the earlier research yields conflicting conclusions about the effect of cohort size on schooling. Second, evidence in two of the previous studies is indirect. Dooley and Gottschalk infer the effect of cohort size on postschool training by examining its effect on the variance in earnings, and Stapleton and Young use a simulation model to test their hypotheses. Third, previous work does not take into account demand-side factors that may change the fraction of individuals who undertake training. That is, previous studies implicitly assume that, once individuals have decided to undertake additional training, slots will be available. This may lead to erroneous conclusions. Suppose, for example, that demographic changes resulted in more individuals applying to college. The fraction actually attending college could still decline if a lower percentage of applicants was admitted due to space constraints.

A fourth reason for added research is that previous efforts do not explore the implications of their assumptions about individuals' expectations. For example, Ahlburg, Crimmins, and Easterlin and Wachter and Kim assume that individuals are myopic. This means that individuals take the current wage structure of the economy as given when making training decisions and do not anticipate changes that will occur because of the size of their own cohort. This implies that new high school grad-

10. Freeman, "Effect of Demographic Factors"; Welch, "Effects of Cohort Size"; Berger, "Changes in Labor Force Composition"; Stapleton and Young, "Effects of Demographic Change"; and J. Peter Mattila, "Determinants of Male School Enrollments: A Time-Series Analysis," *Review of Economics and Statistics*, vol. 64 (May 1982), pp. 242–51.

uates would make the decision about further training based on earnings differentials among slightly older workers already in the market; they would ignore the size of their own age group and its consequences for future wage developments. Wachter and Wascher, Stapleton and Young, and Dooley and Gottschalk, however, assume that expectations are rational. This means that workers make training decisions based on the size of their own birth cohort, the sizes of older and younger cohorts, and the effects of cohort size on the training decisions of other workers and on wages throughout the life cycle. It is not clear, however, what mechanism individuals do use to ascertain the size of their own and other cohorts or to determine the consequences of cohort size when they are making their post–high school training decisions.

A final reason for additional research is that evidence from three of the previous studies is based on aggregate time-series data. This type of analysis is inherently subject to the problem that many determinants of schooling and other training may trend together so that the estimated effects of cohort size may include the influence of other variables. Other factors that may affect schooling choice and wage developments include changes in women's labor force participation rates, the Vietnam war, variations in the real value of the minimum wage, variations in the level of government transfers, and changes in the cost of training. For example, declines in the real value of the minimum wage or increases in the levels of government transfers (such as scholarships and income maintenance programs) may reduce income forgone during the training period and result in higher investment in training. If declines in the real value of the minimum wage and increases in government transfers are positively correlated with cohort size, then the estimated effects of cohort size may be biased upward. A rise in the cost of training over time would bias the effect of cohort size downward for the same reason. Similarly, higher women's labor force participation rates may alter school enrollment and other training decisions, depending on the degree of substitutability between the new female entrants and young workers. While Berger has estimated the elasticity of complementarity between females and different groups of male workers by schooling and ages, little work has been done that disaggregates females by training and experience. Finally, the failure to capture all of the effects of the Vietnam war on school enrollment rates may have biased upward estimates of the effects of cohort overcrowding—for example, efforts to avoid the draft probably resulted in higher college attendance. Each of the studies using time-series data controls for some subset of these problems. However, none includes proxies for all of these possibilities.

Relative Earnings, Schooling, and Demographic Changes

Before statistically analyzing the relation between cohort size, earnings patterns, and educational attainment, it is useful to review briefly the recent historical experience. Trends in the relative earnings of well-educated and poorly educated and younger and older workers are shown in table 1. Not surprisingly, the mean incomes of college-educated workers are substantially higher than those of men and women with only a high school diploma. The first row in table 1 shows that the gap between college graduates and high school graduates has been widening since 1972. Rows 3 and 4 indicate that, while older men earn substantially more than younger men with the same schooling, the gap is larger for those with four years of college than for those with only a high school diploma. Furthermore, although the overall difference in earnings between older and younger males has been growing over time (row 2), young college graduates began closing the gap after 1972. The trends for women contrast sharply with those for men. In particular, younger women tended to gain income relative to older women from 1968 to 1980. However, by 1986 older women, especially those with only twelve years of schooling, began recovering some of their early losses. Since there are substantial differences in earnings by schooling within the younger age group and since both the level and the trend in relative earnings between older and younger cohorts differ by education, the data in table 1 imply that, for both men and women, changes in the training of younger workers could alter the distribution of income both within the younger age group and between age cohorts.

During this same time period, college enrollment rates changed dramatically. Enrollment rates for white male high school graduates rose from 31 percent in 1960 to a high of 43 percent in 1970. They then declined throughout the 1970s to 34 percent in 1980, recovering to 36 percent in 1986. The pattern for white females is significantly different from that for white men. Enrollment rates rose each year from 18 percent in 1960 to 34 percent in 1985.[11]

---

11. Bureau of the Census, *Statistical Abstract of the United States, 1988,* table 233.

Table 1. Ratio of Mean Incomes of Selected Groups, by Sex, Age, and Education, 1968–86

	Mean income ratios							
	Males				Females			
Age and education group	1968	1972	1980	1986	1968	1972	1980	1986
College graduates to high school graduates, both aged 25–34	1.32	1.22	1.22	1.52	1.47	1.40	1.63	1.75
Persons aged 45–54 to persons aged 25–34	1.18	1.26	1.34	1.48	1.16	1.10	1.01	1.05
Persons aged 45–54 to persons aged 25–34, both high school graduates	1.21	1.25	1.31	1.41	1.24	1.19	1.11	1.16
Persons aged 45–54 to persons aged 25–34, both college graduates	1.43	1.68	1.67	1.57	1.35	1.17	1.11	1.10

Source: Calculated from U.S. Bureau of the Census, *Current Population Reports*, series P-60. For 1968, no. 66, table 41; for 1972, no. 90, table 51; for 1980, no. 132, table 51; and for 1986, no. 159, table 35.

Table 2.   Selected Age Distribution Measures, 1945–85

Year	Birth rate per 1,000 population	Ratio of population aged 25–34 to population aged 45–54	Ratio of population aged 15–24 to population aged 45–54	Ratio of labor force aged 25–34 to labor force aged 45–54
1945	20.4	1.37	1.42	n.a.
1950	24.1	1.38	1.27	1.28
1955	25.0	1.28	1.15	1.16
1957	25.3	1.22	1.14	1.08
1960	23.7	1.11	1.19	0.97
1965	19.4	1.02	1.40	0.90
1967	17.8	1.03	1.47	0.93
1970	18.4	1.07	1.56	1.01
1975	14.6	1.30	1.68	1.34
1977	15.1	1.41	1.75	1.51
1980	15.9	1.63	1.86	1.73
1985	15.8	1.86	1.75	1.93

Sources: Column 1: U.S. Bureau of the Census, *Statistical Abstract of the United States, 1988*, table 81. Columns 2 and 3: for 1945–70, *Historical Statistics of the United States; Colonial Times to 1970*, Bicentennial edition (1975), part 1, series A29–42; for 1975, Bureau of the Census, *Statistical Abstract of the United States, 1976*, table 28; for 1977, *Statistical Abstract, 1978*, table 29; for 1980, *Statistical Abstract, 1988*, table 20; and for 1985, *Employment and Earnings*, vol. 33 (February 1986). Column 4: for 1950–80, U.S. Bureau of Labor Statistics, *Handbook of Labor Statistics*, Bulletin 2175 (December 1983), table 3; for 1985, *Employment and Earnings*, vol. 33.
n.a. Not available.

The hypothesis that the baby boom and baby bust could account for such changes in college enrollments and other training depends on the correlation of enrollment rates with the demographic data presented in table 2. Over the postwar years the number of births per 1,000 increased to a high of 25.3 in 1957 and then began falling slowly to a low of 14.6 in 1975. The number has since increased slightly as women in the baby boom generation have begun having children. Correspondingly, the fraction of the population aged 25–34 relative to the population aged 45–54 fell from 1.37 in 1945 to a low of 1.02 in 1965 and then rose to a peak of 1.86 in 1985. The fraction of the population aged 15–24 relative to the population aged 45–54 follows the same general pattern and reflects the onset of the baby bust in 1985. Such changes are also reflected in trends in the age distribution of the labor force, as shown by the last column of table 2.

A comparison of the data shown in table 2 with college enrollment rates suggests that changes in male college enrollments during the 1970s and 1980s could have resulted, in part, from changes in the size of younger cohorts. The decline in college male enrollments during the

1970s and the recovery in 1985 is almost directly inverse to the increase in the size of the cohort aged 15–24 during the 1970s and the decline in 1985. Because women's enrollment rates have monotonically increased over time, there is no such straightforward pattern between their enrollment rates and cohort size.

Data and Empirical Results

The formal statistical analysis in this paper is based on data drawn from the National Longitudinal Study of the High School Class of 1972 (NLS72). The survey was begun in 1972 to obtain information about background characteristics, high school experiences, personal characteristics, and expectations for the future from a nationally representative sample of high school seniors. The sample was reinterviewed in 1973, 1974, 1976, 1979, and 1986 to obtain more up-to-date information about training, labor market experience, and other personal characteristics. (Means and standard deviations for variables used in the analysis are included in appendix table A-1.)

I first examine the determinants of 1979 weekly earnings in order to uncover the types of training that affect earnings. I then estimate the effects of family and other background characteristics and cohort size on whether individuals undertake these types of training. I examined a variety of different cohort-size variables. The two shown in table 3 and used in the analysis are (1) the ratio of the number of individuals aged 15–17 in 1970 (17–19 in 1972) to the number of individuals aged 35–39 in the school district or SMSA (whichever is appropriate) where the individual attended high school,[12] and (2) the ratio of the number of individuals aged 25–29 in 1970 to the number of individuals aged 35–39 in the school district or SMSA where the individual attended high school. The second measure of cohort size is more appropriate if individuals' expectations are myopic, that is, if they expect the current wage structure to persist when they enter the market and if the current wage structure depends on the relative numbers of older and younger workers currently in the labor force.

Unlike earlier analysts, I investigate the impact of *cross-sectional* differences in cohort size rather than the effects of changes in cohort

12. The age group from 35 to 39 was chosen because it is relatively close to the younger group in age and therefore measures the size of an older cohort for which younger workers are more likely to be substituted. Using other older age groups produces similar results. If the individual lived in an SMSA with more than one high school district, the SMSA-wide variables are used. Otherwise, the data measure characteristics of the school district.

Table 3.   Quartile Ranges for Cohort-Size Variables

Age ratio	Lowest quartile	Second quartile	Third quartile	Highest quartile
Men				
15–17/35–39	0.32–1.02	1.02–1.17	1.17–1.36	1.36–3.44
25–29/35–39	0.40–1.10	1.10–1.20	1.20–1.35	1.35–2.95
Women				
15–17/35–39	0.54–0.93	0.93–1.04	1.04–1.16	1.16–3.35
25–29/35–39	0.45–1.01	1.01–1.17	1.17–1.32	1.32–3.17

size over time. Although all individuals in the high school class of 1972 are part of the baby boom generation, there are large variations across labor markets in the relative size of the cohort that these individuals occupy. The extent of this variation is shown in table 3. The variation in relative cohort size across localities is in fact wider than the time-series variation across recent decades. This paper investigates how such differences in relative cohort size across local labor markets affect training decisions.

The data used in this study possess a number of characteristics that make them complementary with previous work. Because the draft ended in 1972, training decisions of males in this sample would not be influenced by efforts to avoid mandatory military service. Hence my analysis is more likely to pick up a pure cohort-size effect. Moreover, because the research analysis relies on cross-sectional differences in cohort size, estimates of cohort effects would not be contaminated by the impact of other factors that change over time, such as women's labor force participation rates, the real value of the minimum wage, the cost of training, and the generosity of government transfers. In addition, the unit of observations is the individual worker and trainee. This closely conforms to the specification implied by human capital theory, since decisions about investment are made at the individual level. The data, therefore, avoid potential problems resulting from aggregation bias.

There are two principal drawbacks from using cross-sectional data to untangle cohort effects on training. First, individuals may make training decisions based on relative wage differences in the nation as a whole rather than in the local labor market. This would be especially true among college-educated workers, for whom the national labor market may be appropriate. This problem does not appear to be important, as will be discussed in more detail below. Second, in addition to indicating differences in birth rates, differences in the cohort-size variables may

Table 4. Effects of Selected Variables on Weekly Earnings, by Sex[a]

Variable	Men[b]	Women[c]
Years of college	0.03677***	0.09194**
	(0.00643)	(0.00790)
Years of vocational training if	0.03468**	0.05728***
no years of college	(0.01469)	(0.02187)
Weeks worked while in	0.00024*	0.00089***
school[d]	(0.00014)	(0.00017)
Weeks worked while not in	0.00065***	0.00191***
school[d]	(0.00012)	(0.00012)
Weeks worked at 1979 job	0.00032***	0.00050***
	(0.00005)	(0.00007)
Months of clerical training	0.00646	0.00123
	(0.00454)	(0.00336)
Months of craftsmen training	0.00679***	−0.00696
	(0.00155)	(0.01006)
Months of operative training	0.01436***	−0.00776
	(0.00363)	(0.01346)
Union member	0.14130***	0.13319***
	(0.01426)	(0.02110)
Lived in rural place or small	−0.05200***	−0.12193***
city	(0.01683)	(0.02200)
Lived in medium-sized city	...	...
	...	...
Lived in large city	0.06244***	0.11337***
	(0.01577)	(0.01880)
Married	0.09855***	−0.12801***
	(0.01366)	(0.01704)
Disabled	−0.09900***	0.05891
	(0.02629)	(0.04397)
Professional worker	0.21914***	0.27973***
	(0.02644)	(0.02913)
Clerical worker	0.12847***	0.11642***
	(0.03057)	(0.02583)
Craftsman	0.21699***	0.22685***
	(0.02745)	(0.06234)
Operative	0.24929***	0.25699***
	(0.02837)	(0.03676)
Laborer	0.08385**	0.13647*
	(0.03339)	(0.07448)
Service worker or other	...	...
Lived in New England	−0.12600***	−0.14957***
	(0.03595)	(0.04179)
Lived in mid-Atlantic state	−0.15100***	−0.08013***
	(0.02325)	(0.02968)

Table 4 *(continued)*

Variable	Men[b]	Women[c]
Lived in south Atlantic state	−0.14400***	−0.03284
	(0.02266)	(0.02816)
Lived in east south central	−0.15800***	−0.7384**
state	(0.02845)	(0.03453)
Lived in east north central	−0.00750	−0.06446**
state	(0.02192)	(0.02748)
Lived in west north central	−0.08110**	−0.13744**
state	(0.02519)	(0.03185)
Lived in west south central	−0.00120	−0.05680
state	(0.02396)	(0.03020)
Lived in mountain or Pacific	···	···
state	···	···
Intercept	5.09872***	4.39149***
	(0.00643)	(0.04031)

 * Significant at 10 percent level.
 ** Significant at 5 percent level.
 *** Significant at 1 percent level.
 a. Sample includes out-of-school workers with positive earnings. Numbers in parentheses are standard errors. Earnings are measured in natural logarithms.
 b. $N = 5,420$; $R^2 = 0.140$
 c. $N = 3,996$; $R^2 = 0.259$.
 d. In 1972–79.

reflect mobility decisions due to variations in the attractiveness of living in different areas. I attempt to control for this problem, as also will be discussed below.

 Regressions showing the types of variables that affect earnings are listed in table 4.[13] These variables fall into four groups: geographic, occupational, demographic, and training and work experience. The results for the geographic variables indicate that earnings increase by size of place and that workers in mountain and Pacific states earn as much as 15 percent more than workers in other regions. Such differences in earnings may result from differences in supply and demand conditions and differences in amenities across localities. Table 4 also shows that professional workers, craftsmen, and operatives are paid at least 20 percent more than service workers, clerical workers are paid at least 13 percent more, and even laborers are paid somewhat more than service workers. Conventional wisdom attributes this pattern of earnings to differences in the relative demand for different types of jobs and to differences in abilities and skills between individuals in different occu-

13. The sample includes out-of-school workers with positive earnings.

pations. The large, positive, and significant effect of union status shows that institutional factors may also affect variations in occupational earnings. In the case of demographic variables, the estimates in table 4 indicate that married men earn more than single men, while married women earn less. One explanation of this finding is that traditional patterns of family responsibilities reduce labor market attachment among married women and raise it for married men.

Years of college and training in vocational schools for those not attending college and various types of work experience significantly raise earnings for both men and women. Surprisingly, the effect of these variables is uniformly higher for women than men.

Other types of training measured in the NLS72 data include on-the-job training, formal registered apprenticeship programs, various manpower programs, correspondence courses, military and other training. Table 4 shows the effect of this type of training on earnings for different kinds of work.[14] The amount of training is measured in terms of the number of months of participation in particular types of training. The coefficients suggest that for men training in craftsmen and operative jobs significantly raises earnings. The importance of this type of training is clear in that the size of the effect of twelve months of this type of training (the coefficients × 12) is larger than the equivalent of either one year of college or fifty-two weeks of work experience. The effects of training in other areas (professional, managerial, service worker, and laborer) did not differ significantly from zero for men and so are not included here.

Women do not appear to benefit from any of these alternative forms of training. This finding may reflect their relative concentration in jobs different from those typically occupied by men, where the payoff to training is small. Alternately, the small effect of training may reflect the effect of intermittent labor force participation among women. Previous training in specific occupations would have a smaller payoff for women than for men since they are less likely to remain continuously employed at the same job.

The coefficients shown in table 4 indicate that college schooling, vocational training among those not attending college, and other training as craftsmen or operative workers can raise weekly earnings.[15] Tables

14. While the NLS72 data determine what type of training program respondents participated in, they do not separately identify the months of training in each type of program.

15. Vocational training had no significant effect on earnings for individuals who attended college.

5–7 present estimates of the extent to which differences in cohort size affect these types of training.

College Attendance

Table 5 shows the effects of a variety of determinants of college attendance. Members of the sample are treated as college attendees if they completed at least one year of college by 1979. Most of the results are consistent with previous work on the effects of family and other background variables on schooling. For both men and women, higher years of parental education raise the probability that offspring will attend college. The coefficient of the father's schooling is higher for sons, while the coefficient of the mother's schooling is larger for daughters. Parental family economic status as measured by family income also has a large positive and significant effect on college attendance for both men and women. This effect probably accounts for the generally small and insignificant coefficient for the father's occupation. In studies where parental income is not observed, such variables usually have a large and important influence on offsprings' schooling. Those who grew up in large cities are more likely to attend college. There are also differences in the probability of attending college across various religious groups. Jews are the most likely to attend college, followed by Protestants and then Catholics. Members of other religious groups or people who report no religious preference are the least likely to attend college. Finally, proxies for family attitudes about school achievement—the presence of dictionaries, encyclopedias, and a regular place at home to study—are all positively correlated with whether the individual attends college.

All of the local labor market characteristics other than cohort size increase the probability that individuals will attend college by 1979, and most are significant at least at the 5 percent level. One possible interpretation that would account for such results is that these variables measure the returns and opportunity costs of training. The average level of male earnings, the percentage of migrants, and the female labor force participation rate may all be associated with greater returns from investment in training. On the other hand, higher unemployment and a higher rate of poverty may signify lower opportunity costs of being out of the labor market.

The cohort-size variable shown in table 5 equals the ratio of the number of men or women aged 25–29 to those aged 35–39 in the school

Table 5. Determinants of College Attendance[a]

Variable	Men	Women
Father's years of schooling	0.1816***	0.1795***
	(0.0203)	(0.0209)
Mother's years of schooling	0.1433***	0.2185***
	(0.0224)	(0.0237)
Father professional worker	0.0972	0.0150
	(0.0708)	(0.0746)
Father clerical worker	0.0936	−0.0078
	(0.0783)	(0.0804)
Father craftsman	−0.1099*	−0.0905
	(0.0655)	(0.0691)
Father operative	−0.1534**	−0.1791**
	(0.0726)	(0.0764)
Father laborer	0.0103	−0.0496
	(0.0752)	(0.0815)
Parental family income[b]	0.0330***	0.0292***
	(0.0087)	(0.0097)
Don't know family income	0.0477	0.0571
	(0.0702)	(0.0675)
Number of siblings	0.0029	−0.0284
	(0.0210)	(0.0225)
Place to study at home[c]	0.1243***	0.0505
	(0.0351)	(0.0374)
Dictionary at home[c]	0.4486***	0.5134***
	(0.1446)	(0.1623)
Encyclopedia at home[c]	0.0638	0.1554***
	(0.0575)	(0.0589)
Protestant	0.3115***	0.2906***
	(0.0418)	(0.0468)
Catholic	0.1788***	0.1570***
	(0.0459)	(0.0524)
Jewish	0.7529***	0.9103***
	(0.1822)	(0.1809)
Grew up in rural place or small city	−0.0372	0.1065**
	(0.0515)	(0.0527)
Grew up in large city	0.1247**	0.1724***
	(0.0570)	(0.0572)
Ratio of persons aged 25–29 to persons aged 35–39, by sex	−0.2809***	0.0210
	(0.1130)	(0.1320)
Mean of male earnings	0.0005**	0.0005**
	(0.0002)	(0.0002)
Percent of population that migrated to area in last 5 years	0.0215***	0.0161***
	(0.0043)	(0.0045)

Table 5   *(continued)*

Variable	Men	Women
Female labor force	0.0139***	0.0028
participation rate	(0.0055)	(0.0061)
Unemployment rate	0.0062	0.0392**
	(0.0161)	(0.0186)
Percent of families below the	0.0185***	0.0116***
poverty line	(0.0068)	(0.0074)
Intercept	−5.1936***	−5.7165***
	(0.6557)	(0.6987)
Likelihood ratio	4,955.45	4,334.81

    * Significant at 10 percent level.
    ** Significant at 5 percent level.
    *** Significant at 1 percent level.
    a. Numbers in parentheses are standard errors. Coefficients are estimated using logit.
    b. In thousands of dollars.
    c. As of 1972.

district or SMSA.[16] As mentioned earlier, this measure of cohort size is appropriate if individuals are myopic, that is, they expect the current wage structure to persist when they enter the market and the current wage structure depends on the relative numbers of older and younger workers currently in the labor force. According to the coefficient in table 5, this measure of cohort size has a negative and significant effect on the probability of college attendance for men but is small and insignificant for women. Thus generational crowding appears to *reduce* average educational attainment among males.

In order to understand what the magnitude of the effect of cohort size for men would imply about the existing time-series variations in birth rates, consider changes in relative cohort size that occurred between 1960 and 1980. In 1960 the ratio of males aged 25–29 to those aged 35–39 was 0.869, while in 1980 the ratio was 1.398.[17] Using the means for the other variables shown in table 5, this change would imply a drop in the probability of attending college of 2.4 percentage points. In the year 2000 the ratio is projected by the Census Bureau to be 0.789.[18] This would imply that, compared with 1980, the probability of attending college would increase by about 2.7 percentage points among

16. The male figure is used in the analysis for men and the female figure is used in the analysis for women. If the total number of persons is used regardless of sex, the results for women remain the same. The coefficients for men also remain roughly the same. However, they are less precisely estimated.

17. Bureau of the Census, 1980 Census of Population: *Characteristics of the Population: General Population Characteristics,* vol. 1, chap. B, table 42.

18. Bureau of the Census, *Characteristics of the Population,* vol. 1, chap. B, table 41.

young males. In 1980 the number of 18-year-old males who attended
college was 653,889, or about 50.7 percent of high school graduates. If
the same fraction of 18-year-old males graduated from high school in
2000 as in 1980 (72 percent) and the fraction of high school graduates
who attended college increased by 2.7 percentage points to 53.4 percent,
then the number of 18-year-old males attending college in 2000 would
be about 634,000. The number is about 5 percent larger than it would
be if cohort size had no effect on educational attainment. A higher
percentage of individuals will be attending college, but the overall number of enrollees will be smaller because the number of 18-year-old males
will have fallen (1,648,000 in 2000 compared with 2,154,000 in 1980).[19]
These findings imply that, although generational crowding reduces male
college attendance, the size of the effect is moderate.

To test the sensitivity of the basic finding, alternative measures of
cohort size were included in the analysis. These included the local fertility rate in 1960,[20] the ratio of number of individuals aged 15–17 in
1970 (17–19 in 1972) to the number of individuals aged 35–39, and
various other ratios using the cohort aged 15–17 compared with older
cohorts. All of these alternatives focused on the effect of the relative
size of the cohort in the areas where the members of the NLS sample
actually lived. None of the coefficients of the alternative measures of
cohort size were significant at the 5 percent level. For example, the first
row of table 6 lists the estimated coefficient for the ratio of the number
of individuals aged 15–17 in 1970 to the number of individuals aged
35–39. The size of this coefficient compared with that for cohort size in
table 5 suggests that workers are indeed myopic, basing their training
decisions on the relative number of older and younger workers already
in the labor market and not on the size of their own age cohort group.

The results of other sensitivity analyses are also shown in table 6. In
the earlier discussion, I argued that the drawbacks of using cross-sectional data to analyze the effects of cohort size are (1) individuals may
make training decisions based on relative wages in geographic regions
larger than the local labor market and (2) in addition to indicating
differences in birth rates, differences in the cohort size variables may
reflect mobility decisions due to variations in the attractiveness of living
in different areas. The first problem does not appear to be important;
the coefficients in the second and third rows of table 6 show that the

19. Bureau of the Census, *Characteristics of the Population*, vol. 1, chap. B, table 41.
20. This is defined as the number of children aged 0–5 per 1,000 women aged 15–44.

Table 6. Effects of Alternative Cohort Size Measures[a]

Variable	Coefficient
Ratio of 15–17-year-old males to 35–39-year-old males	−0.1738 (0.1227)
Ratio of 25–29-year-old males to 35–39-year-old males for those living within 50 miles of original school district in 1979	−0.2304* (0.1371)
Ratio of 25–29-year-old males to 35–39-year-old males for those not living within 50 miles of original school district	−0.2758 (0.1924)
Ratio of 25–29-year-old males to 35–39-year-old males in logit analysis with no other SMSA variables	−0.2337 (0.1081)
Ratio of 25–29-year-old males to 35–39-year-old males, whether applied to college logit analysis	−0.3274*** (0.1231)

* Significant at 10 percent level.
*** Significant at 1 percent level.
a. Numbers in parentheses are standard errors.

estimated effects of cohort size (ratio of men aged 25–29 to men aged 35–39) are the same for those who continue to reside within fifty miles of their high school district in 1979 and for those who moved elsewhere. I attempt to handle the second problem by including variables that would control for variations in the attractiveness of different areas. The local unemployment rate and the fraction of families below the poverty line are measures of the relative demand for labor across different localities. Women's labor force participation rates capture the degree of competition from the largest potential group of other new labor market entrants. The fraction of individuals who moved to the school district or SMSA in the preceding five years directly measures the extent of recent mobility. While these variables had a significant effect on college enrollment rates across localities, any bias resulting from the second problem also appears to be small. The coefficient of cohort size when these variables are omitted from the regression equation is not significantly different from that when they are included (see row 4 of table 6).

A negative correlation between college attendance and cohort size is consistent with the hypothesis that large cohorts reduce incentives for high school graduates to attend college. An alternative explanation for such a finding would be that the fraction of enrollees declines because there are not enough spaces for the number of individuals who wish to attend college. In this case, the negative effect of cohort size would

Table 7.   Determinants of Vocational and Craftsmen Training for Men[a]

Variable	Vocational training	Craftsmen training
Father's years of schooling	0.0983***	0.0725**
	(0.0329)	(0.0363)
Mother's years of schooling	−0.0039	−0.0587
	(0.0363)	(0.0410)
Father professional worker	−0.0299	0.0938
	(0.1125)	(0.1320)
Father clerical worker	−0.1093	0.0426
	(0.1294)	(0.1498)
Father craftsman	−0.0248	0.1804
	(0.0997)	(0.1173)
Father operative	−0.0066	0.1996
	(0.1065)	(0.1239)
Father laborer	−0.0712	0.0205
	(0.1144)	(0.1348)
Parental family income[b]	0.0120	0.0137
	(0.0132)	(0.0145)
Don't know family income	−0.0226	0.0816
	(0.1026)	(0.1120)
Number of siblings	0.0126	0.0158
	(0.0312)	(0.0342)
Place to study at home[c]	0.0196	−0.0323
	(0.0535)	(0.0585)
Dictionary at home[c]	0.2510	0.3149
	(0.1827)	(0.2009)
Encyclopedia at home[c]	0.0923	0.0728
	(0.0853)	(0.0923)
Protestant	0.1425**	0.1195*
	(0.0638)	(0.0683)
Catholic	0.1212	−0.0338
	(0.0688)	(0.0765)
Jewish	−0.6053	−0.4423
	(0.5358)	(0.5339)
Grew up in rural place or small city	−0.0040	0.0745
	(0.0797)	(0.0893)
Grew up in large city	−0.0647	0.0418
	(0.0929)	(0.1031)
Ratio of men aged 25–29 to men aged 35–39	−0.3418**	−0.5075**
	(0.1713)	(0.1948)
Mean of male earnings	−0.0001	0.0003
	(0.0003)	(0.0004)
Percent of population that migrated to area in last 5 years	−0.0123*	0.0082
	(0.0073)	(0.0078)

Effects of Cohort Size   187

Table 7   *(continued)*

Variable	Vocational training	Craftsmen training
Female labor force participation rate	0.0026 (0.0080)	0.0089 (0.0087)
Unemployment rate	−0.0317 (0.0257)	0.0139 (0.0258)
Percent of families below the poverty line	−0.0153 (0.0107)	0.0095 (0.0114)
Intercept	−2.3550** (1.1080)	−2.6993** (1.200)
Likelihood ratio	2,172.86	1,899.43

* Significant at 10 percent level.
** Significant at 5 percent level.
*** Significant at 1 percent level.
a. Numbers in parentheses are standard errors. N = 1,913. Coefficients are estimated using logit.
b. In thousands of dollars.
c. As of 1972.

occur because of constraints on the number of training slots rather than because of changes in choices made by potential trainees.

The results obtained for this analysis suggest that this alternative explanation does not account for the negative correlation between college attendance and cohort size for two reasons. First, as mentioned above, the relevant cohort size variable is the number of individuals aged 25–29 relative to those aged 35–39 and not the actual size of the cohort that would be applying to college at the same time as the NLS sample members. Second, the estimated effects of cohort size on whether individuals apply to college are about the same as the effect for college attendance (see row 5 of table 6).

Training Outside of College

College schooling is not the only type of training that raises subsequent earnings (see table 4). Vocational training among high school graduates and other training in craftsmen and operative jobs perform the same role. Table 7 shows the effect of cohort size on vocational training and craftsmen training that lasted at least six months among men who did not attend college. This training could be received on the job or through formal registered apprenticeship and manpower programs, correspondence courses, and the military. Women are not shown here because there was no effect of cohort size on the vocational training of women who did not attend college.

The coefficients in table 7 show that, aside from the father's education, family and other background characteristics did little to alter individual choices of vocational training or training in craftsmen jobs. However, membership in large birth cohorts lowered the probability of training in postsecondary vocational schools and of acquiring at least six months of training as a craftsman. The size of the effect on vocational training is about the same as the effect for college attendance (see table 5), but the impact on craftsmen training is almost twice as large. If the craftsmen training variable is expanded to include all workers with such training and not just those with at least six months, the size of the estimated effect falls from -0.507 to -0.299 and becomes significant only at the 10 percent level. This suggests that cohort size mainly affects those who train for a relatively long period of time. Cohort size had no effect on the probability of training as an operative.

Effect on Earnings

In general, the findings of this paper imply that, while cohort size has no effect on the training choices of women, it lowers the probability that white men will select training options that require a substantial investment period. This evidence is consistent with Stapleton and Young's hypothesis of less substitutability among old and young male workers with greater levels of postsecondary school training. The Stapleton and Young hypothesis would imply that the lower substitutability results in greater declines in relative wages among men with high levels of post–high school training. In order to escape such negative consequences of membership in a large age cohort, some men alter their training choices to avoid being a member of these groups (that is, those who attend college or obtain vocational or craftsmen training), since they bear the largest part of the burden of cohort size.

The results for women are also consistent with the Stapleton and Young model.[21] According to Freeman and Stapleton and Young, the earnings of young women in the baby boom generation did not fall consistently relative to the earnings of older women, even among col-

21. This is not, however, consistent with Ahlburg, Crimmins, and Easterlin, "Outlook for Higher Education," who find that larger birth cohorts reduce college enrollment rates among both men and women.

lege-educated workers.[22] This implies that the reduced substitutability between younger and older college-educated men that generated the decline in relative male wages does not apply for women. Thus, in deciding on training choices, women have no incentive to avoid college schooling or other possibilities in the face of larger birth cohorts.

My results are consistent with the hypothesis that, in order to avoid losses in relative earnings, young men adjust the amount of training they undertake based on the relative size of the cohort that has most recently entered the labor market. An analysis of the effects of cohort size on young male earnings provides an additional test of this hypothesis. Table 4 shows the results of regressing earnings on training, occupation, and a variety of other characteristics. If cohort size were added to the regression, its coefficient would show the effect of large labor market cohorts on the male earnings if no adjustment in training or occupation were made. As mentioned earlier, previous work would predict a negative relationship. However, a more accurate measure of the overall effect of cohort size on earnings should include any indirect effects through changes in the amount of training. The size of the coefficient of cohort size in a reduced-form regression that excludes training and all other endogenous variables provides just such a measure. If the coefficient of the cohort variable moves closer to zero in this regression, my findings would imply that adjustments in the amount of training enable men to avoid at least some of the negative effects of large cohorts on earnings.

If cohort size is added to the male earnings regression in table 4, its coefficient is -0.034 and it is significant at the 10 percent level. This implies that, holding training constant, cohort size as measured in this paper is negatively correlated with 1979 earnings. Table 8 lists the results of reduced-form earnings regressions for 1979 and 1986. It shows, that, as is generally the case for such analyses, family income is the only background variable that significantly affects male earnings. In addition, it shows that the effect of cohort size on weekly male wages in 1979 and 1986 is negative but insignificant. These results indicate that, in the absence of adjustments in training, large labor market cohorts are negatively correlated with earnings. However, young men successfully escape these negative consequences by adjusting their training choices to

22. Freeman, "Effect of Demographic Factors"; and Stapleton and Young, "Effects of Demographic Change."

Table 8. Determinants of Weekly Earnings for Men, 1979 and 1986[a]

Variable	1979	1986
Father's years of schooling	− 0.00740	0.01328
	(0.00503)	(0.00986)
Mother's years of schooling	− 0.00536	− 0.00807
	(0.00541)	(0.01059)
Father professional worker	0.06914*	0.07119
	(0.03774)	(0.07394)
Father clerical worker	0.09403**	0.02367
	(0.04160)	(0.08165)
Father craftsman	0.04499	0.05188
	(0.03599)	(0.07052)
Father operative	0.04429	0.07637
	(0.03957)	(0.07753)
Father laborer	0.03933	0.05858
	(0.04114)	(0.08061)
Parental family income[b]	0.01335***	0.01426***
	(0.00225)	(0.00442)
Don't know family income	0.12811***	0.23378***
	(0.03683)	(0.07216)
Number of siblings	0.00895	0.00193
	(0.00547)	(0.01073)
Place to study at home[c]	0.01022	0.02122
	(0.01840)	(0.03609)
Dictionary at home[c]	0.03315	− 0.07510
	(0.06470)	(0.12676)
Encyclopedia at home[c]	0.00448	0.00812
	(0.03100)	(0.06076)
Protestant	0.01456	0.03636
	(0.02197)	(0.04305)
Catholic	− 0.01449	0.07878
	(0.02409)	(0.04710)
Jewish	0.07823	0.18830
	(0.06525)	(0.12786)
Grew up in rural place or small city	0.00947	− 0.04874
	(0.02704)	(0.05298)
Grew up in large city	0.05281*	− 0.00815
	(0.02902)	(0.05686)
Ratio of men aged 25–29 to men aged 35–39	− 0.00663	− 0.01266
	(0.02826)	(0.05536)
Mean of male earnings	0.0000293	0.000124
	(0.0000466)	(0.000091)
Percent of population that migrated to area in last 5 years	0.00070	− 0.00061
	(0.00105)	(0.00207)

Table 8   *(continued)*

Variable	1979	1986
Female labor force	−0.00398	0.00249
participation rate	(0.00143)	(0.00280)
Unemployment rate	0.01366***	−0.00378
	(0.00417)	(0.00817)
Percent of families below the	−0.00183	0.00487
poverty line	(0.00178)	(0.00348)
Intercept	5.59268***	5.64527***
	(0.15963)	(0.31276)
R^2	0.0364	0.0190

   * Significant at 10 percent level.
   ** Significant at 5 percent level.
   *** Significant at 1 percent level.
   a. Reduced-form regressions. Numbers in parentheses are standard errors. N = 2,451 (only a portion of the original sample was interviewed in 1986). Earnings are measured in natural logarithms.
   b. In thousands of dollars.
   c. As of 1972.

move out of the most adversely affected groups. Thus, while cohort size alters choices about training, the ultimate consequences for the distribution of male earnings is small both seven and fourteen years past high school.[23]

Summary

Past work suggests that as a cohort's size increases, its relative earnings fall. Since the largest adverse effects of cohort size have been estimated for college-educated men, this finding implies that the effect of cohort size on the distribution of earnings depends, in part, on how cohort size affects education and training choices. My results show that men are less likely to attend college or undertake substantial vocational or craftsmen training if a large cohort has just entered the labor market. The sizes of the estimated effects indicate that the recent baby boom lowered the probability of college attendance between 1960 and 1980 by about two and a half percentage points. They also imply that the forthcoming baby bust will increase college attendance by 5 percent over the level that would be expected in the absence of an effect of cohort size on schooling.

This finding suggests that workers attempt to limit relative earnings

23. A similar conclusion was reached by Stapleton and Young, "Effects of Demographic Change."

losses associated with large cohorts by adjusting their training choices to avoid resembling workers in the most adversely affected groups. The earnings results in this paper provide additional evidence for this view. In the absence of training adjustments, cohort size lowers earnings. In contrast, cohort size has little effect on earnings once the effect of training adjustments is included.

Table A-1. Means and Standard Deviations in National Longitudinal Survey of High School Class of 1972, by Sex

	Men		Women	
Variable	Mean	Standard deviation	Mean	Standard deviation
Dependent variable				
Attended college by 1979	0.536	0.498	0.535	0.499
Log weekly earnings 1979	5.600	0.452	5.085	0.567
Local labor market variable				
Ratio of persons aged 15–17 to persons aged 35–39, by sex	1.231	0.331	1.082	0.269
Ratio of persons aged 25–29 to persons aged 35–39, by sex	1.208	0.322	1.183	0.289
Mean of male annual earnings[a]	1.333	0.272	1.333	0.272
Percent of population that migrated to area in last 5 years	14.528	9.134	14.627	9.129
Female labor force participation rate	46.271	7.669	46.945	7.281
Unemployment rate	4.025	2.177	3.961	2.059
Fraction of families below the poverty line	13.893	8.069	13.734	7.886
Background variable				
Father's years of schooling	12.340	2.365	12.446	2.447
Mother's years of schooling	12.163	1.962	12.116	2.014
Father professional worker	0.249	0.432	0.256	0.436
Father clerical worker	0.107	0.309	0.124	0.329
Father craftsman	0.290	0.453	0.271	0.444
Father operative	0.146	0.354	0.149	0.357
Father laborer	0.115	0.320	0.102	0.303
Parental family annual income[a]	9.804	5.956	8.320	6.333
Don't know family income	0.130	0.337	0.230	0.421
Number of siblings	1.496	1.666	1.549	1.667
Place to study at home[b]	0.568	0.495	0.561	0.496
Dictionary at home[b]	0.978	0.146	0.980	0.136
Encyclopedia at home[b]	0.885	0.318	0.875	0.329
Protestant	0.409	0.491	0.473	0.499
Catholic	0.271	0.444	0.264	0.440

Table A-1 *(continued)*

Variable	Men Mean	Men Standard deviation	Women Mean	Women Standard deviation
Jewish	0.019	0.139	0.024	0.153
Grew up in rural place or small city	0.582	0.493	0.546	0.497
Grew up in large city	0.251	0.433	0.261	0.439
Determinants of weekly earnings				
Years of college	1.438	1.709	1.457	1.705
Years of vocational training if no years of college	0.161	0.474	0.122	0.387
Weeks worked while in school^c	61.013	65.158	54.262	61.790
Weeks worked while not in school^c	225.730	92.904	197.175	93.387
Weeks worked at 1979 job	138.823	124.940	115.474	113.411
Months of clerical training	0.340	1.507	0.887	2.473
Months of craftsman training	1.813	4.627	0.128	0.903
Months of operative training	0.396	1.785	0.074	0.629
Union member	0.315	0.464	0.204	0.403
Lived in rural place or small city	0.238	0.426	0.191	0.393
Lived in large city	0.298	0.457	0.326	0.468
Married	0.558	0.496	0.628	0.483
Disabled	0.066	0.249	0.035	0.185
Professional worker	0.307	0.461	0.308	0.461
Clerical worker	0.118	0.323	0.445	0.497
Craftsman	0.231	0.421	0.021	0.145
Operative	0.182	0.385	0.082	0.274
Laborer	0.076	0.265	0.012	0.112
Lived in New England	0.042	0.201	0.052	0.222
Lived in mid-Atlantic state	0.141	0.348	0.132	0.338
Lived in south Atlantic state	0.155	0.362	0.160	0.367
Lived in east south central state	0.074	0.261	0.083	0.276
Lived in east north central state	0.172	0.377	0.176	0.381
Lived in west north central state	0.097	0.297	0.094	0.293
Lived in west south central state	0.119	0.324	0.119	0.324

Source: The data and tabulation used in this report were made available in part by the Inter-University Consortium for Political and Social Research. The data were originally collected for the National Center for Education Statistics. Neither the original sources of the data nor the consortium bear any responsibility for the analyses or interpretations presented here.

a. In thousands of dollars.
b. As of 1972.
c. In 1972–79.

Comment by Peter Gottschalk

In her paper Linda Datcher Loury explores some important links between cohort size and inequality, a subject of considerable interest to the policy community. These links have gained attention for two very different reasons. First, they suggest behavioral feedback from demographic to economic phenomena. Economists are quick to trace out the effect of exogenous shifts in the labor supply caused by a baby boom: economic theory predicts that the baby boom will depress the wages of those in the large cohort, and that the decline in wages may not be uniform across the wage distribution. Furthermore, theory predicts that there are ways to avoid the impact of cohort size. By increasing training, individual members of a large cohort can differentiate themselves from other baby boomers. The second reason cohort-size links have gained so much attention is that baby booms come and go. Hence if the current increase in inequality reflects the passage of the baby boom, that too will end.

The ephemeral effect of the baby boom, however, also creates a problem in explaining the current increase in inequality of wages. Any explanation based on cohort size will have to contend with the following stylized facts. First, inequality of earnings increased slowly over a long period (see the papers by Burtless and Moffitt in this volume), whereas fertility rates fluctuated considerably over the same period. Second, inequality increased much more rapidly during the 1980s, a period well past the peak of the baby boom, than it had earlier. That the wages of new labor market entrants fell (relative to those of more experienced workers) at the same time as their supply declined suggests that the increase in the skill premiums reflected shifts in demand as well as supply. Any cohort-size story that tries to explain changes in between-group inequality by focusing only on supply will fit the patterns of the 1970s but will not track the recent changes well.[24] All the ideas developed

24. Kevin Murphy and Finis Welch, "Wage Differentials in the 1980s: The Role of International Trade," paper presented at the Mont Pelerin Society General Meeting, September 9, 1988.

earlier to explain increases in inequality during the baby boom will have to be modified in important ways to be consistent with the fact that inequality increased even faster in the baby bust era.

As I argue later, if demographics are to be an important part of the explanation for the changes during the 1980s as well as the 1970s, they will have to focus more on who had children than on the size of the cohorts. The inverted U shape of the fertility profile just does not match the monotonic increase in inequality of wages.

Loury offers a thought-provoking paper on the relation between cohort size and training. In reviewing the literature, she shows that different authors have made different predictions about the amount of training members of the cohort will undertake. She then presents new empirical evidence which suggests that large cohorts invest less than small cohorts. The change in the distribution of training in turn affects the distribution of wages.

For those not familiar with the inequality literature, it may be useful to put this paper into a broader context. A standard way of showing how any factor (including cohort size) influences inequality is to decompose the variance of wages (or log wages) into inequality between groups and within groups using a standard variance decomposition:

$$\sigma^2 = \sum \pi_i \sigma_i^2 + \sum \pi_i (\mu_i - \mu)^2,$$

where μ and σ^2 are the overall mean and variance of wages, μ_i and σ_i^2 are the mean and variance of wages of group i, and π_i is the proportion of people in group i. This identity says that the total variance, σ^2, is equal to a weighted average of within-group variance plus the variance of wages across groups. Changes in cohort size that affect training will therefore have distributional consequences if they change the weights (the π_i's), change the average wages of different education categories (the μ_i's), or change the distribution of wages within educational classes (the σ_i^2's). These are commonly referred to as the effects of changes in weights, changes in between-group inequality, and changes in within-group inequality.

By focusing exclusively on how changes in cohort size affect training, Loury largely ignores the direct impact of cohort size or composition on within- and between-group inequality that would arise even if there were no effect on training. It is therefore important for the reader to recognize that even if cohort size had no effect on training, it would not mean that cohort size doesn't matter. Because she limits her study to the impact of cohort size on training, the author is able to explore one important link between demographics and inequality, but one that may be of secondary importance compared with the direct effect of cohort size on inequality.

Loury further narrows her focus by examining only the impact of cohort size on the weights (the π_i's) and not the effects of training on between- or within-group inequality. Since the educational premium is assumed to be independent of cohort size, cohort size cannot have an effect on inequality between groups.[25] The implicit assumption in the regressions is that each year of college adds an equal percentage (3.7 percent in table 4) to a worker's wages regardless of the cohort's size. Therefore, inequality between education groups cannot be affected by cohort size. Likewise, since cohort size affects neither the returns to other attributes nor the variance of the stochastic component, all variation in wages within groups is assumed to be independent of cohort size.

These restrictions are unfortunate, since most researchers have found that increases in within-group inequality account for the largest proportion of the total change in inequality (for example, see Moffitt's paper in this volume and the article by Grubb and Wilson).[26] Furthermore, the return to education and experience (that is, between-group inequality) changed dramatically during the 1970s and 1980s. Thus, though the paper focuses on an interesting question (the impact of cohort size on the proportion of people in each educational category), much of the action has occurred elsewhere.

I now turn from this general description of where the paper fits into the literature to the specifics of the empirical work. The structure of the paper's empirical section is to contrast time-series evidence with new cross-sectional results. The tabular evidence noted early in the paper focuses on the time-series correlation between cohort size and college enrollment. The author mentions that college enrollment rose during the 1980s, a period in which cohort size declined. The cross-sectional evidence developed later in the paper exhibits a similar negative correlation between cohort size and educational attainment but shows no significant correlation between cohort size and wages in a reduced-form

25. When cohort size is entered in the wage regression, it shifts the wage function equally for all educational levels.

26. W. Norton Grubb and Robert H. Wilson, "Sources of Increasing Inequality in Wages and Salaries, 1960–80," *Monthly Labor Review*, vol. 112 (April 1989), pp. 3–13.

wage equation for men.[27] Thus the cross-sectional evidence is that men "are less likely to attend college or undertake . . . training if a large cohort has just entered the labor market"; however, "cohort size has little effect on earnings once the effect of training adjustments is included."

What should one make of these results? Should one disregard results of studies based on time-series variation in cohort size that contradict the findings of this paper? Loury rightly points out that studies which use variation in cohort size across time potentially suffer from collinearity; that is, cohort size changes over time but so do many other factors, such as cyclical conditions, which also affect training and the distribution of earnings. She suggests using cross-sectional variations in cohort size to avoid the collinearity problem. Although this novel approach has obvious appeal, it introduces a new set of issues.

The key explanatory variable in the cross-sectional work is obviously cohort size. It is measured as the ratio of the number of people aged 15 to 17 (or 25 to 29) to the number of people aged 35 to 39 in the school district where the person attended high school. Hence all the cross-sectional variations in this variable comes from variations in the demographics between school districts. This stands in sharp contrast to previous studies that got variation by comparing people born at different times. The question is whether this variable has sufficient variation to have any explanatory power, and if so, how to interpret the results.

I must admit that I was surprised at the amount of cross-sectional variation in this ratio. The standard deviation for males from table A-1 is roughly one-fourth as large as the mean. Therefore, there is something to move the dependent variable around.

The question is what to make of this variable. It is here that one must clearly distinguish between variations in demographic variables across space and across time. I see two problems with using the measure proposed in this paper. First, I suspect that the demographic makeup of a school district reflects much more than cross-sectional differences in fertility. Going out two standard deviations, one is comparing school districts with ratios of teens to middle-aged persons (15–17 years old as a percentage of 35–39 year olds) of 0.57 to 1.89. It is hard to believe

---

27. While cohort size has a significant negative effect on training (table 5) and training has a significant positive effect on earnings (table 4), the results in table 8 of a "reduced-form equation," which regresses weekly male wages against the exogenous variables in table 5 (but not table 4), shows no significant effect. The rational for this equation and the reconciliation between these results are not developed.

that parents living in similar communities making fertility decisions during identical periods would have had such different fertility patterns.

One suspects that this variable captures other unobservable aspects of the community in which the person went to high school. For example, a growing community composed largely of starter homes would have had a disproportionately high ratio. If that is true, then the cohort-size variable is capturing background characteristics of the community in which the respondent grew up as well as labor supply effects. Although the paper controls for some neighborhood characteristics, I remain skeptical that the cohort-size variable captures pure labor supply effects. The control variables give paradoxical results: the unemployment rate is not significant in the male regression, female labor force participation is significant in the male equation but not in the female equation, and both males and females who went to high school in school districts with high poverty rates are *more* likely to attend college. Furthermore, the positive effect on college attendance of growing up in a poor neighborhood is statistically significant. I am left with the nagging suspicion that community characteristics have not been sufficiently well controlled for to warrant interpreting the key independent variable as a cohort-size variable that captures the effects of differences in labor supply.

The second problem with a cross-sectional approach is that it introduces several new ways of avoiding the effects of demographics. Suppose that, for whatever reason, some school district had an unusually large crop of 15–17-year-olds, which would depress their wages. Admittedly these young people could try to avoid the impact of their cohort size by changing the level or the timing of their educational decisions, as suggested in this paper. But a much less expensive investment would be to move out of the school district to a district with a shortage of workers in their age range. The basic problem is that while it is expensive to escape the effect of changes in cohort size that occur over time, it is easy to escape the effect of differences across space, especially when the geographic areas being studied are so small. The fact that the estimated impact of cohort size is the same for those within fifty miles of their original school district and those living farther away is consistent with the view that the cohort-size variable is not capturing labor supply effects. If it were, those who moved away would have escaped the effects of being in a large cohort. The empirical results, however, show that the effect is similar for those who moved and those who didn't. This suggests that the cohort-size measure captures attributes of the community in which the respondent went to high school whose effects cannot be avoided by simply moving away.[28]

Although I am not convinced that the cost of using cross-sectional variations in cohort size outweighs the benefits, the paper does raise important issues about the diversity of experiences of children born during the baby boom. The changes over time in fertility rates have been so pronounced that we tend to ignore differences between groups which may themselves have important consequences for inequality. For example, while the fertility rates of persons in all age and education groups rose rapidly in the early 1950s and fell dramatically during the 1960s, the fertility rates of college-educated women fell considerably earlier and faster than those of the non-college-educated.[29] This cross-sectional variation of mothers of the same age has important implications for inequality in the future. Since the probability of going to college is considerably higher for children of college-educated parents, the decline in the relative fertility rates of college-educated parents will tend to lower the supply of college-educated children in the next generation. That may well affect the skill premium to attending college, thus affecting not only the weights but also between-group inequality.

We are currently experiencing two offsetting forces that may have profound distributional consequences on the increase in future college enrollment and on earnings inequality. The rapid increase in college enrollments in the 1950s has kept the number of college-educated parents growing sufficiently fast to offset the decline in their relative fertility rates. This increase in the supply of skilled workers has moderated the wage increases of college-educated children. As the growth in college-educated parents slows, the impact of the decline in their relative fertility rates will start being felt in labor markets. As skilled labor markets become relatively tight, one can expect to see supply side–driven increases in the skill premium.

I believe that what is potentially exciting about cross-sectional variation in fertility patterns is not what they tell us about reactions to increases in the absolute size of a cohort but what they tell us about differential patterns within a cohort. If the latter turns out to be important, then demographic factors may turn out to be important during baby busts as well as baby booms.

28. The estimated equation implicitly assumes that the unobservables affecting the decision to attend college are independent of the decision to move. The interpretation of the results would be even more problematic if this assumption was not valid.

29. Rachel Connelly and Peter Gottschalk, "The Effect of Cohort Composition on Human Capital Accumulation across Generations," Department of Economics, Bowdoin College and Boston College, April 1989.

The Distribution of Earnings and the Welfare State

Robert A. Moffitt

SEVERAL studies in recent years have concluded that the distribution of male earnings in the United States has been growing more unequal since the late 1960s.[1] Although several explanations have been advanced to explain this growing inequality, none has been capable of explaining more than a small portion of the trend. One explanation that has not been explored attributes the increasing inequality to the U.S. welfare system, particularly the part of it that provides transfers to the low-income population. By providing disincentives to work and to invest in human capital, welfare programs may have lowered the labor market attachment and earnings levels of workers at the bottom of the earnings distribution.

The notion that transfers may explain part of the rise in inequality has a certain prima facie validity in light of the explosion of the U.S. welfare system that occurred in the late 1960s and early 1970s. Caseloads in aid to families with dependent children (AFDC) tripled, and two major new in-kind transfer programs, food stamps and medicaid, were introduced. At least one well-known social critic, Charles Murray, has argued that these programs had disincentive effects on the incomes of the poor severe enough to have generated the increase in the poverty rate observed in the 1980s.[2] Although Murray does not directly consider the earnings distribution, it follows from his argument that the size of the low-earnings population must have increased as well.

I examine the role of low-income transfers in explaining growing

1. Peter Henle and Paul Ryscavage, "The Distribution of Earned Income among Men and Women, 1958–77," *Monthly Labor Review,* vol. 103 (April 1980), pp. 3–10; Martin D. Dooley and Peter Gottschalk, "Earnings Inequality among Males in the United States: Trends and the Effect of Labor Force Growth," *Journal of Political Economy,* vol. 92 (February 1984), pp. 59–89; and McKinley L. Blackburn and David E. Bloom, "Earnings and Income Inequality in the United States," *Population and Development Review,* vol. 13 (December 1987), pp. 575–609.

2. Charles Murray, *Losing Ground* (Basic Books, 1984).

inequality by reviewing several pieces of evidence. According to the evidence assembled here, there is very little, if any, indication that transfers have played a significant role in causing a rise in inequality. Many of the reasons for rejecting the transfers hypothesis have a larger bearing on the inequality issue: inequality trends accelerated in the late 1970s and early 1980s, just as transfer growth was declining; growing inequality in annual earnings is a result of increasing inequality in hourly wage rates, not annual hours of work; and, perhaps most important, the growth in wage inequality has arisen from an increase in high earners rather than in low earners. In addition, inequality growth has been weaker among black men than among whites, even though the black population has higher participation rates in transfer programs.

I also consider some alternative explanations for the increase in earnings inequality: whether it could be a result of changes in cohort size and the baby boom; whether sectoral shifts from manufacturing to services could be responsible; and whether the Current Population Survey imputation procedure has contributed to a measurement problem. The evidence rejects all of these explanations. Consequently, there appears at present to be no "smoking gun" to explain the increase in earnings inequality in the United States.

Trends in the Distribution of Earnings

The results reviewed here, as well as the evidence discussed throughout the paper, are based upon data from the March Current Population Survey (CPS) files from each year during 1968–88. The CPS in March of each year provides data on work experience and annual wage and salary income (henceforth "earnings") in the year before the survey. Hence the years covered by the surveys are 1967–87. I have used these data in order to maintain comparability with past studies, where the CPS has been the primary source of evidence. Only males are analyzed here because an increasing inequality of earnings for females has not been found in prior work. The bulk of the analysis is also restricted to white males to eliminate the effects of race, although a brief examination of black males is provided. A subsample of the CPS in each year is drawn amounting to approximately 1,600 white men in each, or about 33,000 individuals in all twenty-one years available. Earnings are deflated by the personal consumption deflator (1982 dollars).[3]

3. The personal consumption deflator tracks the CPI-XI (which correctly treats housing expenditure) closely. The analysis sample excludes observations if hours of work in the

Table 1. Standard Errors of the Distribution of the Logarithm of Earnings for White and Black Males, 1967–87

	Whites		Blacks	
Year	Unadjusted	Adjusted[a]	Unadjusted	Adjusted[a]
1967	1.138	0.778	1.227	0.926
1968	1.096	0.759	1.209	0.920
1969	1.202	0.857	1.207	0.941
1970	1.149	0.843	1.176	0.914
1971	1.124	0.845	1.147	0.879
1972	1.097	0.767	1.203	0.939
1973	1.116	0.811	1.215	0.974
1974	1.128	0.815	1.243	1.004
1975	1.172	0.874	1.197	0.947
1976	1.172	0.905	1.167	0.868
1977	1.178	0.855	1.198	0.889
1978	1.065	0.764	1.284	0.977
1979	1.124	0.859	1.224	1.001
1980	1.196	0.933	1.263	1.036
1981	1.234	0.968	1.188	0.985
1982	1.341	1.069	1.296	1.098
1983	1.311	1.012	1.279	1.048
1984	1.248	0.975	1.272	1.021
1985	1.370	1.089	1.280	1.028
1986	1.221	0.998	1.199	0.973
1987	1.267	1.031	1.202	0.946

a. Standard error of a regression of the earnings logarithm on years of education, years of experience, experience squared, and marital status. Experience is defined as age minus education minus six, and marital status is a dummy variable equal to one if the person is married with a spouse present.

Table 1 shows the standard error of the distribution of the logarithm of earnings each year and the standard error after adjustment for several socioeconomic characteristics of white and black men (the results for blacks will be discussed below). Both series show a considerable degree of fluctuation over time. Much of the fluctuation is clearly related to the business cycle, but there is also an unmistakable upward trend. Table 2 shows the results of regressing these time series of standard errors on trend and unemployment variables. Columns 1 and 4 show positive trend coefficients on the margin of conventional significance for the unadjusted series, but significant by conventional levels in the adjusted series. The standard error of earnings is also strongly countercyclical.

The other columns in table 2 show the results of testing for differences

week of the survey or if usual hours per week in the past year (the latter only available after 1975) are greater than seventy, or if age is less than sixteen or greater than sixty-one. Also, observations with earnings of zero are excluded unless explicitly noted otherwise.

Table 2. Time-Series Regressions for the Standard Errors of the Logarithm of the Distribution of Earnings for White Males[a]

	Unadjusted			Adjusted[b]		
Variable	All years (1)	1967–75 and 1976–87 (2)	1967–80 and 1981–87 (3)	All years (4)	1967–75 and 1976–87 (5)	1967–80 and 1981–87 (6)
YEAR[c]						
Overall	0.0047 (0.0032)	...	...	0.0095* (0.0030)	...	...
1967–75	...	−0.0115* (0.0052)	...	...	−0.0053 (0.0050)	...
1976–87[d]	...	0.0127* (0.0034)	...	...	0.0168* (0.0032)	...
1967–80	...	...	−0.0031 (0.0045)	...	...	0.0019 (0.0042)
1981–87[e]	...	...	0.0204* (0.0075)	...	...	0.0247* (0.0070)
UNEMP[f]	0.0020* (0.0102)	0.0300* (0.0085)	0.0304* (0.0104)	0.0188* (0.0096)	0.0280* (0.0082)	0.0290* (0.0097)
Intercept	0.7249	1.8449	1.2523	0.0663	1.0907	0.5786
R^2 (adjusted)	0.54	0.72	0.62	0.74	0.83	0.79

* Significant at 10 percent level.
a. Numbers in parentheses are standard errors
b. See definition in table 1.
c. $YEAR = 67, 68$, etc.
d. The variables in 1976 structural test equation are $[76D_1 + YEAR (1 - D_1)]$ and $[YEAR - 76]D_1$, where $D_1 = 1$ if $YEAR > 76$ and 0 otherwise.
e. The variables in 1981 structural test equation are $[81D_2 + YEAR (1 - D_2)]$ and $[YEAR - 81]D_2$, where $D_2 = 1$ if $YEAR = 81$ and 0 otherwise.
f. $UNEMP$ = adult male unemployment rate.

in the trend effects over time. Columns 2 and 5 show the trend coefficients separately for 1967–75 and 1976–87, while columns 3 and 6 show the corresponding coefficients for 1967–80 and 1981–87. On average, the trends up to 1976 were negative although not always significant, and up to 1980 they were essentially zero or insignificant. The trends after 1976 and after 1980 are strongly positive, the latter also stronger than the former. The evidence thus indicates a very weak trend, if any, in the late 1960s and early 1970s but a positive and accelerating trend in inequality starting at some point in the late 1970s or early 1980s. These patterns of increase in the standard error of the earnings distribution will be the object of interest below.[4]

4. These results hold up under a number of sensitivity tests. First, they are not affected by top coding of earnings in the CPS. Estimates of adjusted and unadjusted standard

A possible explanation for the increasing adjusted standard error is that the variance of earnings is heteroskedastic and is a function of observed individual characteristics such as education, experience, and marital status. For example, the variance of earnings may be systematically lower for college-educated workers than for workers who have not completed high school. If the variance is heteroskedastic and if the composition of the population across observed categories changes over time, the variance will also change.

Appendix table A-1 sheds light on this possibility by showing the results of a regression of the absolute value of the residuals from the year-by-year earnings regressions on selected characteristics.[5] Heteroskedasticity is clearly present, as shown by the significant coefficients on education, experience, and marital status. The inverse experience relation has been noted previously in the human capital literature and has been given a theoretical justification.[6] Interestingly, all coefficient signs are opposite to those in the earnings equation itself, suggesting that the variance of earnings is inversely proportional to its level.[7] In any case, the key result is that the year dummies are still jointly signif-

---

errors obtained from a sample excluding the top 5 percent of the distribution in each year—which eliminates all top-coded observations—generate overall trend coefficients of 0.0047 and 0.0097, respectively, with respective t-statistics of 1.4 and 3.1. Second, the results are not sensitive to outliers. Exclusion of the upper and lower 1 percent of the distribution results in time-trend coefficients for the standard errors almost identical to those shown in table 2. Third, a finer education and experience grid has no effect. Allowing the education coefficient to change over five separate ranges and the experience coefficient to vary over eight separate ranges still leaves a residual standard error that trends upward over time. Fourth, the subsampling of the CPS used to construct the samples used here results in higher standard errors of the time-trend coefficients but no difference in their signs or orders of magnitude. Drawing samples in each year triple in size to those used in tables 1 and 2 yields time-series trend coefficients of 0.0036 and 0.00844 for the adjusted and unadjusted standard errors, respectively, with respective t-statistics of 1.8 and 5.1. Fifth, obtaining adjusted standard errors from the residuals of a regression pooled across all years instead of separate regressions by year still leaves upward-trending residual standard errors.

5. If a regression equation is $y = X'\beta + \epsilon$ and $\text{Var}(\epsilon) = (Z'\alpha)^2$, then a regression of $|\hat{\epsilon}|$ on Z' will yield consistent estimates of $c\alpha$, where c is an unknown constant. See George G. Judge and others, *The Theory and Practice of Econometrics* (Wiley, 1980), pp. 133–34.

6. Jacob Mincer, *Schooling, Experience, and Earnings* (Columbia University Press, 1974), chap. 6.

7. This observation suggests that the increasing standard error of earnings may have been a result of a falling real mean earnings. Indeed, over the twenty-one time-series observations available, the mean of earnings and the unemployment rate explain 50 percent of the variance of the earnings standard error.

icant and still trend upward over time. Thus heteroskedasticity cannot explain the increasing standard error of earnings.

The Transfers Hypothesis

The hypothesis this chapter addresses is that the increasing inequality of male earnings, even when controlled for observed individual socio-economic characteristics, is a result of the U.S. transfers system. It is first necessary to determine the direction of the trends in participation and benefits in the various transfer programs over the past twenty years. In addition, it must be determined which groups are eligible for benefits in the first place. The remaining issue is what theories of behavior might provide a conceptual link between eligibility for benefits and male earnings levels.

The U.S. Welfare System

The most widely known cash transfer program for the poor in the United States is the AFDC program. It is, for the most part, a program only for female heads—the term used here to refer to female heads of family with children under eighteen present. An unrelated male can be present in the household, but he must not contribute to the support of the family. To be eligible for benefits a family must have income and assets below certain specified levels, which are set separately in each of the fifty-one U.S. states and jurisdictions.

Table 3 illustrates the growth of the AFDC caseload. The program's greatest growth was in the decade between 1965 and 1975, when the number of families on the rolls more than tripled. This phenomenal growth was followed in 1975–85 by a period of slow growth in the number of families on the rolls and a decline in the number of individual recipients. The decline is attributable in part to the 1981 Omnibus Budget Reconciliation Act (OBRA), a Reagan administration bill that restricted eligibility for the program.

In approximately half the states, husband-wife families that have children under eighteen and meet the low income and asset conditions for AFDC are also eligible for benefits. However, the breadwinner of the family (usually the husband) must be unemployed and must have a suitable history of labor attachment and earnings similar to that required for eligibility for unemployment insurance. Caseload growth in the program, called AFDC-UP (UP for unemployed parent), is also shown in

Table 3. Average Monthly Caseloads of the Major Income-Tested Transfer Programs, Selected Years, 1960–85

Millions

Program	1960	1965	1970	1975	1980	1985
AFDC[a]						
Families	0.8	1.0	2.2	3.5	3.7	3.7
Recipients	3.0	4.3	8.5	11.3	10.8	10.9
AFDC-UP						
Families	0	0.06	0.08	0.10	0.14	0.26
Recipients	0	0.36	0.42	0.45	0.61	1.13
Food stamp recipients	0	0.4	4.3	17.1	21.1	19.9
Medicaid recipients						
Total[b]	0	0	15.5	22.0	21.6	22.2
Adults with						
dependent children	0	0	3.4	4.5	4.9	5.5
Dependent children	0	0	7.3	9.6	9.3	9.8

Sources: AFDC program: U.S. Social Security Administration, *Social Security Bulletin: Annual Statistical Supplement, 1988*, p. 334. AFDC-UP program: for 1965. U.S. National Center for Social Statistics. *Public Assistance Statistics*, series A-2 (July 1965), table 8; for 1970–85, *Background Material and Data on Programs within the Jurisdiction of the Committee on Ways and Means*, prepared for the House Committee on Ways and Means, 101 Cong. 1 sess. (GPO, 1989), p. 559. Food stamp recipients: SSA, *Social Security Bulletin: Annual Statistical Supplement, 1988*, p. 336. Medicaid recipients: for 1970, National Center for Social Statistics, *Medicaid: Fiscal Year 1970*, series B-5 (1970), table 1; for 1975–85, *Background Material . . . Ways and Means*, p. 1141.

a. Includes AFDC-UP (unemployed parent).

b. Includes aged, blind, and disabled, as well as dependent children and their adults.

table 3. As the table shows, the caseload has always been small in AFDC-UP, largely because of its stringent eligibility requirements, although there has been a recent spurt of growth. However, even at present the caseload is only 7 percent of that of AFDC as a whole.

The most important development in the transfer system in the 1970s was the emergence of in-kind transfers. The food stamp program provides food coupons to families with low income and assets regardless of family type or marital status, and hence is the closest thing in the country to a universal transfer program. There is also widespread evidence that the coupons are treated by recipients as though they were equivalent to cash, in which case the program's in-kind nature is only nominal. The program was begun in the mid-1960s by Congress as a federal program with benefits set at the national level. As table 3 shows, the program was quite small in 1965, shortly after its introduction, but grew rapidly in the 1970s. By 1985 there were almost twice as many food stamp recipients as AFDC recipients, although expenditures were only about 50 percent greater because food stamp benefits are much lower than AFDC benefits.

The medicaid program is the major source of health benefits for the poor, providing a basic set of medical services to eligible families. The program is federally subsidized and regulated but administered by the states, which have some leeway in defining the set of services offered. However, eligibility for the program is highly restricted in most states because AFDC eligibility is usually required for men and women who are neither aged nor disabled. As a consequence, poor husband-wife couples are generally not eligible for medicaid, nor are most poor female heads who do not wish to be on AFDC. The major exception occurs in thirty-eight states that allow medicaid benefits for any family that has a major medical expense and is willing to use up its private assets (to "spend them down," in the parlance) until it is effectively poor. But these recipients constitute only a small percentage of the caseload.

As table 3 indicates, the program was of no consequential magnitude until 1970 (its enabling legislation was passed in 1965), but its growth has also leveled off since 1975. The total caseload is even greater than that of food stamps, largely because the elderly and disabled constitute a large fraction of the medicaid caseload. Female heads and their children constitute about two-thirds of all medicaid recipients, reflecting the close tie to AFDC recipiency mentioned above, although they are responsible for only 27 percent of spending.

This simple examination of the trends in the U.S. transfer system raises immediate questions regarding the possible role that transfers could play in increasing inequality in the distribution of earnings. For example, it is clear from the table that the explosive growth of the transfer system occurred in the late 1960s and early 1970s rather than during the 1980s, in contrast to the pattern of increase in inequality of earnings. The only possible exception to this generalization is the food stamp program, which, unlike AFDC and medicaid, continued to grow significantly into the 1980s.

In addition, the eligibility rules of AFDC and hence of medicaid imply that most males will be ineligible for their benefits. The exceptions occur in the states with AFDC-UP but, as the evidence indicates, caseloads in that program have been quite small over the entire period. The only program for which sizable numbers of men are eligible is food stamps, the program that continued growing in the 1980s.

To determine the extent to which males could have been affected by food stamps as well as other transfers, 1984 data on the receipt of transfers by both single parents and husband-wife couples are shown in table 4. Husband-wife couples received virtually no transfers. Only 18 percent of two-parent families received any type of benefit at all, and

Table 4. Transfers Received, by Family Type, 1984
Percent

Transfer	Nonelderly single-parent families	Nonelderly two-parent families
No program	44.5	81.8
Food stamps only	3.6	1.9
Medicaid only	1.1	0.9
AFDC, medicaid only	2.3	0.6
Food stamps, medicaid only	0.5	0.3
AFDC, medicaid, food stamps only	15.4	1.2
AFDC, medicaid, food stamps, and other benefit	11.0	0.5
AFDC, medicaid, and other benefit (not food stamps)	1.0	0.3
Cash transfers only [a]	9.7	7.6
Housing assistance only	3.3	0.9
Other[b]	7.6	4.0
Total	100.0	100.0

Sources: Daniel H. Weinberg, "Filling the 'Poverty Gap,' 1979–1984; Multiple Transfer Program Participation," Technical Analysis Paper 32 (U.S. Department of Health and Human Services, March 1986), tables 3, 4; and unpublished data provided by Daniel Weinberg.
a. Includes unemployment insurance, general assistance, and other cash programs.
b. Other combinations of programs.

almost half of those that did so received cash transfers other than AFDC, medicaid, and food stamps—primarily unemployment insurance. As a result, even though such families are eligible for AFDC-UP in some states and for food stamps in all states, their rates of recipiency are very low. This is in contrast with the patterns for single-parent families, more than half of whom receive at least one form of benefit and 20 to 25 percent of whom receive AFDC, food stamps, and medicaid.[8]

Other transfer programs received by husband-wife couples are also unlikely to be of importance to the earnings distribution. General assistance, which is included in the categories of "cash transfers only" and "other" in table 4, is very rarely received and even then only by men with little possibility of labor force attachment. Unemployment insurance, which is the transfer most frequently received by men, is potentially more important. However, recipiency rates of unemployment insurance have fallen since the early 1980s, about the same time as earnings

8. Single men have higher food stamp recipiency rates, about 5 percent, but even these are still quite low. See Thomas Fraker and Robert Moffitt, "The Effect of Food Stamps on the Labor Supply of Unmarried Adults without Dependent Children," Mathematica Policy Research, Washington, D.C., 1989.

Table 5. Monthly Benefit Levels in Transfer Programs, Selected Years, 1969–87

Year	AFDC[a]	Benefit level (1982 dollars) Food stamps[a]	Medicaid[b]	Sum[c]	Ratio of benefit to female earnings (percent) AFDC	Sum	Ratio of benefit to male earnings (percent) AFDC	Sum
1969	515	233	n.a.	n.a.	66	n.a.	34	n.a.
1971	513	214	n.a.	n.a.	60	n.a.	33	n.a.
1973	485	218	n.a.	n.a.	53	n.a.	30	n.a.
1975	490	247	169	652	55	73	31	41
1977	485	246	187	654	52	70	31	42
1979	448	233	180	613	46	63	28	39
1981	410	221	185	576	42	59	28	39
1983	387	244	212	593	39	60	26	39
1985	396	237	184	582	40	59	24	35
1987	391	227	n.a.	n.a.	n.a.	n.a.	24	n.a.

Sources: AFDC benefits: for 1969, unpublished appendix to Richard A. Kasten and John E. Todd, "Transfer Recipients and the Poor during the 1970s," in Richard J. Zeckhauser and Derek Leebaert, eds., *What Role for Government? Lessons from Policy Research* (Duke University Press, 1983); for 1971–87, data from Office of Family Assistance. Food stamp benefits for 1969–71, personal communication from Dr. Thomas Fraker; for 1973–87, *Background Material and Data on Programs within the Jurisdiction of the Committee on Ways and Means*, prepared for the House Committee on Ways and Means, 101 Cong. 1 sess. (GPO, 1989), p. 1126. Medicaid benefits: data from U.S. Health Care Financing Administration. Weekly female and male earnings: computed from Current Population Surveys.
n.a. Not available.
a. Maximum amount paid for a family of four with no other income.
b. Insurance value for a family of four.
c. Food stamps plus 70 percent of AFDC (because the food stamp program taxes 30 percent of it away) plus 36.8 percent of the medicaid benefit to convert it to a cash-equivalent value.

inequality was increasing.[9] Finally, pension, social security, and disability income are received by many older men in the U.S. population and have been held to be responsible for the decline in labor force attachment among such men. However, the earnings inequality figures presented above excluded men over the age of 61, making it unlikely that social security could have significantly affected the earnings distribution. In addition, earnings inequality has increased among young men as well as old.

One factor that has been omitted from this discussion, however, is the growth of benefit levels in the system. Even if recipiency rates are low, and even if they did not grow excessively in the late 1970s and early 1980s, a high rate of benefit growth could have significantly affected the earnings of those who are recipients. Table 5 shows real benefit growth in AFDC, food stamps, and medicaid over 1969–87. As the table indicates, real AFDC benefits actually fell over the 1970s, in contrast to the trend in earnings inequality. The food stamp benefit was ap-

9. Gary Burtless, "Why Is Insured Unemployment So Low?" *Brookings Papers on Economic Activity*, 1: 1983, pp. 225–49.

proximately constant in real terms, no doubt because it is indexed to inflation, while the real medicaid benefit rose and then declined. However, these trends are rather misleading because both food stamps and medicaid were not as widespread in 1969 as in 1985. Comparing the 1969 AFDC benefit of $515 with the 1985 total combined transfer of $582 shows that there was real growth in the effective total benefit over the period, but the growth was not large.

A possibly more relevant question is the trend in the ratio of real benefits to earnings, shown in the table separately for both male and female earnings. Interestingly, the ratios declined over the entire period, a reflection of benefit growth that was even slower than earnings growth. Further, there was essentially no change between the ratio of AFDC alone in 1969 and the ratio of total benefits in 1985. Thus, once again, the prima facie evidence on trends in the transfer system does not appear to explain the growth in earnings inequality.

Behavioral Models for the Transfers Hypothesis

Economists have done considerable research on the effects of transfer programs on individual labor market behavior. This research provides the first source of information that might be used to evaluate the transfers hypothesis. However, the bulk of this literature is not germane to the issue at hand because most of it is concerned with the AFDC program and hence with female heads of family. This literature shows that the AFDC program has had disincentive effects on the work effort of female heads, for example, but this would not explain how transfers might affect male earnings.[10]

As noted previously, low-income men are eligible for food stamps. The only study of the work disincentives of food stamps on male work effort estimated that the program reduced hours of work by approximately 6 percent.[11] However, the study was concerned with only single men, not the larger group of married men. In any case, the low rates of food stamp recipiency noted above make any effect in this direction rather unlikely. The same is true for AFDC-UP, for which there have been no work disincentive studies.[12]

10. Robert Moffitt, "Work and the U.S. Welfare System: A Review," University of Wisconsin–Madison, Institute for Research and Poverty, Special Report 46 (April 1988).

11. Fraker and Moffitt, "Effect of Food Stamps."

12. There has been only one study of medicaid, which found it to have no effect on labor supply. Rebecca M. Blank, "The Effect of Medical Need and Medicaid on AFDC Participation," *Journal of Human Resources*, vol. 24 (Winter 1989), pp. 54–87.

Even if the problem of male ineligibility for the major programs is ignored, there is also the issue of whether the increase in earnings inequality has been generated by an increase in inequality of hourly wages or an increase in inequality of hours of work (that is, labor supply). The research literature on the effects of transfer programs has been almost exclusively concerned with their effects on labor supply, not the hourly wage rate; and the major economic theory underlying the literature—the standard static model of labor supply—takes the market hourly wage to be fixed. The decomposition of earnings inequality into its wage and labor supply components has not been formally examined, although there has been some attention paid through a comparison of inequality among year-round, full-time workers with that among all workers. I will discuss this further below.

To the extent that the increase in earnings inequality has arisen from an increase in wage inequality, some theory other than the standard labor supply theory must be invoked to obtain an effect. The conventional economic theory for wage rate determination is human capital theory. The empirical literature in human capital is vast, but the subset that deals with the effects of transfer programs on wage rates is virtually nonexistent. I know of only one study of the AFDC program, which addressed effects for only female heads.[13] The study indicated that participation in the AFDC program depresses hourly wages by about 20 percent, but the effect disappears fairly rapidly after the recipient leaves AFDC. In any case, the only evidence available for the potential effects of transfers on male wage rates comes from the income maintenance experiments, where no statistically significant effects of income maintenance payments were detected.

An avenue through which AFDC and medicaid could affect male labor market behavior is that of marital status and female headship. If the AFDC program reduces marriage rates by decreasing the rate of marital formations and increasing the rate of marital dissolutions, and if married men have different labor market attachments than unmarried men, an AFDC effect could result. The evidence on the latter relationship has been frequently examined in the literature on labor supply and human capital, where it has universally been found that married men have both greater levels of labor supply and higher wage rates than

13. Robert Moffitt and Anuradha Rangarajan, "The Effect of Transfer Programmes on Work Effort and Human Capital Formation: Evidence from the U.S.," in Andrew Dilnot and Ian Walker, eds., *The Economics of Social Security* (Oxford University Press, 1989), pp. 116–36.

unmarried men. The evidence on the former relationship is, however, much more tenuous. Although most of the studies of the effect of AFDC on marital status conducted in the 1970s showed a mixed pattern of results, and therefore no strong evidence of an effect, the better studies that have been conducted more recently show statistically significant effects.[14] However, as is widely recognized in the literature, the magnitudes of the effects are far too small to explain the dramatic increases in female headship that have occurred over the past twenty years, especially in light of the slow growth of real benefits for most of that period.

Nevertheless, there have been no studies conducted that explicitly examine the existence and strength of a possible connection between male labor force attachment and AFDC related to marital status. Therefore it is possible that some of the increase in earnings inequality could have arisen from this source. A fortiori, there have been no studies of whether any such effect would fall more heavily on male labor supply or on male wage rates.

Tests of the Transfers Hypothesis

This discussion suggests that the transfers hypothesis does not have strong prima facie support. Nevertheless, there are several ways that its strength can be measured and its explanatory power tested by an examination of the available data.

Source of the Increase in Earnings Inequality

First and most obviously, it must be determined whether the increase in the standard error of the logarithm of earnings has arisen from an expansion of the lower tail or the upper tail of the earnings distribution. The transfers hypothesis has credibility only if the lower tail has expanded. There is mixed evidence on this issue in the past studies of inequality, so I reexamined it.

14. Sheldon Danziger and others, "Work and Welfare as Determinants of Female Poverty and Household Headship," *Quarterly Journal of Economics,* vol. 97 (August 1982), pp. 519–34; David Ellwood and Mary Jo Bane, "The Impact of AFDC on Family Structure and Living Arrangements," in Ronald Ehrenberg, ed., *Research in Labor Economics,* vol. 7 (JAI Press, 1985), pp. 137–207; and Robert Hutchens, "Welfare, Remarriage, and Marital Search," *American Economic Review,* vol. 69 (June 1979), pp. 369–79.

Table 6. Measures of Subcomponents of the Earnings Distribution for White and Black Males, Selected Years, 1967–87

Year	Percent with earnings 50% below median	Percent with earnings 50–150% of median	Percent with earnings above 150% of median	Ratio of percentile points to median earnings			
				10%	25%	75%	90%
			Whites				
1967	23.0	58.4	18.6	0.13	0.58	1.37	1.89
1969	25.5	54.8	19.7	0.13	0.50	1.38	1.90
1971	25.3	56.2	18.5	0.15	0.50	1.38	1.87
1973	24.1	56.9	19.0	0.14	0.52	1.36	1.81
1975	24.2	53.3	22.4	0.15	0.54	1.50	2.00
1977	25.6	51.7	22.7	0.14	0.47	1.47	2.04
1979	24.1	52.0	23.9	0.16	0.51	1.45	2.02
1981	26.4	45.6	28.0	0.12	0.47	1.60	2.22
1983	26.7	44.4	28.9	0.11	0.47	1.58	2.18
1985	27.4	44.9	27.6	0.10	0.44	1.56	2.19
1987	25.9	47.3	26.8	0.15	0.50	1.63	2.29
			Blacks				
1967	25.2	46.2	28.6	0.11	0.49	1.64	2.09
1969	26.0	47.2	26.8	0.13	0.46	1.51	1.95
1971	23.7	51.6	24.7	0.13	0.53	1.36	2.00
1973	26.1	47.7	26.2	0.12	0.50	1.57	2.02
1975	26.5	46.2	27.3	0.11	0.45	1.58	2.07
1977	23.6	46.9	29.5	0.11	0.53	1.59	2.16
1979	26.0	45.8	28.2	0.14	0.52	1.66	2.22
1981	27.2	50.0	22.8	0.13	0.48	1.47	2.08
1983	27.5	44.6	27.8	0.10	0.41	1.57	2.18
1985	27.0	43.5	29.6	0.10	0.44	1.61	2.30
1987	27.1	41.5	31.4	0.12	0.48	1.67	2.22

Table 6 shows trends in two measures of the source of the increase in earnings inequality for white and black men (the results for blacks will be discussed below). The first three columns show the percentages of the sample with earnings below 50 percent of the median, between 50 percent and 150 percent of the median, and above 150 percent of the median. Interestingly, almost all of the increase in inequality has come from an extremely large increase in the upper tail of the distribution. In 1967 only about 19 percent of white men had relatively high earnings, whereas in 1987 almost 27 percent did, an increase of almost 50 percent. The middle portion of the earnings distribution has declined correspondingly, from 58 percent to 47 percent of the work force. The lower tail, however, has changed little, if at all; there is no clear evidence of a trend in the percentages, and a regression of the figures in table 6 on a trend variable yields a coefficient of marginal significance.[15]

The next four columns present the ratios of several of the percentile points of the earnings distribution to median earnings. Once again, while the ratios at the seventy-fifth and ninetieth percentiles have increased strongly, the ratio at the tenth percentile has remained stable. The ratio at the twenty-fifth percentile has declined slightly, which may be evidence of a slippage in the distribution in the range between 10 percent and 25 percent. But since transfer programs should be expected to affect the very bottom of the distribution the most, neither this evidence nor that in the first four columns supports the transfers hypothesis.[16]

The different relative growth rates of the upper and lower tails of the earnings distribution also represent different growth rates in the real level of earnings. This arises primarily because the median level of earnings itself grew very little over the period, from about $16,500 in 1967 to $16,700 in 1987 (1982 dollars). The real twenty-fifth percentile earnings level dropped over the same period from $9,500 to $8,400, whereas the real seventy-fifth percentile earnings level rose from $22,600 to $26,800. Thus the percentile earnings points are "fanning out" over time.[17]

Importance of the Labor Supply

Because the major theories of transfer effects posit an effect that works through labor supply, it should be determined whether the increase in earnings inequality has arisen from an increase in the inequality of labor supply rather than from an increase in the inequality of wage rates. Another issue related to labor supply is the purely statistical

15. Including both a time trend and an unemployment rate, the time-trend coefficient for the first column of table 7 is 0.00005 ($t = 1.63$). A similar finding was reported in Marvin H. Kosters and Murray N. Ross, "The Distribution of Earnings and Employment Opportunities: A Re-examination of the Evidence," American Enterprise Institute, Washington, D.C., September 1987. No adjustment to the raw CPS medians has been performed here.

16. Time-series regressions of the last four columns on a trend and unemployment rate give trend coefficient estimates of 0.0004 (s.e. = 0.0009), −0.0031 (s.e. = 0.0016), 0.0112 (s.e. = 0.0022), and 0.0212 (s.e. = 0.0039) for the bottom through top medians, respectively.

17. This result, as well as many of the others in this chapter, is also found by Burtless in his chapter in this volume.

Table 7. Standard Errors of the Distribution of the Logarithm of Hourly Wages and Annual Hours Worked for White and Black Males, Selected Years, 1967–87

Year	Whites		Blacks	
	Wages[a]	Hours[b]	Wages[a]	Hours[b]
1967	0.704	0.595	0.807	0.663
1969	0.788	0.643	0.684	0.618
1971	0.742	0.636	0.635	0.649
1973	0.700	0.619	0.755	0.660
1975	0.725	0.637	0.656	0.650
1977	0.660	0.665	0.653	0.712
1979	0.760	0.558	0.801	0.644
1981	0.768	0.552	0.654	0.660
1983	0.831	0.683	0.713	0.666
1985	1.021	0.590	0.723	0.683
1987	0.910	0.544	0.676	0.646

a. Hourly wages computed by dividing annual earnings by annual hours.

b. Annual hours estimated by product of survey work hours and estimate of weeks worked in prior year, estimated by midpoint of weeks-worked category in 1967–74 and an equivalent midpoint assignment from the continuous weeks-worked variable in 1975–87.

argument that changes in the composition of the male labor force induced by labor market entrants and withdrawals have artificially increased the variance of the earnings distribution observed for workers.

Table 7 shows the standard errors of the distribution of the logarithms of hourly wages and annual hours worked.[18] All of the increase in earnings inequality appears to be a result of increases in wage inequality. The standard error of wages clearly trends upward, at least in the second half of the period. Likewise, the standard error of annual hours shows either no change or a decline over the period.[19] This result immediately rules out the majority of theories of transfer program effects, which are, as discussed previously, based upon labor supply responses.[20]

18. The results for two alternative definitions of wages and hours, shown in appendix table A-2, are identical. Different definitions are necessary because over the years the CPS has treated weeks worked in various ways, sometimes grouping it into intervals and sometimes not, and because only survey week hours were available in the early years of the CPS, while the preferable prior-year usual weekly hours were used in the later years. The detailed definitions are given in the notes to table 7 and appendix table A-2. However, the "usual" weekly hours in the prior year is not unambiguously superior because it is evident from the data that respondents rounded off their values to the nearest integer divisible by five. Much less evidence of such rounding is apparent in the survey week hours.

19. Identical results for regression-adjusted standard errors were obtained. This implies that changes in the covariance matrix of education, experience, and marital status have not contributed to the increase in inequality.

20. The declining variance of annual hours of work is consistent with the growth of part-time and part-year work over the period, as found, for example, by Blank in her chapter in this volume. Such growth lowers the mean of annual hours of work but has no necessary implication for its variance.

Table 8. Time-Series Regressions for the Standard Errors of the Logarithms of Hourly Wages and Annual Hours Worked for White Males

Variable	Wages			Hours		
	All years (1)	1967–75 and 1976–87 (2)	1967–80 and 1981–87 (3)	All years (4)	1967–75 and 1976–87 (5)	1967–80 and 1981–87 (6)
YEAR						
Overall	9.16* (4.16)	...	...	−6.62* (1.52)	...	...
1967–75	...	−9.38 (7.42)	...	...	−8.92 (3.23)	...
1976–87	...	18.26* (4.76)	...	...	−5.49* (2.07)	...
1967–80	...	...	−2.36 (5.68)	...	...	−9.38* (2.30)
1981–87	...	...	32.16* (9.46)	...	...	−1.11 (3.83)
UNEMP	4.85 (13.42)	16.40 (12.08)	20.31 (13.04)	21.25* (4.89)	22.68* (5.24)	24.96* (5.27)
Intercept	41.24	1,323.80	815.63	1,017.00	1,175.96	1,202.47
R^2 (adjusted)	0.39	0.56	0.54	0.49	0.48	0.53

Source: See table 2. Coefficients in regressions multiplied by 1,000. Numbers in parentheses are standard errors.
* Significant at 10 percent level.

Time-series regressions for the standard errors in table 7 are shown in table 8. As the results indicate, the standard error of wages trends upward significantly over the period after cyclical control, but the standard error of hours falls. The results also show separate trends for wages and hours before and after 1976 and 1981 (the results for alternative definitions are similar). They indicate that the standard errors of wages actually fell in the early years and did not rise until the later years. This conforms with the results obtained for earnings. Finally, separate regressions (not shown) of the absolute values of the regression residuals on year dummies show upward time trends.

As noted above, a separate hypothesis related to labor supply is that transfers have changed the fraction of the sample working and therefore the standard errors of earnings are affected by selection bias. Employment rates for white men have fallen from 0.861 in 1967 to 0.817 in 1987. However, as long as the earnings distribution is log concave, such a decline in employment rates will act to decrease, not increase, the conditional variance of earnings. Thus the selectivity-bias hypothesis cannot explain the rising inequality of earnings.

The selection-bias hypothesis implies instead that the "true" standard error of the earnings distribution increased even more than originally shown in table 1. Assuming normality for the natural logarithm of earnings, the standard error of log earnings is biased downward by the square root of the factor $1 + \rho^2\lambda(v - \lambda)$, where $\lambda = f[F^{-1}(1 - p)]/p$, $v = F^{-1}(1 - p)$; p is the probability of working; f and F are the unit normal density and distribution functions, respectively; and ρ is the correlation coefficient between the ln wage and hours of work. Using a maximum value of 0.50 for ρ and using $p = 0.861$ and $p = 0.817$ in 1967 and 1987, respectively,[21] implies that the standard error of earnings in 1967 should be 1.190 instead of 1.138 and in 1987 it should be 1.335 instead of 1.267. Thus the increase in the standard error of log earnings is virtually identical even after adjustment for selection bias.

Marital-Status Effects

If the AFDC-medicaid eligibility restriction to female heads has had an indirect effect on men working through marital status, changes in marital status should explain the increasing variance of the wage rate. Since marital status has indeed fallen, it should have induced some growth in the lower tail of the earnings distribution, provided that unmarried men have lower wages than married men. As table 9 indicates, this is indeed the case. Being married has had a positive effect on wages in every year in the data. Although the magnitude has varied considerably, no doubt mostly a result of sampling error (there is no evidence of a trend either up or down), the differential has been as high as 33 percent. In addition, the decline in the fraction married has increased the standard error of the marital status "distribution" by about 8 percentage points from 1967 to 1987 (from 39.9 to 47.6). Nevertheless, even taking the maximum possible effect of 33 percent as the true effect, the increase in the standard error of marital status has been responsible for only 0.025 of the 0.206 increase in the wage standard error shown in table 7.[22] Thus the effect has been trivial.

---

21. For derivation of these formulas and approximate values of ρ and p, see Michael Keane, Robert Moffitt, and David Runkle, "Real Wages over the Business Cycle: Estimating the Impact of Heterogeneity with Micro Data," *Journal of Political Economy*, vol. 96 (December 1988), pp. 1232–66.

22. The direct contribution of marital status to the wage standard error in each year is equal to the product of the first two columns in table 9. That product would have changed by 0.025 if the coefficient had been 0.329 in both 1967 and 1987.

Table 9. Regression Coefficients and Standard Errors of Marital Status and Total Benefits for White Males, Selected Years, 1967–87

| Year | Marital status | | Total benefits[a] | |
	Coefficient[b]	Standard error[c]	Coefficient[d]	Standard error
1967	0.302	0.399	0.397	165
1969	0.188	0.424	0.512	134
1971	0.108	0.419	0.426	139
1973	0.251	0.436	0.336	141
1975	0.329	0.436	0.303	143
1977	0.196	0.457	0.336	124
1979	0.215	0.462	0.775	111
1981	0.077	0.469	0.198	106
1983	0.068	0.464	0.729	98
1985	0.325	0.477	0.656	94
1987	0.232	0.476	n.a.	n.a.

n.a. Not available.

a. Benefit in each state in each year equals sum of food stamps, 70 percent of AFDC, and 36.8 percent of medicaid (cash-equivalent value).

b. Coefficient in each year in a log wage regression on a dummy variable equal to one if the individual is married with a spouse present.

c. Standard error of the dummy variable (not of its coefficient).

d. Multiplied by 1,000.

Another piece of evidence relevant to this hypothesis can be gleaned from the examination of heteroskedasticity discussed above, the results of which are reported in appendix table A-1. That examination revealed that heteroskedasticity is indeed present with respect to marital status—specifically, that married men have higher standard errors of earnings than do unmarried men. Since the percentage of white men who are married fell between 1967 and 1987, this implies that the overall standard error of earnings should have increased. However, the magnitude of the effect can explain only one-quarter, at most, of the increase in male earnings inequality during that period.[23]

Even if no explicit behavioral theory of the effects of transfers on male earnings is supported by the data, it may be that some behavioral mechanism has been overlooked. Therefore it is worth examining the degree to which transfer benefit levels in AFDC, food stamps, and

23. The coefficient on marital status in appendix table A-1 is −0.264. Since the percentage of white men who are married fell from 74.5 in 1967 to 69.1 in 1987, this implies that the dependent variable in the appendix regression (the absolute value of the regression residual) rose by approximately 0.033 over the same period. But the 1987 year-dummy coefficient in the regression implies that the dependent variable was 0.118 higher in 1987 than in 1967, about four times greater than 0.033.

medicaid are correlated with the degree of earnings inequality both in cross section and in time series.

An examination of this issue can be conducted in the same manner as was just presented for marital status. First, table 9 shows the coefficient on a variable for the total welfare benefit (AFDC plus food stamps plus medicaid) in a wage regression for each year. Surprisingly, the coefficients are positive in all cases, implying that higher benefits raise wage rates. This positive correlation may be a spurious result of an association between the wage level in a state and how high that state sets welfare benefits. However, even if this is the case, the coefficients in the table show no trend, implying that this spurious correlation has not changed over time. Therefore, the trend in the effect of welfare benefits on wage rates cannot contribute to an explanation of changing earnings. In any case, the table also shows the standard error of the welfare benefit across the sample, which arises from cross-state inequality in welfare benefits. As the results indicate, such inequality has actually decreased. Therefore, the trend in welfare benefits should have decreased, not increased, inequality in earnings (see footnote 22 for the type of calculation involved).

Second, a more direct test of the benefits hypothesis can be conducted by testing whether the variance of the error term is correlated with the cross-sectional benefit variation. When the benefit sum is included in the residual regression reported in appendix table A-1, its coefficient is almost identical to zero and its t-statistic is 0.234. Moreover, the upward trend in the year-dummy coefficients remains. Thus once again the transfers hypothesis fails to accord with the data.

Tests of the Hypothesis for Black Men

The analysis up to now has concerned only white men. A brief examination of black men is warranted because the black population has higher rates of participation in most of the low-income transfer programs, and hence the various arguments for the transfers hypothesis given above may carry more weight.

Tables 1 and 7 provide basic evidence indicating that this is not the case. For blacks, unlike whites, the standard error of earnings has not risen over the period. Furthermore, there has been no significant trend in the standard errors of hourly wages or annual hours worked. These conclusions are confirmed in appendix table A-3, which shows the coefficients of time-series regressions of these standard errors on a trend and the unemployment rate. While the earnings and wage trends are always positive, their magnitudes are only one-fourth or one-fifth of those for white males (see table 2), and they are never statistically significant at conventional levels. Separate results (not shown) presenting separate trends before and after 1976 and 1981 show positive post-1976 effects for the wage that are approximately one-third the magnitude of those for whites ($t = 1.3$), but there are no post-1981 effects or any effects for earnings.[24]

Table 6 shows trends in the distributional indicators based upon median earnings. As was the case for whites, there is little, if any, indication of an increase in the lower tail of the earnings distribution of black men. The fraction of the work force with earnings less than 50 percent of the median exhibits no strong and apparent upward trends, nor do the ratios of the tenth and twenty-fifth percentile points to the median show any strong and apparent downward trend over the period. In fact, time-series regressions of these three series on trend and cycle yield small and insignificant trend coefficients, with t-statistics no higher than 0.919. On the other hand, the upper tail of the distribution has clearly grown. This is evident from the growth in the percentage of the sample with earnings above 150 percent of the median as well as from the growth in the ratios of the seventy-fifth and ninetieth percentile points to the median. Time-series regressions for the latter two series yield positive and significant trend coefficients with t-statistics of 2.6 and 4.7, respectively.

The source of the marked difference between black males and white males is not obvious, especially given the current emphasis in many policy discussions of the growth of a black underclass. There is no evidence of any such growth in the CPS distributions of earnings. One possible statistical explanation is that the black-white difference arises from a differential selectivity bias in employment rates, for black male rates have fallen considerably faster than white male rates over the period. Black male employment rates in the 1967 sample used here were 0.858, about equal to that of white men, but they had dropped twice as much by 1987, to 0.744. However, if the selection-bias adjustment factor shown above is applied to these figures, the selection-bias hypothesis fails to explain the racial difference. The "true" standard error of earnings in 1967 is, according to these calculations, 1.283 instead of 1.227

24. Using the full sample of black men from the CPS instead of the subsample increases the post-1976 trend coefficient to approximately one-third of that of white men and its t-statistic to 2.0. However, the other trend coefficients remain insignificant.

and in 1987 is 1.279 instead of 1.202. Thus the adjustment partially eliminates the decline in the black male standard error, but does not cause it to increase.

Also, inequality in the black male earnings distribution has traditionally been at a higher level than that for white males, regardless of trend. However, the data in table 1 reveal that the level of inequality among white males has risen to approximately equal that among black males, a result that may be related to the more general convergence of black and male earnings documented extensively elsewhere.

Other Hypotheses

If transfer programs do not provide an explanation for the upward trend in earnings inequality, what does? I examine three alternative explanations: baby boom cohort effects, industry effects, and, in a more statistical vein, changing trends in the imputation of earnings in the CPS.

Baby Boom Cohort Effects

Earnings functions have undergone several major changes in the1970s and 1980s that could be related to the inequality of earnings. The effects of education on earnings, for example, fell over the 1970s but have risen during the 1980s. In addition, the entry of baby boom cohorts over the 1970s depressed earnings at early ages and hence steepened the experience slope of the earnings profile. In the 1980s, as the growth rate of entry-cohort sizes lessened, experience slopes flattened.

The evidence that I have gleaned thus far does not provide any obvious support for a connection between these trends and the increasing inequality of earnings. First, as the data in tables 1 and 2 indicated, the upward trend in earnings inequality remains even after education and experience are controlled for. Further, the upward trend is retained even if education and experience are allowed to have separate effects in each year, thus allowing the changes in cohort size to alter the year-specific education and experience differentials in an arbitrary fashion (see also footnote 4 for the results of a finer education and experience grid). Put differently, the upward trend in earnings inequality has arisen from an increasing variance within education and experience cells, not across them. Second, the usual supposition is that the baby boom should have increased the variance of earnings by widening skill differentials in general, yet the time-series evidence goes in the opposite direction: the largest increases in earnings inequality occurred in the 1980s, just as the baby boom effects were disappearing.

A question related to the baby boom hypothesis is how earnings inequality has changed for successive birth cohorts over the last twenty years. An increase in overall earnings inequality could arise in two different ways: each birth cohort that enters the labor market could have a different average level of earnings from its first through its last year than did the previous cohort, or each birth cohort that enters could have the same average earnings in its first year as the immediately preceding cohort but an increased variance of earnings over the course of its career. In any given year, the former explanation implies that there has been a growing inequality in earnings levels across individuals of different ages, whereas the latter explanation implies that the relative average earnings levels of each cohort have remained unchanged but inequality within each age group has increased. The baby boom hypothesis is of the first type, for it assumes that average earnings levels of certain cohorts have changed over their entire lifetimes because of their large relative population size.[25]

Appendix table A-4 contains results of regressions that shed light on this issue. The equations reported there show whether different cohorts have experienced higher average levels of earnings in all years of their lifetime, from their first to their last, or whether different cohorts have experienced changes in the way earnings inequality varies over their lifetime. The estimates imply that both factors are important in explaining the rise in overall earnings inequality. The increased inequality that recent cohorts have experienced as they have entered the labor market has not remained fixed over their lifetimes: for each cohort, inequality has increased as its members have grown older. This implies that the increase in overall inequality has not been purely a result of cohort effects: forces have been operating year by year on all cohorts to make inequality for all of them increase at the same time.

---

25. In statistical terminology, the question is whether the increase in overall earnings inequality has arisen from an increase in the "between-cohort" variance or the "within-cohort" variance. A related question is whether there has been an increase in the between-individual variance or the within-individual variance (that is, the amount of year-to-year earnings fluctuation over an individual's lifetime). Panel data are needed to answer this latter question. Since the CPS files provide data from repeated cross sections rather than a panel, the question cannot be addressed here.

Industry Effects

A frequently mentioned hypothesis for the increasing variance of earnings is that it has been a result of the decline of manufacturing jobs and the increase in service-sector jobs in the U.S. economy. Presuming that the former pay higher wages than the latter, such a shift could be expected to increase the size of the lower tail of the earnings distribution, ceteris paribus.

As shown above, the increased variance of earnings is more a result of an increase in the upper tail than in the lower, thus casting some doubt on the explanatory power of the sectoral hypothesis. In addition, the timing of the increase in earnings inequality does not correspond to the timing of the sectoral shifts, for the decline in manufacturing was much more severe in the 1970s than in the 1980s. In the data used here, the percentage of the white male work force working in manufacturing declined from 33 percent in 1967 to 25 percent in 1977, but then fell only to 24 percent in 1987. The percentage working in the service sector rose from 15 percent to 19 percent and then to 20 percent over the same three years, again showing greater change in the earlier period.

Nevertheless, a simple test of the sectoral hypothesis can be conducted by examining whether the increase in the variance of earnings has occurred between or within sectors. Following the same procedure as that above, wages can be regressed upon education, experience, marital status, and sectoral dummies for manufacturing and services. The year-by-year estimated standard errors of the regression residuals can then be regressed upon a time trend and an unemployment rate. The results show that almost all the upward trend in wage inequality still remains. The overall time-trend coefficient is 0.0085 ($t = 1.9$), only slightly slower than the 0.0095 shown in table 2. The post-1976 trend coefficient is 0.018 and the post-1981 coefficient is 0.028, both larger than their counterparts in table 2. Thus the evidence for the sectoral shifts hypothesis does not appear to be strong.

CPS Imputations

A more technical explanation for the trend in earnings inequality is that it is a statistical artifact of the CPS imputation procedure for earnings and income. The CPS "hot deck" procedure has been subject to considerable criticism for leading to biased estimates of earnings regressions, although not all analysts agree on the magnitude of the problem.[26] Some evidence indicates that underreporting is greatest in the lower and upper tails of the earnings distribution and is smallest in the middle. If the CPS hot deck procedure introduces artificial noise into the earnings distribution, it may increase the measured variance of that distribution. In addition, if income nonreporting has been increasing over time, as many assume that it has, an increased earnings variance could result.

Appendix tables A-5 and A-6 provide evidence on this possibility from the white male data used in this paper. Table A-5 shows the rates of nonreporting of earnings in the CPS samples since 1975, the earliest year that nonreporting is available in the CPS public use files. The table shows that nonreporting has not in fact increased and appears, if anything, to have decreased over the period. Table A-6 shows the results of regressions for the absolute value of the residuals from two wage equations. In the first, a dummy variable for imputed earnings was included as a regressor along with education, experience, and marital status. In the second, all observations with imputed earnings were excluded from the wage equations. Neither of these methods is unbiased if there are in fact biases in the hot deck procedure, but the results should nevertheless indicate how sensitive to imputation in general are the findings for increasing wage inequality.

The estimates reported in table A-6 indicate that an upward trend in the wage standard error remains regardless of the method of controlling for imputation. In fact, the estimates are close to those obtained previously without any control for imputation. Thus the weight of the evidence clearly points toward little or no role for biases in the CPS hot deck procedure in explaining the increase in wage and earnings inequality.[27]

Summary

The results reported here address the hypothesis that transfer benefits have been responsible for the growing earnings inequality in the United

26. Lee Lillard, James P. Smith, and Finis Welch, "What Do We Really Know about Wages? The Importance of Nonreporting and Census Imputation," *Journal of Political Economy*, vol. 94, pt. 1 (June 1986), pp. 489–506; and Martin David and others, "Alternative Methods for CPS Income Imputation," *Journal of the American Statistical Association*, vol. 81 (March 1986), pp. 29–41.

27. A very similar finding was reported in Lynn Annette Karoly, "A Study of the Distribution of Individual Earnings in the United States from 1967 to 1986," Ph.D. dissertation, Yale University, 1988.

States. None of the evidence supports the hypothesis. Benefits are generally available only to female heads of family, not men, yet the increasing inequality has been concentrated among males; the increase in inequality has occurred more in the upper tail of the wage distribution than in the lower; the increase has been entirely a result of increases in the inequality of hourly wage rates, not in hours of work, ruling out any transfer-related labor supply effects; changes in male marital status, possibly a result of the transfer system, can explain only a trivial amount of the increase; and direct correlations between transfer benefits and inequality go in the opposite direction to that of the hypothesis in both time series and cross section. In addition, the increase in earnings inequality has been present only for white men, not black men, and neither cohort effects, sectoral shifts, nor CPS income nonreporting can explain the increase for white men.

Table A-1. Regression of Residuals on Selected Characteristics of White Males and Year Dummies[a]

Characteristic	Coefficient[b]	Characteristic	Coefficient[b]
Education	−0.015	Year dummies	
	(0.001)	1977	0.028
Experience	−0.025		(0.025)
	(0.001)	1978	−0.022
Experience^{2c}	0.052		(0.025)
	(0.003)	1979	0.037
Marital status	−0.264		(0.025)
	(0.010)	1980	0.082
Year dummies			(0.025)
1968	−0.003	1981	0.105
	(0.024)		(0.025)
1969	0.013	1982	0.109
	(0.024)		(0.025)
1970	0.022	1983	0.135
	(0.024)		(0.025)
1971	0.018	1984	0.110
	(0.024)		(0.025)
1972	−0.021	1985	0.162
	(0.024)		(0.025)
1973	0.005	1986	0.115
	(0.025)		(0.025)
1974	0.009	1987	0.118
	(0.024)		(0.025)
1975	0.044	Intercept	1.112
	(0.025)		
1976	0.028		
	(0.025)		

a. Dependent variable = absolute value of residuals from year-by-year regressions of the log of earnings on education, experience, experience squared, and marital status (see table 1 for definitions).

b. Numbers in parentheses are standard errors.

c. Multiplied by 100.

Table A-2. Standard Errors of the Logarithm of Hourly Wages and Annual Hours Worked for White Males, under Alternative Definitions, Selected Years, 1967–87

	Definition 1[a]		Definition 2[b]	
Year	Wages[c]	Hours	Wages[c]	Hours
1967	0.704	0.595	...	...
1969	0.788	0.643	...	...
1971	0.742	0.636	...	...
1973	0.700	0.619	...	...
1975	0.711	0.650	0.712	0.755
1977	0.650	0.663	0.683	0.755
1979	0.760	0.540	0.737	0.669
1981	0.770	0.577	0.783	0.773
1983	0.830	0.687	0.832	0.802
1985	1.013	0.587	0.980	0.747
1987	0.903	0.538	0.902	0.724

a. Annual hours worked estimated by product of survey week hours and estimate of weeks worked in prior year, estimated by midpoint of weeks-worked category in 1967–74 and continuous weeks-worked variable in 1975–87.
b. Annual hours estimated by product of "usual" weekly hours in prior year and weeks worked in prior year.
c. Hourly wages computed by dividing annual earnings by annual hours.

Table A-3. Time-Series Regressions for the Standard Errors of the Distribution of Earnings, Hourly Wages and Annual Hours Worked, for Black Males[a]

	Earnings			Annual hours
Variable	Unadjusted	Adjusted	Hourly wages	worked
YEAR	0.0022	0.0034	0.0037	0.0001
	(0.0022)	(0.0028)	(0.0028)	(0.0018)
UNEMP	0.0034	0.0093	−0.0160*	0.0022
	(0.0072)	(0.0089)	(0.0089)	(0.0058)
Intercept	1.0357	0.6614	0.5040	0.6536

* Significant at 10 percent level.
a. Numbers in parentheses are standard errors.

Table A-4. Regression of Residuals on Cohort and Other Characteristics, White Males[a]

Variable	Coefficient
Education	−0.0008
	(0.0014)
Experience	0.0017
	(0.0044)
Experience[2b]	0.0002
	(0.0076)
Marital status	−0.1026*
	(0.0095)
Cohort[c]	0.0045*
	(0.0011)
Cohort × experience	−0.0002*
	(0.0001)
Cohort × experience[2b]	0.0007*
	(0.0002)
Intercept	0.3494

* Significant at 10 percent level.
a. Residuals taken from year-by-year log wage regressions. Numbers in parentheses are standard errors.
b. Multiplied by 100.
c. Birth year minus 1900.

Table A-5. Percentage of White Male Work Force with Imputed Earnings, 1975–87

Year	Percent	Year	Percent
1975	15.8	1982	13.5
1976	13.0	1983	13.7
1977	15.3	1984	15.2
1978	18.7	1985	13.9
1979	15.6	1986	13.8
1980	15.5	1987	13.9
1981	14.4		

Table A-6. Regressions of Residuals Adjusted for Imputation[a]

Variable	Imputation dummy in wage equation	Wage equation estimated on non-imputations only
Education	−0.0047	−0.0052
	(0.0018)	(0.0019)
Experience	−0.0071	−0.0075
	(0.0015)	(0.0017)
Experience[2b]	0.0172	0.0176
	(0.0035)	(0.0038)
Marital status	−0.0804	−0.0605
	(0.0122)	(0.0132)
Year dummies[c]		
1976	0.037	0.025
	(0.025)	(0.026)
1977	−0.022	−0.027
	(0.025)	(0.027)
1978	−0.025	−0.019
	(0.024)	(0.027)
1979	0.034	0.036
	(0.025)	(0.027)
1980	−0.098	−0.025
	(0.025)	(0.027)
1981	0.021	0.023
	(0.025)	(0.027)
1982	0.058	0.051
	(0.025)	(0.027)
1983	0.050	0.057
	(0.025)	(0.027)
1984	0.049	0.052
	(0.025)	(0.027)
1985	0.099	0.072
	(0.025)	(0.027)
1986	0.069	0.052
	(0.025)	(0.027)
1987	0.055	0.055
	(0.025)	(0.027)
Intercept	0.587	0.579

a. Numbers in parentheses are standard errors.
b. Multiplied by 100.
c. 1975 omitted.

Comment by Edward M. Gramlich

Robert Moffitt tackles the question of whether the growth of welfare programs has been responsible for the increasing inequality of the earnings distribution. Before being asked to discuss the paper I would not have found the hypothesis very plausible, and I now find it even less so. I summarize the case he makes against transfers as causal agents and interject some queries of my own along the way. Since I too believe that transfers are innocent, I cannot quarrel with Moffitt's overall interpretation of the evidence. All I can do is to mention a few more leads he might have pursued to make the case even more overwhelming.

The Dependent Variable

The topic of the volume is the fact that the distribution of white male earnings is becoming less equal. The standard error of the log of earnings in the CPS rose from 1.138 in 1967 to 1.267 in 1987. Moffitt fits annual cross-sectional regressions to a set of human capital variables and finds that the standard error of these regressions has also increased, from 0.778 in 1967 to 1.031 in 1987. He then regresses both the unadjusted and the adjusted, or regression, standard errors on a cyclical variable and a series of time trends for the entire period and various subperiods. The cyclical variable raises the standard error, as one would expect, but the key fact is that the trends are positive too—very much so, and very significant, both for 1976–87 and for 1981–87. There seems little doubt that the standard error of the white male earnings distribution has increased, both unadjusted and adjusted for time-series variables, cross-sectional variables, and heteroskedasticity, and that a lot of that increase has occurred lately.

This raises a number of questions. First, Moffitt says early on that he is not looking at the distribution of female earnings because that variance has not increased. True, but there may still be some merit in examining the question. If transfers are to affect anything, it should be the distribution of female earnings, for the simple reason that women are the ones who get transfers. And even though the distribution of female earnings has not become less equal, there could be offsetting effects. Moreover, some of the tests could be done, or the methodology could be verified, from an examination of the female earnings distribution.

Second, in focusing exclusively on changes in the variance of white male earnings, it is easy to forget that this variable obscures the influence of changes in the mean. It turns out that the mean of real earnings for white men barely grew over the past two decades. Hence a rising variance could imply that lower-tail male earnings are actually declining in real terms. It seems that this is happening at the twenty-fifth percentile but not at the tenth percentile. The reason for the difference and what to make of it are not clear. Should one focus attention on the variance statistics, as Moffitt does, or simply on levels of real earnings or wages for the lower tail? In investigating the transfers hypothesis, my preference would be for the latter. Transfers affect only a small portion of the overall earnings distribution, and there seems to be no logical reason to focus on what changes in transfers can do to the overall distribution, even to the mean and variance of it. Why not just focus on earnings or wages at the relevant portion? For better or worse, Moffitt did not do the analysis this way. He has enough persuasive evidence that his choice of analytical mode will not prove important, but I wish he had focused more on the actual levels in the relevant part of the earnings distribution.

Given the focus on the overall variance, the next question is whether the variance is increasing symmetrically or differentially on the high or low side. Moffitt examines this by computing the percentage of the sample with earnings below 50 percent of the median and above 150 percent of the median. He finds a sharp growth in the latter, little change in the former. He then computes the ratio of earnings at various percentile points to the median. Earnings at the tenth percentile are in about the same ratio to the median, and earnings at the twenty-fifth percentile have slipped, giving rise to the puzzle noted above. But the main news is that upper-tail earnings have risen quite sharply compared with the median. This finding obviously should make us doubt that transfer programs can be an important causal force, for the obvious reason that upper-tail workers do not get transfer payments.

The final question is whether the story is roughly the same once hours worked are separated from average hourly earnings. If the growth in transfers were to have affected the distribution of earnings, one would think it would work through the labor supply term—hours worked—and not through average wage rates. And again Moffitt finds that the standard error of hours worked has actually declined over the period, both unadjusted and in a regression of the sort run before. On the other hand, the standard error of average hourly earnings has increased sharply over the period, unadjusted and in a regression, and, as before, particularly in the 1976–87 and 1981–87 subperiods. The finding that all the increases in earnings inequality have come through the wage term, not the hours term, should again make one wonder how transfers can be the driving force. But again, to nail the case down completely, it would have been helpful for Moffitt to compute, analyze, and interpret the behavior of the actual series on lower-tail hours worked.

The Independent Variables

The transfer programs Moffitt looks at are those for low-income recipients: AFDC, food stamps, and medicaid. In terms of caseloads, most of the expansion of these programs occurred in the late 1960s and early 1970s, well before the earnings distribution began to widen. Moreover, both eligibility rules and the actual numbers show that most males are not even eligible for benefits in any but the food stamp program, and the recipiency rates are low. In 1984, for example, only about 3 percent of nonelderly two-parent families, the families that male workers almost certainly must come from, received benefits from any of these antipoverty programs.

At this point one could question why Moffitt confined himself to antipoverty transfer programs. About 18 percent of nonelderly two-parent families received some transfer benefit, the most prevalent being unemployment insurance. Although the properties of the earnings distribution discussed above make unemployment insurance just as unlikely as the driving force as antipoverty transfers, Moffitt could at least have examined the question. People who might have believed that the growth of transfer programs partly explained the increasing inequality of earnings would have been much more likely to believe this about unemployment insurance than about antipoverty transfers.

But Moffitt also shows that properly measured, even the antipoverty transfers did not grow over the two-decade period. Even with the early expansion of all three programs, the fact that AFDC gives the largest benefits and its real benefits have declined steadily over the period means that the trend ratio of real transfer benefits to earnings also declined steadily over the period.

Linkage Theories

These facts about the behavior of both the dependent and independent variables make it quite unlikely that any prosecuting attorney could find that transfer growth caused earnings inequality. But there are all sorts of judges and juries in the world, and Moffitt took a shot at coming up with some more creative causal links.

One possibility involves the family split issue. If transfer growth led to family splits, and if married men earn more than unmarried men, transfer growth could lead to an increase in earnings inequality. While this argument might win points for creativity, it cannot win many for logic. First, the effect of transfer programs on the overall proportion of married and unmarried men is minuscule. Second, although it is true that married men earn more than unmarried men, who can believe that if a married man splits up with his spouse, his earnings will fall noticeably? Surely the married-unmarried wage differential represents in large measure personal differences, which would remain whatever was going on with transfer programs. Finally, as Moffitt shows, even if all the married men's wage premium vanished as the married men split, and even if all the splits were occasioned by transfer growth, the effect would still be small.

Moffitt's second shot was to throw the real benefit variable into his annual cross-sectional log wage equation to see if there was some mysterious link he had not thought of. There was not.

Overall Assessment

The case is so overwhelming that antipoverty transfers did not cause the increase in earnings inequality that it is hardly worth summarizing:

—There was no transfer growth in real or relative terms.

—Only a tiny share of male worker families get transfers anyway.

—The observed increase in earnings inequality is mainly on the high side of the distribution, where no males get transfers.

—The only earnings inequality observed is for wages, which are unlikely to be influenced by transfers, and not for hours worked.

—The link through family splits is implausible and empirically negligible.

—There is no other direct empirical link.

My only complaints about his argument are minor, but I still would have had him at least examine the evidence for women's earnings for actual levels of the lower tail variables, and for transfers such as unemployment insurance.

Conference Participants

with their affiliations at the time of the conference

LAURI BASSI
*U.S. Department of Labor and
Georgetown University*

ROBERT BEDNARZIK
U.S. Department of Labor

McKINLEY L. BLACKBURN
University of South Carolina

REBECCA M. BLANK
*Woodrow Wilson School and
Massachusetts Institute of Technology*

DAVID E. BLOOM
Columbia University

BARRY BLUESTONE
University of Massachusetts

KATHARINE L. BRADBURY
Federal Reserve Bank of Boston

GARY BURTLESS
Brookings Institution

DAVID CRAWFORD
U.S. Department of Labor

RICHARD B. FREEMAN
*Harvard University and
National Bureau of Economic Research*

PETER GOTTSCHALK
Boston College

EDWARD M. GRAMLICH
University of Michigan

KAREN HOLDEN
University of Wisconsin—Madison

MICHAEL HORRIGAN
U.S. Department of Labor

MARVIN H. KOSTERS
American Enterprise Institute

LINDA DATCHER LOURY
Tufts University

MARILYN MANSER
U.S. Bureau of Labor Statistics

ROBERT A. MOFFITT
Brown University

ISABEL V. SAWHILL
Urban Institute

WAYNE VROMAN
Urban Institute

ROBERTON WILLIAMS
Congressional Budget Office

236

Index